Indigenous Peoples, the United Nations and Human Rights

editor

Sarah Pritchard

Zed Books Ltd • The Federation Press

1998

To the memory of Rob Riley,
a champion of justice for Indigenous people.
Born Moora, 10 December 1954, died Perth, 1 May 1996.

Published in the United Kingdom, North America, Europe and Africa by

Zed Books Ltd
7 Cynthia St
London N1 9JF
United Kingdom
Ph: (0171) 837 4014
Fax: (0171) 833 3960

Published in Australasia and the rest of the world by

The Federation Press
PO Box 45, Annandale, NSW, 2038
71 John St, Leichhardt, NSW, 2040
Australia
Ph: (02) 9552 2200
Fax: (02) 9552 1681

National Library of Australia Cataloguing-in-Publication:

Indigenous peoples, the United Nations and human rights.

ISBN 1 86287 259 7.

1. United Nations. 2. Aborigines, Australian – Civil rights. 3. Human rights.
I. Pritchard, Sarah.

342.940872

Typeset by The Federation Press, Leichhardt, NSW
Printed by Ligare Pty Ltd, Riverwood, NSW

Contents

Abbreviations

ATSIC	Aboriginal and Torres Strait Islander Commission
CAT	Committee against Torture, also Convention against Torture and Other Cruel, Inhuman or Degrading Treatment or Punishment
CEDAW	Committee on the Elimination of Discrimination against Women, also Convention on the Elimination of All Forms of Discrimination against Women
CERD	Committee on the Elimination of Racial Discrimination, also Convention on the Elimination of All Forms of Racial Discrimination
CESCR	Committee on Economic, Social and Cultural Rights
CHR	Commission on Human Rights
CROC	Committee on the Rights of the Child, also Convention on the Rights of the Child
CSD	Commission on Sustainable Development
ECOSOC	Economic and Social Council
FAO	Food and Agriculture Organization of the United Nations
HRC	Human Rights Committee
HREOC	Human Rights and Equal Opportunity Commission
ICCPR	International Covenant on Civil and Political Rights
ICESCR	International Covenant on Economic, Social and Cultural Rights
ICJ	International Court of Justice
ILO	International Labour Organisation
NAILSS	National Aboriginal and Islander Legal Services Secretariat
NGO	Non-Governmental Organisation
UN	United Nations
UNCED	United Nations Conference on Environment and Development
UNESCO	United Nations Educational, Scientific and Cultural Organization
UNICEF	United Nations Children's Fund
UNDP	United Nations Development Programme
UNEP	United Nations Environment Programme
UNHCR	United Nations High Commissioner for Refugees
WGIP	Working Group on Indigenous Populations
WHO	World Health Organization

Preface

The present publication arose out of a conference held in Sydney, Australia in June 1995. The conference was designed to increase awareness of the United Nations (UN) human rights system, especially amongst Indigenous Australians. The organisers of the conference were particularly concerned to enhance knowledge about how UN human rights standards and procedures might be used to advance the human rights of Indigenous peoples.

While international control procedures are no substitute for national mechanisms for the protection of human rights, they have an important supplementary role to play in supervising conformity with internationally mandated standards. There are situations in which it is important to focus international attention on countries' domestic human rights performance. A number of recent cases in Australia have indicated some of the possibilities for pursuing rights under international procedures. The *Toonen* case taken to the UN Human Rights Committee by activists for gay and lesbian rights in Tasmania resulted in Commonwealth legislation (the *Human Rights (Sexual Conduct) Act* 1994) purporting to override the discriminatory Tasmanian laws, and eventually to Tasmanian legislation (*Criminal Code Amendment Act* 1997) amending the offending provisions of the *Tasmanian Criminal Code*. On 3 April 1997, the Human Rights Committee found the detention of a Cambodian boat person for a period of four years to be arbitrary and contrary to Australia's obligations under the International Covenant on Civil and Political Rights.[1] At the time of writing, the Australian Government's response to the adverse decision is awaited.

The conference was organised by the Aboriginal Education Program and the Aboriginal Law Centre at the University of New South Wales. Thanks are due to Professor Garth Nettheim, Terri Libesman, Brenda and Craig Stores, and Pia Almond. Financial support was provided by the Aboriginal and Torres Strait Islander Commission (ATSIC), the Central Land Council, the Northern Land Council, the Office of the Aboriginal and Torres Strait Islander Social Justice Commissioner, the Evatt Foundation, the Department of Prime Minister and Cabinet, and the Attorney General's Department. Assistance in the form of documentation

---

[1] *A v Australia*, UN Doc CCPR/C/59/D/560/1993 (30 April 1997).

was provided by Christopher de Bono of the United Nations Information Centre in Sydney, Bill Barker and Victoria Walker of the Department of Foreign Affairs and Trade, Margaret Swieringa of the Human Rights Sub-Committee of the Joint Standing Committee on Foreign Affairs, Defence and Trade, and Kathy Leigh and Libby Bunyan of the Attorney-General's Department.

The conference would not have been possible without the advice and encouragement of the eminent speakers. We thank Philip Alston, Bill Barker, Libby Bunyan, Hilary Charlesworth, Mick Dodson, Elizabeth Evatt, Kathy Leigh, Garth Nettheim, Deborah Nance, John Scott-Murphy, Chris Sidoti, Margaret Swieringa and Pat Walsh. We are particularly indebted to the Secretary of the Committee on the Elimination of Racial Discrimination, Michael O'Flaherty. Sessions were chaired by Jean Carter, Geoff Clarke, Chicka Dixon, Mick Dodson, Mark McKenzie, Damien Miller, Darryl Pearce, Aden Ridgeway, Rob Riley, Patricia Turner, Kevin Williams and George Villafor.

We also thank Justice Michael Kirby, then President of the New South Wales Court of Appeal, and now a Justice of the High Court of Australia, and Robert Tickner, former Minister for Aboriginal and Torres Strait Islander Affairs, for their thoughtful speeches at the conference dinner. Justice Kirby paid particular tribute to the work of NGOs:

> The NGOs are the engine room for getting things done. . . We should all be in NGOs. As free citizens we should all be trying to do what we can to stir the pot of injustice. We should not be ashamed to ask embarrassing questions. It is our right. We should insist upon doing so, both in national forums and also in the international community. At the level of NGOs we should play our part. NGOs can change the world. They can make a difference.

Justice Kirby described a number of developments at the level of international organisations, particularly in the Commission on Human Rights, which have contributed to the building of a better world:

> No longer can people do wrong things, seemingly safe in the secrecy of wrongs. Tyrants, autocrats and even democratic governments that are neglectful and do not do what they should are brought to the bar of the international community. They are made to answer.

The former Minister for Aboriginal and Torres Strait Islander Affairs, Robert Tickner, spoke of his first visit to the UN's Working Group on Indigenous Populations:

I was struck by the common bonds of solidarity and common experiences that bound together Indigenous peoples from around the world. The parallels between the loss of land, the oppression of governments, the denial of human rights and the conflicts with resource companies were striking.

The former minister offered some observations on the potential of UN processes to advance the human rights of Indigenous people:

> There seems to be a certain degree of inevitability about the way in which UN processes will be used to advance the domestic agenda for human rights for Indigenous people. . . People may well criticise the United Nations for its failings. But for all those failings, it is the best hope that humanity has. We need to work to improve it and to use it for all it is worth to advance the human rights of Indigenous people.

Finally, we thank Chris Holt and Diane Young of Federation Press for their support during the production of the book and Kathy Fitzhenry and Helen Williams for their wonderfully insightful and efficient editorial work. At the University of New South Wales, Lisa de Ferrari, Damien Miller, Robyn Gilbert and Maria Giuffre provided assistance with the manuscript.

The present publication is dedicated to the memory of Rob Riley, elected at the age of 27 Chairperson of the National Aboriginal Conference and appointed to head the Aboriginal Issues Unit of the Royal Commission into Aboriginal Deaths in Custody. At the June 1995 conference, Rob Riley addressed the following comments to Michael O'Flaherty, Secretary of the UN Committee on the Elimination of Racial Discrimination:

> I think it is important for us to be informed as to the measures indigenous peoples can take at a domestic level, and then how we might be able to take these issues to international forums. When issues get a bit heated and emotional, people trot out the line: "We'll take Australia to the International Court". We need to have a better idea of the procedures that exist and how we might use them.

It is hoped that this book will make a modest contribution to enhancing understanding of how UN processes might be used to advance the human rights of all people, especially the world's Indigenous peoples.

Sarah Pritchard, Olga Havnen and Anne Martin, August 1997

Notes on contributors

Philip Alston is Professor of International Law at the European University Institute in Florence. He was previously Professor of Law and Director of the Centre for International and Public Law at the Australian National University. He was an official of the United Nations Centre for Human Rights at Geneva from 1978 to 1984, and on the faculty of Harvard Law School from 1984 to 1989 and the Fletcher School of Law and Diplomacy at Tufts University from 1985 to 1989 and in 1993. He has been a Member of the UN Committee on Economic, Social and Cultural Rights since 1987, and Chairperson since 1991, and was Discrimination Commissioner for the Australian Capital Territory from 1992 to 1994.

Hilary Charlesworth is Professor of Law at the University of Adelaide and Visiting Professor in the Research School of Social Sciences at the Australian National University. She was a part-time Commissioner of the Australian Law Reform Commission on its reference into Equality before the Law. She is a member of the Australian Council for Women and a Hearing Commissioner of the Human Rights and Equal Opportunity Commission. She holds Arts and Law degrees from the University of Melbourne and a doctorate from Harvard Law School.

Michael Dodson is the first Aboriginal and Torres Strait Islander Social Justice Commissioner appointed under the *Human Rights and Equal Opportunity Legislation Amendment Act (No 2) 1992* (Cth). After completing a Bachelor of Law and a Bachelor of Jurisprudence at Monash University in 1979, he worked with the Victorian Aboriginal Legal Service. In 1981 he became a barrister at the Victorian Bar, in 1984 Senior Legal Advisor and in 1990 Director of the Northern Land Council. He was Counsel Assisting the Royal Commission into Aboriginal Deaths in Custody from 1988 to 1990. Mick was a Deputy Chair of the Technical Committee for the 1993 International Year of the World's Indigenous People and is Chair of the Board of Trustees of the United Nations Indigenous Voluntary Fund.

Elizabeth Evatt AO LLB (Syd), LLM (Harv) was until 1994 President of the Australian Law Reform Commission and Deputy President of the Australian Industrial Relations Commission. She was first Chief Judge of the Family Court of Australia from 1976 to 1988, and a member of the United Nations Committee on the Elimination of Discrimination against

Women from 1984 to 1992, before becoming its Chairperson from 1989 to 1991. She is currently a member of the United Nations Human Rights Committee.

Garth Nettheim is currently Visiting Professor in the Faculty of Law at the University of New South Wales, where he was Professor of Law from 1971 to 1996. He is Chair of the Indigenous Law Centre and the Australian Human Rights Centre at the University of New South Wales, and a member of the Executive Committee of the Australian Section of the International Commission of Jurists. He is editor of the title "Aborigines" in the *Laws of Australia*, an editor of the *Australian Indigenous Law Reporter* and co-author, with Heather Macrae and Laura Beacroft, of *Indigenous Legal Issues: Commentary and Materials*, 2nd ed, Law Book Company, Sydney, 1977.

Michael O'Flaherty BCL, BPh, STB, MPhil, ASIR has served as Secretary of the UN Committee on the Elimination of Racial Discrimination. He has worked extensively with non-governmental organisations and is a consultant in Human Rights Law and Practice to the Law Society of Ireland. His publications include *The International Covenant on Civil and Political Rights: International Human Rights Law in Ireland* (with Liz Heffernan), Brehon, Dublin, 1995, and *Human Rights and the UN: Practice before the Treaty Bodies*, Sweet and Maxwell, London, 1996.

Sarah Pritchard is an Australian Research Council Postdoctoral Research Fellow in the Faculty of Law at the University of New South Wales, where she teaches courses in Human Rights Law and International and Comparative Indigenous Legal Issues. She is Director of the Australian Human Rights Centre, and is associated with the Diplomacy Training Program and the Indigenous Law Centre. She is an editor of the *Australian Indigenous Law Reporter* and contributor of the sub-title "Aborigines and International Law" to the *Laws of Australia*. She completed a doctoral thesis at the University of Tuebingen on the international legal protection of ethnic minorities, and has worked with Aboriginal organisations at the United Nations since 1986.

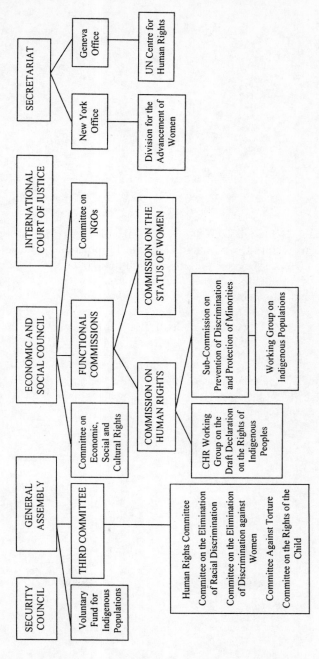

UN Human Rights System and Indigenous Peoples

Part I

Introduction

1

The significance of international law

Sarah Pritchard

Why do advocates for Indigenous rights need to know about international law?

The purpose of this collection is to consider how the UN human rights system might be used to advance the human rights of all people, but especially Indigenous individuals and communities. The focus is on practical outcomes, and some might consider it strange to find a technical discussion of international law. Some might consider it questionable given international law's historical role in legitimising the expansion of colonial empires and the acquisition of title to the territories of Indigenous peoples. At the end of the twentieth century, however, international law is no longer the exclusive domain of European powers with imperial agendas.

As States become increasingly interdependent and struggle to contend with complexities resulting from technological change, cooperative approaches to the solution of problems affecting all members of the inter-national community become more and more compelling. Protectionist sentiments and ethnic and regional antagonisms and loyalties will no doubt continue to challenge the logic of interdependence and cooperation. However, it is clear that globalisation has become a major factor for change in international relations and will continue to generate new issues for the international agenda and a greater capacity to solve them. There is in place today a substantial framework of rules and structures which permeate every aspect of international relations. As the former Australian Minister for Foreign Affairs, Gareth Evans, has noted, without these rules and structures, much of contemporary international intercourse would be inconceivable.[1] There will continue to be rapid growth in cooperative multilateralism and law-making amongst States.

An important dimension of the contemporary development of international legal regimes is the creation of processes which non-State actors can use to secure recognition of their interests. Not only States but other actors such as international organisations, non-self-governing peoples and individuals have been recognised as subjects of rights in international law. Newly independent countries and non-State actors have recognised that international law can be a force for justice and have challenged the international community to develop and implement cooperative strategies to tackle systematically issues not previously thought to require international cooperation. These include peace, overpopulation, hunger, debt and environmental degradation. In recent years, issues surrounding the continuing subjection of Indigenous peoples have been added to this agenda. Indigenous peoples' organisations have been extremely effective in their efforts to secure recognition by the international legal system of the rights which arise from their specific historical and contemporary experiences.

One of the liveliest issues on the internationalist agenda is human rights. In the area of human rights, the rhetoric of concern is being translated into action, both in multilateral forums and in bilateral relations. In recent years, many governments have invested considerable diplomatic resources in the area of human rights. According to the former Australian Minister for Foreign Affairs, for example:

> Australia has always taken its international responsibilities very seriously. . . we have regarded the international instruments to which we adhere as committing us to more than just good intentions. Once we subscribe to an international treaty we abide by its requirements in every detail. We similarly take pains to observe to the full the rules of international customary law.[2]

In a pleasing development, British Foreign Secretary Robin Cook has announced that the British Government will put human rights "at the heart of [British] foreign policy".[3] In a major speech delivered on 17 July 1997, "Human Rights into the Next Century", the Foreign Secretary

---

1   G Evans, *Cooperating for Peace: The Global Agenda for the 1990s and Beyond*, Allen and Unwin, Sydney, 1993, p 41.

2   G Evans and B Grant, *Australia's Foreign Relations in the World of the 1990s*, Melbourne University Press, Melbourne, 1991, p 143.

3   R Cook, Foreign Secretary, London, 12 May 1997.

outlined his vision for putting human rights at the centre of British foreign policy:

> If every country is a member of an international community, then it is reasonable to require every government to abide by the rules of membership. They are set out in the Universal Declaration of Human Rights. . . . These are rights which we claim for ourselves and which we therefore have a right to demand for those who do not yet enjoy them.

Announcing a dozen steps to implement the government's commitment to raise international human rights standards, the Foreign Secretary continued:

> If Britain is to carry credibility when we talk to other governments about their observance of human rights, we must command respect for our own human rights record. . . . A key constitutional commitment of the government is to incorporate the European Convention on Human Rights into British law. And we have launched a review of the UK's position with regard to the Protocols of the UN Covenants and the ILO Conventions to which we have not acceded, as well as the reservations we have recorded when signing other human rights treaties.[4]

Despite such fine and laudable sentiments, it is clear that the value of international human rights regimes will depend ultimately on pressure from well-informed and vigilant non-governmental constituencies. The case of Australia serves to illustrate the deep ambivalence of governments towards their international obligations. These include governments which profess a particular commitment to international human rights regimes. Notwithstanding an affirmation of internationalism in Australia's recent human rights diplomacy, Australia has been, as Justice Michael Kirby has observed, one of the few countries to stand substantially outside the body of human rights jurisprudence which has been developing since the end of the Second World War. In a small number of cases, international statements of human rights have been enacted as part of domestic law. However, even where this has occurred, there are only very weak mechanisms for ensuring compliance with those standards.[5] Australia has no bill of rights around which human rights jurisprudence might have

---

4   Speech by the Foreign Secretary, Mr Robin Cook, Locarno Suite, Foreign and Commonwealth Office, London, 17 July 1997.

5   See generally H Charlesworth, "Australia's Split Personality: Implementation of Human Rights Treaty Obligations in Australia" in P Alston, M Chiam (eds), *Treaty-Making and Australia: Globalisation Versus Sovereignty*, Federation Press, Sydney, 1995, pp 129-140.

developed. Nor is there a regional human rights mechanism which might influence domestic law into conforming with international thinking on human rights issues.[6]

A significant step to redress Australia's detachment from the international discussion of human rights was taken in 1991, with the accession by Australia to the Optional Protocol to the International Covenant on Civil and Political Rights (ICCPR). This development enables the UN Human Rights Committee to receive and examine complaints that Australia has failed to comply with the human rights standards recognised in the ICCPR. Thus, Australian courts are now subject to the scrutiny of an international body armed with a growing body of jurisprudence and supported by the weight of international opinion.[7]

In *Mabo v Queensland (No 2)*, the Australian High Court explicitly endorsed the development of Australian law in conformity with the expectations of the international community. Brennan J, with whom Mason CJ and McHugh J agreed, said:

> Whatever the justification advanced in earlier days for refusing to recognise the rights and interests in land of the indigenous inhabitants of settled colonies, an unjust and discriminatory doctrine of that kind can no longer be accepted. The expectations of the international community accord in this respect with the contemporary values of the Australian people. The opening up of international remedies to individuals pursuant to the Optional Protocol to the International Covenant on Civil and Political Rights brings to bear on the common law the powerful influence of the Covenant and the international standards it imports. The common law does not necessarily conform with international law, but international law is a legitimate and important influence on the development of the common law, especially when international law declares the existence of universal human rights.[8]

The full impact of these developments on Australian law remains to be seen. At the very least, courts will increasingly bring Australian law into conformity with internationally mandated standards in the interpretation of legislation and the development of common law. In the *Teoh* decision of 7 April 1995, the High Court again took the lead where the government had failed to ensure domestic implementation of Australia's

---

6   M Kirby, "Implications of the Internationalisation of Human Rights Law" in P Alston (ed), *Towards an Australian Bill of Rights*, Centre for International and Public Law/Human Rights and Equal Opportunity Commission (HREOC), Canberra, 1994, pp 267, 268.

7   Ibid, p 296.

8   *Mabo v Queensland (No 2)* (1992) 175 CLR 1.

international human rights obligations. The issue was whether ratification of the Convention on the Rights of the Child creates a legitimate expectation that government agencies will take its principles into account in making decisions affecting children. The Court held that ratification of a human rights treaty in itself, even in the absence of legislation incorporating its provisions into domestic law, creates a legitimate expectation that the Commonwealth Government will act in accordance with the treaty. In a joint judgment, Mason CJ and Deane J said:

> [R]atification by Australia of an international convention is not to be dismissed as a merely platitudinous or ineffectual act, particularly when the instrument evidences international accepted standards to be applied ... in dealing with basic human rights affecting the family and children. Rather, ratification of a convention is a positive statement by the executive government of this country to the world and to the Australian peoples that the executive government and its agencies will act in accordance with the Convention.[9]

In a statement on 10 May 1995, the then Attorney-General and the Minister for Foreign Affairs announced the intention of the former government to enact legislation to override the *Teoh* decision:

> We state on behalf of the Government, that entering into an international treaty is not reason for raising an expectation that government decision-makers will act in accordance with the treaty if the relevant provisions of the treaty have not been enacted into domestic Australian law. It is not legitimate, for the purpose of applying Australian law, to expect that the provisions of a treaty not incorporated by legislation should be applied by decision-makers. Any expectation that may arise does not provide a ground for review of a decision. This is so, both for existing treaties and for future treaties that Australia may join.[10]

This response was designed to impede the ability of courts and decision-makers to take into account international human rights jurisprudence. As Hilary Charlesworth noted at the time, Australia had not only failed to fulfil its international obligations under the Convention on the Rights of the Child, but also intended to prevent the judiciary from deriving domestic significance from our international actions.[11] Australia's brashly asserted international commitment to human rights crumbled at the suggestion of domestic political discomfort.

---

9 *Minister for Immigration and Ethnic Affairs v Teoh* (1995) 183 CLR 273.

10 "International Treaties and the High Court's Decision in Teoh", Joint Statement by the Minister for Foreign Affairs, Senator Gareth Evans, and the Attorney-General, Michael Lavarch, 10 May 1995.

11 Charlesworth, note 5, at 140.

The former government's response to *Teoh* created an anomalous situation. In order to place itself amongst good international company and appear a fearless advocate of human rights, it was prepared to accept individual complaint mechanisms under international human rights treaties. Domestically, however, it actively sought to prevent Australian courts from importing the growing body of human rights jurisprudence into domestic law. One likely consequence of such an approach will be that Australians, deprived of protection of their human rights at the domestic level, will have little choice but to seek relief in international bodies.[12]

Action by the Australian Government to defeat any expectation that domestic decision-makers will act consistently with international standards reveals the profoundly equivocal attitude of domestic law-makers to international human rights regimes. International human rights standards have profound implications for many of the issues with respect to which non-governmental actors are seeking justice. For NGOs generally, and Indigenous peoples in particular, the human rights system has become an increasingly important arena for reminding governments of their internationally mandated obligations. A basic knowledge of international law is necessary in the armoury of those concerned to secure recognition and protection of the rights of Indigenous peoples everywhere.

What is international law?

International law, or the Law of Nations, is the body of rules and principles binding upon States in their relations with one another at the international level. According to this definition, the State is of primary importance as the main actor or "subject" of international law.

In the development of international law, great importance has been attached to the consent of States. The concept of consent finds frequent application: obligations arising from agreements and from customary rules depend on consent; the jurisdiction of international tribunals requires consent; membership in international organisations is not

---

12 In a joint statement on 25 February 1997, the Minister for Foreign Affairs and the Attorney-General and Minister for Justice indicated on behalf of the current Coalition Government that contrary to the decision in *Teoh*, "the executive act of entering into a treaty does not give rise to legitimate expectations in administrative law" ("The Effect of Treaties in Administrative Decision-Making", Joint Statement by the Minister for Foriegn Affairs and the Attorney-General and Minister for Justice, 25 February 1997).

compulsory; and the powers of organs of international organisations to make and enforce decisions depend on the consent of member States.

The international legal system is not like the domestic legal systems of States. There is no supreme law-making authority (legislature or parliament) which, on a continuous or regular basis, makes laws binding on States. Treaties are concluded on an ad hoc basis. They must be signed and ratified by each State party. They do not create obligations binding on those States which do not consent to them. Generally speaking, resolutions and declarations of the General Assembly are without binding force.

In general, the international judiciary is without compulsory jurisdiction. States may voluntarily accept the jurisdiction of the International Court of Justice. Many treaties also provide for the resolution of disputes by arbitration.

Finally, there is no real executive power for the enforcement of international legal rights. There is no standing international police force, although in some circumstances the Security Council has particular powers.

Some important doctrines of international law

Sovereignty

A consequence of the view that international law is based on the consent of States is the doctrine of sovereignty. According to this doctrine, States exercise supreme political authority within their territories and in relation to their citizens. There is no power which can impose itself upon a State. Related to the notion of the sovereignty of States is the duty on the part of States to refrain from intervention in the internal affairs of other States. Matters within the internal competence of States are said to be within their reserved domain or domestic jurisdiction. Article 2(7) of the Charter of the UN states the duty of non-intervention in "matters which are essentially within the domestic jurisdiction of any State".

Through increasing membership in international organisations, conclusion of treaties and development of rules of customary law, there has been a reduction of matters within the domestic jurisdiction of States. Traditionally, for example, a State's treatment of its citizens was considered to be a matter within the domestic jurisdiction of that State and not regulated by international law. As a result of developments in international law in connection with the protection of individuals, the domestic jurisdiction reservation does not apply to questions concerning the promotion and protection of human rights. Articles 55 and 56 of the UN Charter affirm that human rights are a legitimate issue for consideration at the international level. More recently, the World Conference on Human Rights, held in Vienna in June 1993, asserted that "the promotion and protection of all human rights is a legitimate concern of the international community".[13]

Equality of States

Related to the notion of sovereignty is the doctrine of equality of States. According to this doctrine, all States are equal, regardless of size, population and resources. When a matter arises to be settled by vote, for example in the UN General Assembly, each State has a right to vote and all votes have the same weight. The doctrine of equality of States is not always applied in practice. Thus, permanent membership of the UN Security Council is presently restricted to five States.

Territorial integrity

Also connected with rules concerning the sovereignty and equality of States is the principle of the territorial integrity of States. This principle has two aspects. The first aspect is concerned with threats to the territorial integrity of States which arise in the course of their relations with other States. Article 2(4) of the UN Charter calls upon States to refrain in their international relations from the threat of use of force against the territorial integrity of any State.

The second aspect of the principle of territorial integrity is concerned with threats to the territorial integrity of States which arise from movements of identifiable groups for national independence. Relevant to this aspect is the doctrine of *uti possidetis*. In the practice of African States, in particular, the doctrine of *uti possidetis* has been invoked to insist that the frontiers of colonial administrative divisions be maintained as the boundaries of newly independent successor States. In Africa, adherence to borders inherited from colonisation has been largely motivated by a concern to promote the stability of new States and to advance processes of national consolidation.

---

13 See the *Vienna Declaration and Programme of Action*, adopted by the World Conference on Human Rights, Vienna, 25 June 1993, para 4.

The principle of self-determination is also relevant to the independence aspirations of groups within "post-colonial" States. In its "Friendly Relations Declaration" of 1970,[14] the UN General Assembly sought to clarify the relationship between this aspect of the principle of territorial integrity and the principle of self-determination of peoples. The Friendly Relations Declaration states that it shall not be understood to support any action which would impair the territorial integrity of any States:

> conducting themselves in accordance with the principles of equal rights and self-determination of peoples ... and thus possessed of a government representing the whole people belonging to the territory without distinction as to race, creed or colour.[15]

What is a State?

Article 1 of the Montevideo Convention on the Rights and Duties of States (1933) provides that a State in international law should possess the following characteristics:

1. a permanent population;
2. a defined territory;
3. a government;
4. the capacity to enter into relations with other States.

As a practical matter, a newly emerging State must also gain the formal recognition of other States.

Subjects of international law

Subjects of international law are those entities capable of possessing international rights and duties and with the capacity to maintain those rights by bringing international claims. Such entities are also referred to as international legal persons and are said to possess international legal personality. Subjects of international law are not identical in their purposes and functions, nor in the extent of their rights and duties.

---

14 *Declaration on Principles of International Law Concerning Friendly Relations and Co-operation among States in Accordance with the Charter of the United Nations*, adopted without a vote by the General Assembly on 24 October 1970 (General Assembly Resolution 2625 (XXV)).

15 See also para 3 of the *Vienna Declaration and Programme of Action*, adopted by the World Conference on Human Rights, Vienna, 25 June 1993.

States are considered the primary subject of international law. International organisations are also recognised as capable, under certain conditions, of enjoying the status of subjects of international law. The most important international legal person of this type is the UN. States and international organisations represent the normal types of legal persons on the international plane. However, the complexities of international relations make it increasingly difficult to restrict international personality to "normal types". A growing number of entities possess personality for particular purposes. It is widely accepted, for example, that the populations of "non-self-governing territories" within the meaning of Chapter XI of the UN Charter[16] have legal personality of a special type.

Separate legal personality is distinct from protected status. In some cases, minorities within States may be guaranteed particular standards of treatment under an international agreement. It does not follow that groups so protected possess legal personality, especially where they are without procedural rights before an international forum. The boundary between protected status, with no separate personality, and a special status with a limited legal capacity, is not easily drawn.

Traditionally, individuals were not considered capable of enjoying rights and duties at international law independent of the will of sovereign States. As a result of the development of law of human rights, individuals have also been recognised, within a limited sphere, as subjects of international law.

Sources of international law

Unlike in national legal systems, there is no supreme law-making authority on the international plane. However, sources of international law do exist, even though they are less obvious than sources of national

---

16 Chapter XI is entitled "Declaration Regarding Non-Self-Governing Territories". In Article 73 members of the UN: "recognise the principle that the interests of these inhabitants are paramount, and accept as a sacred trust the obligation to promote to the utmost, . . . the well-being of the inhabitants of these territories, and, to this end . . . to develop self-government". The ill-defined obligation in Article 73, together with Resolutions 1514 and 1541, adopted by the General Assembly in 1960, provide the basis upon which many formerly colonised peoples in Africa, Asia and the Pacific have attained independence.

law. Article 38 of the Statute of the International Court of Justice enumerates the main sources of international law. In deciding international disputes submitted to it, Article 38 directs the International Court of Justice to apply:

1. international conventions (or treaties), whether general or particular, establishing rules expressly recognised by States;
2. international custom, as evidence of a general practice accepted as law;
3. the general principles of law recognised by civilised nations; and
4. judicial decisions and the teachings of the most highly qualified publicists of the various nations, as subsidiary means for the determination of the rules of law.

Treaties as a source of law

In the area of human rights, express agreements constitute the most significant source of international law. Various terms are used to describe such agreements. These include treaties, conventions, covenants, instruments, pacts and protocols. A treaty is defined by the Vienna Convention on the Law of Treaties (1969) as:

> an international agreement concluded between States in written form and governed by international law, whether embodied in a single instrument or in two or more related instruments and whatever its particular designation.[17]

The law of treaties concerns the incidents of obligations resulting from express agreements. The basis principle of treaty law is reflected in the maxim *pacta sunt servanda*; that is, agreements are binding upon the parties to them and must be performed by them in good faith.

States can become parties to treaties with one other State (bilateral) or treaties involving more than two States (multilateral). Australia is a party to over 1300 treaties, 900 of which are bilateral, and the remainder multilateral.[18]

In concluding a multilateral treaty, the following procedures are generally observed:

---

17 Article 2.
18 See Department of Foreign Affairs and Trade, *Human Rights Manual*, AGPS, Canberra, 1993, p 26.

Adoption

The outcome of negotiations is generally the adoption of the text of the treaty in an international forum. Upon adoption, the treaty becomes "open for signature".

Signature

By signing a treaty, a State indicates its intention to become a "party" to the treaty. Whilst signature often constitutes the first step in becoming a party, it does not establish consent to be bound by the terms of the treaty.

Ratification/accession

Ratification and accession are the formal acts by which States establish, on the international plane, their intent to be bound by a treaty. These acts generally occur once necessary domestic legislative or executive action has been completed. In Australia, treaties can only be entered into with the approval of the Federal Executive Council, that is by action of the Governor General in Council. In theory, at least, there is no need for parliamentary approval before Australia becomes bound by an international treaty.

Once adopted, the treaty remains open for signature for a specified period of time. This period of time generally allows for ratification by the number of States stipulated as necessary for the treaty's "entry into force". Ratification is completed by a formal exchange or deposit of the instrument of ratification with the Secretary-General of the UN in New York.

Accession is the process by which a State becomes party to a treaty it did not sign. Accession may occur before or after a treaty has entered into force.

Customary international law

Express agreements are not the only source of international law. In the area of human rights, international custom can constitute a significant source of law. Customary international law is associated with the concept of "State practice". This is the notion that binding rules of international law can be discerned in the ways States habitually behave with one another. The elements of custom are:

1. uniform and consistent State practice over time; and
2. the belief that such practice is obligatory (*opinio juris*).

13

In determining whether an alleged rule has gained the status of customary international law, it is necessary to consider whether there is sufficient evidence of both State practice and the subjective acceptance of an obligation so to act (opinio juris). Evidence of custom can be found in, amongst other places, bilateral treaties, voting patterns on resolutions, ongoing references to particular resolutions of the UN General Assembly, the conclusions of international conferences and drafts adopted by the International Law Commission.

Rules of customary international law have similarities with Aboriginal customary law. In very general terms it is said that Aboriginal customary law is the body of rules, values and traditions accepted in traditional Aboriginal societies as establishing standards and procedures to be followed and upheld.[19]

Human rights norms may acquire the status of customary law and become binding on States, even where a State is not party to a particular treaty, or where a rule is found in documents which are not treaties. For example, the Universal Declaration of Human Rights, adopted by the UN General Assembly in 1948, is not a legally binding treaty. However, it establishes an internationally recognised catalogue of human rights standards that are binding on States irrespective of their membership in treaty regimes. Similarly, Resolution 1514,[20] adopted by the UN General Assembly in 1960, is cited in support of the view that self-determination has become a binding rule of international law. This resolution provided the legal basis for the process of decolonisation.

Related to the concept of customary international law is that of *ius cogens*. Rules of *ius cogens* are also referred to as "peremptory" norms of general international law. These are rules of customary law so fundamental that they cannot be departed from or set aside by treaty. They can be modified only by a subsequent norm of general international law having the same character.[21] Commonly asserted examples of *ius*

---

19 See K Maddock, "Aboriginal Customary Law" in P Hanks and B Keon-Cohen (eds), *Aborigines and the Law: Essays in Memory of Elisabeth Eggleston*, George Allen and Unwin, Sydney, 1984, p 212 at pp 230-232; see also P Hennessy, "Aboriginal Customary Law" in *The Laws of Australia*, Law Book Co, Sydney, 1995, Subtitle 1.2, at [1].

20 Resolution 1514 (XV), Declaration on the Granting of Independence to Colonial Countries and Peoples, adopted by the General Assembly on 14 December 1960.

21 Vienna Convention on the Law of Treaties 1969, Article 53.

cogens include the prohibitions of slavery, genocide, racial discrimination and the use of force by States, as well as the principle of self-determination.

Enforcement of international law

Settlement of inter-State disputes

In the period since the establishment of the UN, the use of force by individual States has become unlawful as a means of settling disputes. Members of the UN are enjoined to seek a peaceful settlement of inter-State disputes, in accordance with Chapter 6 of the UN Charter. Article 33 of the Charter lists various mechanisms for the peaceful settlement of disputes, including negotiation, inquiry, mediation, conciliation, arbitration and judicial settlement. Exceptionally, in situations posing a threat to international peace and security or constituting aggression, the UN Security Council is empowered to authorise enforcement action in accordance with Chapter 7 of the UN Charter.

The most important means of "judicial settlement" is resort to the International Court of Justice (ICJ), sometimes referred to as the "World Court". This avenue is open only to States. According to Article 34 of the Statute of the International Court of Justice, only States can be parties in cases before the ICJ. Unlike domestic courts, the jurisdiction of which is compulsory, the ability of the ICJ to hear a case depends upon States consenting to submit to its jurisdiction, either by referring a particular case to the ICJ, by entering into a treaty which provides for referral of disputes to the ICJ,[22] or by expressly recognising the ICJ compulsory jurisdiction, which only applies to particular categories of disputes.[23]

The ICJ may also provide an advisory opinion on a legal question, when requested by the General Assembly or the Security Council. With the authorisation of the General Assembly, other organs of the UN and its specialised agencies may also request advisory opinions. The court's advisory jurisdiction is intended to assist the political organs of the UN (that is, the General Assembly and the Security Council) in facilitating

---

22 Statute of the International Court of Justice, Article 36(1).

23 Statute of the International Court of Justice, Article 36(2). See further Department of Foreign Affairs and Trade, *Human Rights Manual*, AGPS, Canberra, 1993, pp 34-36.

the settlement of disputes and to provide guidance on problems of law arising within the scope of the activities of organs and specialised agencies.

Protection of human rights

Individuals and groups are without "standing" to bring a case before the ICJ. In the area of human rights, specific procedures have been developed to secure the protection and promotion of international human rights standards. These procedures — UN Charter-based and treaty-based — are the subject of the contributions to the present collection.

How international law becomes domestic law

Each State has its own constitutional procedures for giving effect to international obligations in the domestic sphere.

Treaties

In some countries, treaties form part of the law of the land as soon as they are entered into. In counties such as Australia, the executive may enter into a treaty, but the treaty does not create rights in domestic law until parliament has passed "enabling" legislation. The requirement for legislation is known as the requirement for an "act of transformation". However, even in the absence of legislation, international law, including treaty law, is a legitimate and powerful influence on the development of the common law.[24]

In federal systems, the requirement of transformation can create particular difficulties. Implementation of the provisions of international treaties sometimes necessitates the enactment or amendment of laws in areas traditionally within the constitutional competence of the States and Territories. Section 51(xxix) of the Constitution of Australia vests in the Commonwealth an "external affairs" power. This has been interpreted by the High Court to include the power to conclude treaties on behalf of Australia and to legislate as appropriate in implementation of such obligations.[25]

---

24 *Mabo v Queensland (No 2)* (1992) 183 CLR 1.

25 *Koowarta v Bjelke-Petersen* (1982) 153 CLR 168; *Commonwealth v Tasmania (Tasmanian Dam* case) 158 CLR 1.

Before proceeding to accession or ratification, the Australian Government generally engages in consultations with the States to ensure the existence of a legislative framework which conforms with international obligations. However, domestic conflicts arising from Federal/ State relations cannot be invoked as an excuse for failure to implement obligations arising under international treaties. According to Article 27 of the Vienna Convention on the Law of Treaties 1969, a State cannot plead provisions of its own law, or deficiencies in that law, in answer to a claim against it for a breach of its obligations under international law.

Customary international law

In contrast to treaties, rules of customary law are considered to be part of the law of the land and therefore binding even in the absence of an act of transformation.[26] This principle is subject to the qualification that customary rules are incorporated only in so far as they are not inconsistent with an Act of parliament or a prior decision of a court of final authority.[27]

---

26 *Polites v Commonwealth* (1945) 70 CLR 60; *Chow Hung Ching v R* (1948) 77 CLR 449.

27 *Wright v Cantrell* (1943) 44 SR (NSW) 45; *Polites v Commonwealth* (1945) 70 CLR 60.

2

Linking international standards with contemporary concerns of Aboriginal and Torres Strait Islander peoples

Mick Dodson

Before we move headlong into the technicalities of international law, I would like to bring right to the forefront of our minds the ultimate meaning of human rights. Not the laws and provisions and mechanisms. Not even the statistics of death, disease and inequality. But the runny eyes, the angry, frustrated faces, the lost knowledge, the desecrated land and the hopelessness.

This is the bottom line – one you all know: our peoples are facing such dire problems that our very survival is seriously under threat.

Two – you also know: the promises that Australian governments have for two hundred years shown consistent reluctance and apparent inability to fully respect and uphold our rights.

This failure becomes even more offensive when one considers how Australia postures on the international stage as a great champion of human rights. Since the inception of the UN, Australian diplomats and politicians have played key roles in developing human rights standards and mechanisms, and have strongly advocated the importance of all governments respecting human rights. The double standards are glaringly obvious, and frankly I'm tired of regaling governments for their domestic failures. Now is the time for us to take their words and commitments at face value and insist that they are translated into realities that we can live and not just hear about.

Three: it makes absolute sense for us to take our grievances beyond this country to a higher authority. My first session at the UN Working Group on Indigenous Populations was a moment of tremendous insight and recognition. I was sitting in a room, 12,000 miles away from home, but if I'd closed my eyes I could just about have been in Maningrida or Doomadgee or Flinders Island. The people wore different clothes, spoke in different languages or with different accents, and their homes had different names. But the stories and the sufferings were the same. We were all part of a world community of Indigenous peoples spanning the planet; experiencing the same problems and struggling against the same alienation, marginalisation and sense of powerlessness. We had gathered there united by our shared frustration with the dominant systems in our own countries and their consistent failure to deliver justice. We were all looking for, and demanding, justice from a higher authority. That famous phrase at the beginning of the UN Charter, "We the people of the United Nations", started to take form for me. I recognised that the people back home were part of the peoples of the world who are the subjects of universal human rights.

As members of the world's peoples, we are the subjects of international law. We are entitled to be the full and equal beneficiaries of that law and make claims over our rights. That holds true whether we live in New York or Bolivia or Murray Bridge. Moreover, when Australia joined the UN and ratified the relevant instruments it explicitly accepted that this is the case. Unfortunately this fact seems to upset some of the more reactionary sectors of Australian society which insist that our appeals to international protection of our human rights threaten Australia's sovereignty. The strange thing is, these very same people are desperate to keep up with the latest international developments in technology, television and takeaway. It strikes me as a strangely convenient irony that these all too keen internationalists suddenly discover their national pride when it comes to the abuse of human rights. But their arguments are as feeble as their morality and thinly hide the real sentiment behind their resistance. That is: "No one tells us how to run our country. And if we want to bash our poofters and vilify our coons, that's our sovereign right." Both the sentiment and its manifestations must be firmly rejected. "Sovereign right" does not mean, and must never be permitted to mean, an unfettered licence to abuse or neglect the rights of minorities or the marginalised.

Despite its aspirations to the latest and the best, when it comes to human rights scrutiny, this country takes full advantage of its geographic isolation. It hides away at the bottom of the South Pacific convinced and insisting that Indigenous affairs are an entirely domestic matter and no one else's business. We are not convinced. And nor is the international human rights regime. Now we must make it our work to ensure that Australia's human rights business is the world's business. Our governments may be desperate for Australian products to export and to lower the budget deficit. However, the ugly truth about this country's underbelly is one thing that they are not so keen to export – and if we hit the market in the right way, they might actually start trying to stop manufacturing human rights abuses.

This project of fully utilising the international human rights system is hampered by several myths about international law and the jurisdiction of the UN. I would like to take this opportunity to dispel the most harmful of those myths.

Myth number one: the UN imposes alien and foreign laws on Australians.

Fact: the only international instruments to which any Australian can appeal are those which Australia has formally agreed to uphold. The only provisions of international instruments which have any bearing in Australia are those which Australia has said will be matched by Australian law and practice. Before complaints can be taken to the UN, Australia has ample opportunity to meet its commitments to ensure that domestic laws and policies are adequate to the standards set in international instruments to which it is a party. In all instances complaints can only be taken where domestic laws and practices fall short of such standards and all domestic remedies have failed. In other words, where Australia has failed to meet its own commitments. There is no question of appealing to some particularly radical standards beyond those already deemed acceptable by the Australian Government. This is not a matter of calling in some strange and alien body.

Myth number two: international law is the panacea to all our problems.

Hopeful, but one to be quickly dispelled. One need look no further than to the limited powers which the international community actually has to enforce its findings. Or look to who it is that makes up the UN: it is nation States. And that means that its operations are, in the main, guided by the interests of nation States and their interpretation of correct and proper action or intervention. It takes little imagination to realise that few States are going to initiate criticisms of other States which may well be reflected back at their own practices. There is no better or more tragic illustration of these limitations than the UN's 50-year failure to adequately address the specific concerns of the world's Indigenous peoples or the violation of our rights. If there exists a magic wand which could be waved over domestic governments to cure all evils and make them good, it is certainly not international law. Or at least not yet. That is why NGOs have to keep on pushing and agitating through their governments, and directly through international fora, and insist that the body of international law does what it set out to do: protect and promote the rights of all peoples. The Working Group on Indigenous Populations, and the Draft Declaration on the Rights of Indigenous Peoples, are two of the key avenues to pursue this course. In addition, we have to get a lot wiser about accessing the spectrum of the international system, whether they be the treaty bodies, the World Bank, General Agreement on Tariffs and Trade, or the Security Council.

The third myth is the other side of the coin to the second. It is that international human rights law is variously: a fancy waste of time; incomprehensible gibberish designed by international lawyers and bureaucrats to fill up resolutions; good for a dinner speech, and a nod and a wink if you're a foreign minister; and good for a junket to Geneva if you're an Indigenous person.

Well, the fact is that with all its many imperfections, international law is the most highly developed body of human rights law that exists. Or perhaps more accurately, the most highly developed body which is recognised by the Australian State. Fifty years ago the nations of the world decided to try to create a system which would safeguard future generations from the scourge of war which they had known. And since then countless people have turned their minds and hearts to developing that system with the hope that it would free the world not only from war and genocide, but from the gamut of systematic human rights violations. You could say it's an ambitious plan. Nevertheless, we already have some proof of the positive influence which international law can have on the way in which Australia conducts its domestic affairs.

Just scan some of the "better moments" in Australian law — I refrain from saying the great moments, because I do not actually believe that from our point of view there have been any. That aside, the *Racial Discrimination Act* 1975 (Cth), the *Land Rights (Northern Territory) Act* 1976 (Cth), the High Court's 1992 decision on native title — all of them were firmly grounded in, if not derived from, international law. This is all about strategy, and using every tool available to do what every Indigenous Australian knows has to be done. To get our kids well and educated and housed; to get our young adults out of detention centres and our men and women out of lock-ups and prisons; to get us off the front pages as sensationalist news and into our own lives and living healthy cultures.

So let's get pragmatic. The system of international law is not perfect — far from it. But while we agitate for improvement we're fools if we don't get on with the business of making maximum use of what are some potentially very powerful tools. And the first step towards that is to know them, understand them, and link them to what is most close to home.

Which is what I'd like to do now. I'd like to indicate a few points where peoples' grievances might be picked up in the provisions of international instruments.

You may be an Aboriginal woman. As a woman at some time you might expect a baby. As an Aboriginal woman, you might expect that your baby will be three times more likely to die than the baby of any other Australian woman. You may be an Aboriginal man. You can plan on living 20 years less than other Australian men. You may be one of the 20 percent of Aboriginal children in the Northern Territory who is malnourished.[1] Or if you are a four-month-old Torres Strait Islander baby, you will by now have begun to suffer hearing impediments. I could continue by detailing the statistics on diabetes, heart disease, suicide, kidney failure or alcohol-related death. If you are, or know any one of these people, you might want to have a look at one of the following.

Start with the most fundamental human right. The right to life. Because what we are talking about are unambiguous violations of that right. Article 6 of the International Covenant on Civil and Political Rights (ICCPR) states that "every human being has the inherent right to life". Where an individual believes their rights under the ICCPR have been violated and the government of the country in which they live has failed to address the violation, they can lodge a complaint to the UN Human Rights Committee (HRC) under the First Optional Protocol to the ICCPR.

After 25 years of reports observing the same, if not worsening, conditions, parroting the same recommendations, and receiving the same shocked reaction and promises, we have given "exhausting domestic remedies" a new meaning. If the diseases don't kill us then trying to get some action most likely will. In its comment on the meaning of Article 6, the HRC has made it clear that the right to life is not limited in its meaning to arbitrary killing, but places an obligation on the State to establish conditions consistent with respect for the right to life. I would

---

1   Findings based on a study of infants under two by paediatricians Dr Alan Ruben and Dr Alan Walker of the Royal Darwin Hospital and cited in "AMA demands action over black children famine" *Australian*, 18 April 1994.

say that the 20,000 or more Aboriginal people who live in communities with totally inadequate or contaminated water supplies do not enjoy such conditions.

The International Covenant on Economic, Social and Cultural Rights (ICESCR) provides that everyone has the right "to the enjoyment of the highest attainable standard of physical and mental health".[2] In fact, the section dealing with health could have been written for the very problems I am talking about. It provides that States must take steps to reduce the stillbirth and infant mortality rate, and ensure the healthy development of the child; they must take steps to improve environmental health, to prevent, treat and control endemic and epidemic disease, and to ensure that medical services are available to the sick.

Although the ICESCR does not have a mechanism for individual complaints, the Australian Government is required to provide reports on its implementation every five years. The Committee on Economics, Social and Cultural Rights, under the leadership of a distinguished Australian human rights activist and scholar, Professor Alston, has made it perfectly clear to States that sweeping statements will not be an acceptable form of reporting, and has developed rigorous reporting guidelines. Current standards should be compared with previous indicators, information should be provided on specifics such as infant mortality, access to safe water and life expectancy. And perhaps most importantly from our point of view, States should report "if there are any groups in your country whose health situation is significantly worse than the majority population".[3]

Although technically it is only governments who are required to report, NGOs can provide information to the Committee on Economic, Social and Cultural Rights concerning alleged violations, and the Committee can then ask suitably probing and embarrassing questions of the government. Professor Alston has been extremely progressive in developing mechanisms and procedures to ensure that the views of NGOs can be given voice during the examination of country reports. I am sure the Committee would not be averse to receiving information from some

---

2   Article 12.

3   Alston, P, "The International Covenant on Economic, Social and Cultural Rights" in UN Centre for Human Rights and UN Institute for Training and Research, *Manual on Human Rights Reporting under Six Major International Human Rights Instruments United Nations*, New York, 1991, p 43.

of you on matters omitted by the Australian Government in its upcoming official report on the implementation of the ICESCR.

The Convention on the Rights of the Child (CROC), also ratified by Australia, is similarly explicit about health, spelling out children's rights to the highest attainable standards of health and to facilities for the treatment of illness. It specifically mentions infant and child mortality, primary health care, adequate nutrition and clean drinking water, pre- and post-natal health care, health education and preventative health.[4] Again there is no mechanism for individuals to take specific complaints to the CROC Committee, but as with the ICESCR, they can provide information to the CROC Committee which can be raised in response to the Australian Government's five-yearly obligatory reports. The CROC Committee can recommend to the General Assembly that the Secretary-General be requested to undertake specific studies on issues concerning CROC.[5] I would suggest that the Australian Government might be less than pleased if the next visit by the Secretary-General was for the purpose of scrutinising the welfare of our communities, rather than to open conferences.

Staying with health, the glaring disparities between Indigenous and non-Indigenous health are obvious grounds for complaint under the Convention on the Elimination of All Forms of Racial Discrimination (CERD), also ratified by Australia. Article 2 lays down the general prohibition on racial discrimination, and Article 5 explicitly requires that States parties guarantee the right to public health and medical care without discrimination.[6] In late 1992 Australian accepted the competence of the CERD Committee to receive complaints from individuals or groups of individuals claiming violations of CERD.

Another obvious area where the human rights of Indigenous Australians are being abused is in the criminal justice system. And here I include not only deaths in custody, but our appalling over-representation in the prison population, and prison conditions. Again start with the right to life and Article 6 of the ICCPR. Recalling the HRC's comments on the meaning of this article, one would be hard pressed to prove that the conditions in which many of our people are incarcerated meet the criterion of being "consistent with respect for" the right to life. Placing a

---

4   Article 24.

5   Article 45(c).

6   Article 5(c)(iv).

human being in conditions which are likely to induce suicide, and the flagrant disregard for this eventuation may well breach Article 6.[7]

The obscene number of Indigenous people in prisons are no strangers to solitary confinement, forcible separation from family, community and country, with no opportunity for communication, squalid conditions, refusal of medical care, and humiliating treatment. All may be grounds for complaint to the HRC under Articles 7 and 10 of the ICCPR, which respectively provide that:

> No one shall be subjected to torture or cruel, inhuman or degrading treatment or punishment.

> All persons deprived of their liberty shall be treated with dignity and humanity and with respect for the inherent dignity of the human person.

I hardly think that having prison officers dangle pairs of socks in front of you with suggestions that you could become the next death in custody qualifies as treatment with dignity and humanity. And while I'm at it, I do not think that being kept stewing for three days in the back of a paddy wagon doing the tour of remote communities in north Western Australia en route to a trial judge meets the requirements of either Article 10, or Article 9, which requires that persons charged be promptly brought before a qualified judge.

In order to elaborate the precise meaning of these articles, the HRC takes guidance from the "UN Standard Minimum Rules for Prisoners". We could do a quick check on whether those rules are being applied to the hundreds of Indigenous people serving time in lockups in remote communities right now. Is the watch-house in Mornington Island a healthy, well-ventilated and well-lit cell with adequate space as in Rule 10? Is the kid in Murray Bridge who was locked up and refused his asthma medicine receiving adequate medical care as in Rule 24? Is shoving a suicidal prisoner in a cell and poking him every two hours the local version of specialist psychiatric service as in Rule 22?

Perhaps the gravest area of grief for Indigenous people is what is happening to our young people, and their treatment by the juvenile justice system. The gross over-representation of young Aboriginal people in the juvenile corrective institutions is well known to us all. Just to remind you,

---

7   For an extensive discussion on the application of international law to prison issues and deaths in custody see John Hookey, "Aboriginal Deaths in Custody: International Issues", consultant's report to the Royal Commission into Aboriginal Deaths in Custody, Aboriginal Law Centre, University of NSW, 1990.

across Australia it is by a factor of 22.[8] Clearly this raises issues under CERD. The discriminatory response that the juvenile justice system has to our young people raises even more questions. Why are our kids in Western Australia 25 percent of those arrested and 67 percent of those in detention centres?[9] Why are one in three young people referred to children's panels, but only one in eight Aboriginal children? Why are they arrested when their non-Aboriginal counterparts receive summonses? Why are they detained in custody when others are granted bail? Questions you well may wish to put to the CERD Committee when it is considering Article 5, which provides for equality before the law and guarantees equal treatment before courts and tribunals.

If you happen to know one of the 85 percent of young Aboriginal people who report being hit, punched, kicked or hit with a baton, phone book or torch by police, or of the 80 percent of those who reported racist abuse by police,[10] or any of the kids who spend most of their young lives in detention centres away from their family and community with no cultural education, perhaps you had better not tell them that the overarching principle required in the treatment of juveniles is that they must be assured "a meaningful life in the community which will foster a process of personal development and education".[11] And will the kids in boot camps thousands of kilometres from their home receive the "care, protection, and all necessary individual assistance — social, educational, vocational, psychological, medical and physical — that they require in view of their age, sex and personality"?[12] Tell them that Australia promised to uphold these principles when it ratified CROC[13] or that they are the internationally accepted and endorsed standard minimum rules and you're likely to only add to their sense of hopelessness. At least if you tell them that they are also known as "the Beijing Rules" they

---

8   Cunneen, C, and T Liebesman, *Aboriginal People and the Law in Australia*, Butterworths, Sydney, 1995, p 62.

9   Wilkie, M, *Aboriginal Justice Programs in Western Australia*, Crime Research Centre, Nedlands WA, 1991, p 150.

10 Cunneen, C, *A Study of Aboriginal Juveniles and Police Violence, Report Commissioned by the National Inquiry into Racist Violence*, Human Rights Australia, Sydney, November 1990, p 2.

11 United Nations Standard Minimum Rules for the Administration of Juvenile Justice (the Beijing Rules), 1.2.

12 Ibid, 13.5.

13 See in particular Articles 37 and 40.

may get a good laugh. Because that's about how far away those rules might be from their reality.

However, we would do well to remind the Australian Government that it sponsored those rules, and that they were adopted by the UN General Assembly. Better still, you might also think about providing information to the HRC or to the CROC Committee suggesting that Australia is doing less than well in upholding the most basic principles: diversion from custody, institutionalisation as a sanction of last resort, and separation from adults. For starters they might be interested to know that over two-thirds of young Aboriginal people in Western Australia are received into adult prisons despite explicit requirements that juvenile prisoners be separated from adult prisoners.[14] Or that in 1990, 90 percent of Aboriginal boys and 97 percent of Aboriginal girls in Western Australia served their sentences in police lockups.[15]

I doubt that once you have started you'll be scratching around for material, but you might want to include in your communications some information on some less than satisfactory aspects of the law. As you may know, when the Western Australian Parliament introduced the *Crime (Serious and Repeat Offenders) Sentencing Act* in early 1992, the then Human Rights Commissioner demonstrated in graphic terms how the law was in flagrant breach of several articles of the ICCPR and CROC. It was not hard to predict that his words would fall on deaf ears in Western Australia, but they might have been of interest to the HRC. That notorious Act has now lapsed, but it has been replaced by the *Young Offenders Act* 1994. Here again, the Parliament of Western Australia had little problem with pushing through an Act which it had been advised was in breach of Australia's international treaty obligations. Of particular concern are the provisions concerning sentencing of so called serious and repeat offenders. The Act explicitly states that when sentencing these young people, who are overwhelmingly Aboriginal, it should "give primary consideration to the protection of the community ahead of all other principles".[16]

Now I don't want to skip over that. The highest principle spelled out again and again in instruments dealing with young people is that the primary consideration must be the "best interests of the child". That

---

14 Broadhurst, RG, et al, *Crime and Justice Statistics for Western Australia: 1990*, Crime Research Centre, Nedlands WA, 1991, Table 5.3.

15 Ibid, Table 5.7.

16 Section 125.

principle holds in all cases. Always. You could not ask for a more explicit breach of the principle. In addition, in directing courts to diverge from standard principles when sentencing these young people, the Act contravenes both the ICCPR[17] and CROC,[18] which explicitly forbid arbitrary sentencing. Once again, I doubt that this information will be conveyed by the Australian Government in its forthcoming report to the HRC or the CROC Committee.

One very significant area that you might like to look into is the possibility of pressing land rights claims under Article 27 of the ICCPR.

> In those States in which ethnic, religious or linguistic minorities exist, persons belonging to these minorities shall not be denied the right, in community with the other members of their group, to enjoy their own culture, to profess and practice their own religion, or to use their own language.

Although this is a fairly general article, providing that minorities shall enjoy the right to enjoy their own culture, the HRC has indicated that in the case of Indigenous peoples, enjoyment of this right may require positive legal protection of traditional lands.[19] The HRC has made some fairly explicit statements concerning the way in which developments that prevent Indigenous peoples' hunting, fishing or living according to their culture on their traditional lands may be in breach of Article 27.[20]

I hope that I've given you ample food for thought. And I haven't even started to cover the territory. The 20,000 Aboriginal people without adequate water,[21] the 5,000 homeless Indigenous families,[22] the 14,000 Aboriginal people in Western Australian remote communities who live without proper sewerage systems, power sources, or other essential

---

17 Article 9.

18 Article 37(b).

19 General Comment No 23 (50), adopted by the Committee at its 1314th meeting, 6 April 1994.

20 In particular, see *Lansmann v Finland*, Communication No 511/1992, UN Doc CCPR/C/52/D/511/1992 (8 November 1994), where the complainant alleged that quarry developments interfered with traditional hunting rights and so breached Article 27.

21 Figures from Federal Race Discrimination Commissioner, Water; A report on the Provision of Water and Sanitation in Remote Aboriginal and Torres Strait Islander Communities, AGPS, Canberra, 1994, p 12.

22 Jones, RM, *The Housing Needs of Indigenous Australians*, CAPER Research Monograph No 8, 1991.

services.[23] These people, along with the children who don't get pre-school, let alone secondary or higher education, could all find suitable provisions under the ICESCR and CERD.

When I say they could find them, that is largely a hypothetical statement. There are undeniably huge impediments which the average person faces in using the mechanisms of international instruments. The fact that they are there means absolutely nothing if you have no way of understanding them or using them. It is of little use the Australian Government recognising the competence of committees to hear individual complaints if it is going to do nothing about helping individuals become competent to make those complaints. This was recognised by the Royal Commission into Aboriginal Deaths in Custody and, in its official response, the Commonwealth Government committed itself to provide funds for educational programs, two of which are being developed by my office. And I will endeavour to make them effective. However, by no stretch of the imagination are existing funding levels adequate to do the job comprehensively.

I must also comment on an issue of which everyone in this country should be made aware, namely the fact that the Commonwealth used some of this royal commission money to set up an Optional Protocol Unit, not for people whose rights are being violated, but for the government to defend itself. This is a scandal that must be exposed and corrected. I have no objection to the government's defending itself – it has every right to do so. However, money earmarked to protect the rights of the most abused peoples in this country must not be the funding source.

So I close where I began. It's not perfect. It's far from perfect. But I'd suggest that Indigenous Australians could do a lot worse than have a few billion people of the international community on our side.

---

23 Report of the Western Australian Government on Western Australia's 151 most remote communities, reported in the *West Australian*, Editorial, 12 June 1994.

Part II

The UN Charter-based human rights system

3

The UN Charter-based
human rights system: an overview

Garth Nettheim

Introduction

The present chapter is concerned with the UN Charter-based human
rights system, as distinct from the treaty-based system.

A State may avoid treaty obligations by declining to ratify human
rights treaties. The ratification record by States in the Asia-Pacific region
is not impressive. It does not follow that such States are immune from
international critical scrutiny. How can this be, if States are sovereign
entities subject only to such obligations to other States as they voluntarily
accept? The answer lies in the fact that most States are members of the
UN. They became members by ratifying a treaty – the Charter of the UN.

Do they thereby assume obligations in the human rights field under
that Charter? Initially the answer that would have been given on behalf of
most governments was negative. While the UN Charter did speak of
obligations in regard to human rights, such obligations were nowhere
specified. Moreover, Article 2(7) makes it quite clear that the UN may
not intervene in matters within the domestic jurisdiction of a State. The
sole exceptions are in regard to situations within Chapter 7 of the Charter,
that is, where there is a threat to the peace, a breach of the peace, or an
act of aggression.

Yet today it is broadly accepted that a State may be under obligations
in regard to human rights solely by reason of its membership of the UN
and its obligations under the Charter. In fact the practice of the UN
organs generally has evolved so as to read Article 2(7) as not excluding

international discussion or condemnation of conduct by a State with respect to those within its boundaries.

For the most part, however, the UN Charter does not spell out what are human rights and what will amount to violations of those rights. Where then can the specific obligations assumed by States who are members of the UN find definition? There has occurred an evolution in thinking about the Universal Declaration of Human Rights so that, by 1968, it could be argued that a consensus had crystallised that it constituted a part of customary international law. There is an alternative theory upon which the same force can be given to the provisions of the Universal Declaration of Human Rights; that alternative theory is that the Universal Declaration represents an authoritative interpretation of the references to human rights in the UN Charter.

There has also been an evolution of processes within the UN system, and it is these which are significant in case of a State such as Burma which has not accepted obligations under most parts of the treaty-based regime. Under Article 68 of the Charter, the Economic and Social Council (ECOSOC) established a Commission on Human Rights (CHR) comprising some 53 members, all representing States. The CHR is assisted by a Sub-Commission on Prevention of Discrimination and Protection of Minorities which, despite its title, operates across the broad spectrum of human rights concerns. It comprises 26 members who are (supposedly) independent experts and not representatives of governments. In all the work of the Sub-Commission and the CHR, NGOs play a major role. Draft instruments proceed from the CHR via ECOSOC to the General Assembly. The Charter bodies are not solely concerned with standard-setting — designing treaties under which supervision of human rights at State level is entrusted to treaty committees. The Charter bodies have developed a major role in overseeing human rights. The role of these bodies is, as noted, particularly important in relation to States that have not ratified human rights treaties. But they may also be relevant in relation even to States such as Australia which have ratified most of the core human rights treaties.

Methods of work

The Security Council, the International Court of Justice and the Trusteeship Council may all exercise functions which relate to human rights. So may specialised agencies such as the UN High Commissioner for Refugees and the International Labour Organisation. Most of the general human rights work, however, goes through the Charter bodies. At the peak is the General Assembly.

General Assembly

The General Assembly comprises representatives of all member-States and meets in New York between September and December each year. It is at the General Assembly that key human rights treaties are adopted and opened for signature, but the General Assembly adopts resolutions on a whole host of matters. The General Assembly functions through a number of committees. Its Third Committee deals with social, humanitarian and cultural matters. Most of the agenda items come up from ECOSOC. The General Assembly has also established standing subsidiary bodies of its own including the Special Committee on Decolonization and committees to deal with apartheid and Israeli practices in the occupied territories.

The Economic and Social Council (ECOSOC)

ECOSOC comprises 54 representatives of States. As well as receiving its own mandate under the Charter, ECOSOC is authorised by the Charter to set up commissions in human rights and other fields. ECOSOC has established the Commission on the Status of Women and the CHR. ECOSOC receives and considers annual reports from these functional commissions.

The Commission on the Status of Women

The Commission on the Status of Women has been particularly effective in developing international instruments on such matters as nationality and matrimonial rights, as well as the broad-based Convention on the Elimination of All Forms of Discrimination against Women (CEDAW). There is momentum to avoid the "ghettoisation" of women's human rights in the Commission on the Status of Women and CEDAW, and to require all UN bodies to consider gender-specific issues in their work.

The Commission on Human Rights (CHR)

The CHR comprises 53 representatives of States. It meets in Geneva between January and March each year. Since it was set up in 1946 it has evolved from a standard-setting body into one which can also respond to human rights violations and pursue a wide range of measures to handle human rights. The CHR makes studies, prepares recommendations, drafts international instruments, investigates allegations of human rights violations and deals with communications. Only the 53 member-States may vote, but other States, specialised agencies and intergovernmental organisations may participate on invitation. Particularly important is the work of NGOs in consultative status with ECOSOC.

The Sub-Commission on Prevention of Discrimination and Protection of Minorities

The CHR receives particular assistance from the Sub-Commission on Prevention of Discrimination and Protection of Minorities (the Sub-Commission). It is not confined to matters of discrimination and minorities, but has a general human rights mandate. The Sub-Commission consists, not of representatives of States, but of 26 independent experts. It meets in Geneva in August each year and reports to the CHR. Both the CHR and the Sub-Commission use working groups of their members for various purposes.

Communications

The capacity of the system to respond to violations of human rights in particular places has evolved over time. Initially, in the face of Article 2(7) of the Charter, any UN activity in relation to bad human rights situations needed to be predicated on a finding that they constituted threats to inter-national peace and security (for example, South Africa and Rhodesia). However, from the earliest days of the UN, people began writing to the Secretary-General drawing attention to violations of human rights. For years, such letters were effectively ignored on the basis that there was nothing that the UN could do. The Secretariat simply compiled an annual list of complaints received.

In 1959 under ECOSOC Resolution 728F a halting step forward was made. ECOSOC confirmed that the CHR had no power to take any action in regard to complaints concerning human rights, but the Secretary-General was asked to provide to both the CHR and the Sub Commission two lists: a non-confidential list containing a brief indication of the substance of each communication "which deals with the principles involved in the promotion of human rights"; and a confidential list containing a brief indication of the substance of other communications concerning human rights. Members of the CHR and the Sub-Commission were entitled, on request, to consult the originals of communications in the first list. Writers of communications were to receive a response that, apart from this procedure, there was no power to take any action. Member States were to receive copies of communications about them, without divulging the identity of the author. Replies from States might, on request, be circulated to members of the CHR (but not to authors).

In 1967 the UN was ready for a further advance with the adoption of ECOSOC Resolution 1235. This authorised the CHR and the Sub-Commission to examine communications on the lists prepared under Resolution 728F. Even higher hopes were initially held for ECOSOC Resolution 1503, adopted in 1970, which established what has become known as the "confidential procedure". Resolution 1503 authorised establishment of a 5-person Sub-Commission working group to consider "all communications, including replies of Governments thereon, received by the Secretary-General under Resolution 728F". Their purpose was to select out, from the vast number of communications received (350,000 in 1989) those, together with replies of governments, if any, "which appear to reveal a consistent patterns of gross and reliably attested violations of human rights and fundamental freedoms".

There are three levels of qualifier: the violations have to be "reliably attested", they have to be "gross", and they have to form a "consistent pattern". The Sub-Commission has drawn up Rules of Procedure for deciding which communications to accept for examination. Those communications, and replies of governments, if any, which have been so identified by a majority of the working group are then considered, together with "other relevant information", by the Sub-Commission as a whole. The Sub-Commission then decides in closed session whether or not to refer to the CHR "particular situations" (not the communications as such) which appear to reveal a consistent pattern of gross and reliably attested violations.

The CHR in 1974 established its own working group on communications to screen the "situations" referred to the CHR by the Sub-Commission. Governments involved are invited to submit any observations. The working group prepares draft decisions. The CHR as a whole considers these "situations" in closed session attended by the government concerned. The CHR may determine that it requires a "thorough study". It may also decide that it shall be the subject of investigation by an ad hoc committee, but only with the express consent of the State concerned. This has never been done. Instead, if the CHR simply decides to keep a situation under review it may send written questions to the government, or send a CHR member or a staffer to make direct contacts. CHR announces the names of countries which are under consideration.

Only a couple of dozen communications each year are sufficiently detailed to receive serious consideration by the Sub-Commission's working group. The Sub-Commission may refer to the CHR some 8 to 10 "situations" each year. The communications that do best in the process are those that are prepared by lawyers or researchers for NGOs that send representatives to the Sub-Commission to ascertain what is happening and to lobby members (as governments do). The process is slow, complex, secret, and vulnerable to political influence at various stages. It does provide a way of exposing governments to political pressure, but a choice may need to be made as to whether the government in question may respond better to the public procedure involved in Resolution 1235. In many cases, a problem government can be moved out of "confidential procedure" into the "public procedure" – Myanmar (Burma) is a recent example.

Resolution 1235 authorised establishment by the CHR of a regular agenda item: "Question of violation of human rights and fundamental freedoms". The CHR and the Sub-Commission were authorised to examine information relevant to "gross violations" contained in communications. In practice, the resolution has provided the basis in both the CHR and the Sub-Commission for an annual debate on human rights violations around the world. Such debates are not confined to matters brought forward on communications. Both bodies regularly adopt resolutions expressing concern about violations in particular places.

Working groups and special rapporteurs

Under authority of Resolution 1235 there has also been the development of very important special procedures. Before 1975 there were a few such special procedures to maintain critical scrutiny in respect of Southern Africa and Israeli-occupied territories. Since 1975 there have been a number of country mechanisms established, initially for Cuba and then for a succession of other countries. These special procedures may take the form of working groups of the members of the CHR or "special rapporteurs", that is, individual experts.

There was a further evolution in 1980. There was a proposal to appoint a "country rapporteur" for Argentina to look largely at the phenomenon of "disappearances" under the military junta. Argentina strongly resisted the proposal, so the CHR resolved on the establishment of the first "thematic procedure", the Working Group on Enforced or

Involuntary Disappearances. Other thematic procedures have since been established on other significant topics. The following chart lists the CHR thematic procedures as in 1994:

- Enforced disappearances (working group)
- Summary and arbitrary executions (special rapporteur)
- Torture and inhuman treatment (special rapporteur)
- Activities of mercenaries (special rapporteur)
- Religious intolerance (special rapporteur)
- Sale of children (special rapporteur)
- Arbitrary detention (working group)
- Displaced persons (expert)
- Racism, racial discrimination and xenophobia (special rapporteur)
- Right to development (working group)
- Freedom of opinion and expression (special rapporteur)
- Violence against women (special rapporteur)
- Independence of the judiciary (special rapporteur)

The Sub-Commission, too, has established working groups on topics such as slavery, detention and Indigenous populations. As noted, both the CHR and the Sub-Commission have working groups to deal with communications under Resolution 1503.

Working groups, special rapporteurs and experts are also regularly established to develop policy, to carry out studies, and to draft new instruments. A primary agenda item for the Sub-Commission's Working Group on Indigenous Populations (WGIP) was the "evolution of standards" which, to date, has produced the Draft Declaration on the Rights of Indigenous Peoples. In 1995 the CHR established its own open-ended working group to consider that draft and to take matters further. If a declaration emerges from the CHR it will proceed via ECOSOC to the General Assembly's Third Committee.

Participation of NGOs

The WGIP is particularly flexible in allowing NGOs and Indigenous individuals to participate in its work. In bodies higher up in the system only NGOs with consultative status are permitted to participate. Even in the WGIP, NGOs with consultative status have stronger rights and entitlements than others. The only Australian Indigenous NGOs with consultative status with ECOSOC are the Aboriginal and Torres Strait

Islander Commission (ATSIC) and the National Aboriginal and Islander Legal Services Secretariat (NAILSS).

When the CHR resolved to establish its own working group to consider the WGIP's Draft Declaration, Australia made a special effort to ensure that Indigenous peoples would be able to participate. CHR Resolution 1995/32 adopts a midway process. It will not be sufficient for organisations simply to have their representatives turn up on the day. Organisations need to apply in writing for registration. The letter of application should set out the organisation's name, address and contact person, its aim and purposes, its programs and activities, and a description of its membership.

To become an NGO with consultative status with ECOSOC, organisations need to work within ECOSOC Resolution 1296. The process is detailed and applications are considered only every second year. An alternative is to seek access to UN procedure through existing accredited NGOs. There are numbers of non-Indigenous NGOs which may be willing to allow Indigenous peoples' organisations to operate under their umbrella, for example, Survival International, Anti-Slavery Society, Minority Rights Group, and the International Commission of Jurists. Within Australia, ATSIC and NAILSS may be happy to work with others.

To date, Australian Indigenous peoples' organisations have concentrated on the WGIP, which is relatively accessible. A few have targeted the Sub-Commission, which is helpful because the WGIP report and resolutions may need lobbying support at that level. Few have attempted to influence the CHR and that will be difficult, as this is where representatives of governments have greater powers.

Conclusion

The WGIP, and the higher level processes dealing with its work, have been the principal focus in the Charter-based system for Australian Indigenous peoples' organisations. Such organisations may feel little need to range further afield in the Charter-based system when Australia is so fully engaged in the treaty-based system. But it is useful, at least, to know that other mechanisms and procedures exist in the Charter-based system. Indigenous peoples' organisations in the United States (which has not been fully engaged in the treaty-based system) have used Charter-based procedures such as communications under Resolution 1503. Some of the thematic procedures of the CHR are relevant to the concerns of Indigenous peoples. It is very important for organisations developing an international strategy to know what these procedures are and how to use them, and to be able to establish priorities.

4

Working Group on
Indigenous Populations:
mandate, standard-setting activities
and future perspectives

Sarah Pritchard

Establishment of the Working Group on
Indigenous Populations

In contrast to the International Labour Organisation, the UN was slow to undertake action in the field of Indigenous rights. Article 27 of the International Covenant on Civil and Political Rights, adopted by the General Assembly in 1966, contains a regime for the protection of ethnic, religious and linguistic minorities. However, this was not intended to apply to Indigenous peoples.[1]

During the early 1970s, an international Indigenous lobby emerged. The earlier view that Indigenous peoples were to be integrated or assimilated had become unacceptable. The limited relevance of UN activities to the situation of Indigenous peoples could no longer be overlooked. In May 1971 the Economic and Social Council (ECOSOC) authorised the Sub-Commission on Prevention of Discrimination and Protection of Minorities (the Sub-Commission) to make a study of the

---

1   During the debates on Article 27 in the Third Committee of the General Assembly, the Australian delegate stated that Aborigines were "too primitive" to be considered minorities: UN Doc A/C 3/SR 1104 (14 November 1961), para 26.

40

problem of discrimination against Indigenous populations and to suggest measures for eliminating such discrimination.[2] In August 1971 the Sub-Commission appointed José R Martinez Cobo as Rapporteur to carry out such a study.[3] Before the study was completed, the Sub-Commission was authorised to establish a Working Group on Indigenous Populations (WGIP) to review developments pertaining to the human rights of Indigenous populations and to give attention to the evolution of standards concerning the rights of such populations.[4]

In the 1982 resolution authorising the establishment of a working group on Indigenous populations, ECOSOC entrusted the WGIP with two tasks:

1. Review developments pertaining to the promotion and protection of the human rights and fundamental freedoms of indigenous populations;

2. Give special attention to the evolution of standards concerning the rights of such populations.

The WGIP held its first session at Geneva from 9 to 13 August 1982, immediately prior to the 1982 session of the Sub-Commission. It has since met annually for up to two weeks except in 1986, when the financial crisis facing the UN caused the postponement of sessions of the Sub-Commission and its subsidiary bodies.

Composition, location and work methods

The WGIP is composed of five independent experts elected every two years by the Sub-Commission. These five members are also members of the Sub-Commission and represent the five geographic regions of the world. At the WGIP's fourteenth session in 1996, these members were:

- Chairperson Ms Erica-Irene Daes (Greece),
- Mr Miguel Alfonso Martinez (Cuba),
- Mr Volodymyr Boutkevitch (Ukraine),
- Mr Ribot Hatano (Japan),
- Mr El-Hadji Guisse (Senegal).

---

2   ECOSOC Resolution 1589 (L), 21 May 1971, para 7.

3   Sub-Commission Resolution 8 (XXIV) of 18 August 1971. The full report, entitled *The Study of the Problem against Indigenous Populations*, is issued in consolidated form as UN Doc E/CN 4/Sub 2/1986/7 and Add 1 to 3.

4   ECOSOC Resolution 1982/34, 7 May 1982.

The WGIP is located at the lowest level of the UN human rights hierarchy. On the way to the General Assembly, its recommendations must pass through the Sub-Commission, the Commission on Human Rights (CHR) and ECOSOC.

Indigenous peoples and their organisations have been very successful in securing the adoption of flexible methods of work in the WGIP. At its first session in 1982, rules of procedure were adopted which allow all interested persons to address the WGIP and permit the submission of information from any source. A UN seminar in January 1989 witnessed the equal participation of Indigenous peoples and nominees of States, as well as the election of an Indigenous participant as Rapporteur.[5] Indigenous representatives Ms Rigoberta Menchu Tum and Mr Mick Dodson were elected Vice-Chairpersons of the Technical Meeting convened to elaborate a plan of action for the International Year of the World's Indigenous People in 1993.[6] In April 1997, Mick Dodson was elected Chairperson of the UN Voluntary Fund for Indigenous Populations.

These methods of work have brought about a reasonably wide representation of Indigenous peoples and consideration of substantive issues affecting their organisations and communities. The creation in 1985 by the General Assembly of a Voluntary Fund for Indigenous Populations has also assisted Indigenous participation in the WGIP's deliberations.[7]

Questions of definition

The issue of definition was raised at the first session of the WGIP in 1982. One government delegation sought to distinguish between situations of relatively recent immigration, as in the Americas, Aoteoroa (New Zealand) and Australia, and situations involving historical coexistence and political integration, as in Asia. The WGIP resolved to defer consideration of definition, noting the importance of both objective

---

5   See *Report of a Seminar: The Effects of Racism and Racial Discrimination on the Economic and Social Relations between Indigenous Peoples and States* (16 to 20 January 1989), UN Doc HR/PUB/89/5.

6   UN Doc E/CN 4/1992/AC 4/TM 2/3, annex; see also *Evaluation of the International Year: Interim Report of the Coordinator of the International Year of the World's Indigenous People: Note by the Secretariat*, UN Doc E/CN 4/1994/AC 4/TM 4/2.

7   See General Assembly Resolution 40/31.

criteria, such as historical continuity, and subjective factors including self-identification.[8]

At the WGIP's second session, the Chairman asked the Secretariat to submit a discussion draft based on the study of Special Rapporteur Martinez Cobo. Martinez Cobo's definition provides:

> Indigenous communities, peoples and nations are those which, having a historical continuity with pre-invasion and pre-colonial societies that developed on their territories, consider themselves distinct from other sectors of the societies now prevailing in those territories . . . They form at present non-dominant sectors of society and are determined to preserve, develop and transmit to future generations their ancestral territories, and their ethnic identity, as the basis of their continued existence as peoples, in accordance with their own cultural patterns, social institutions and legal systems.[9]

Martinez Cobo defines an Indigenous person as:

> one who belongs to these Indigenous populations through self-identification as Indigenous (group consciousness) and is recognised and accepted by these populations one of its members (acceptance by the group).

To date, attempts to restrict the term "Indigenous" to those peoples colonised by peoples who, in comparatively recent times, arrived from overseas have not been successful. The resolution of the Sub-Commission in connection with the establishment of the Voluntary Fund for Indigenous Populations refers to the need "to secure a broad geographical representation".[10] UN activities during 1993, the International Year of the World's Indigenous People, included seminars and conferences "in all the areas where indigenous peoples live . . . Latin American countries, North America, Australia, Nordic countries, and Asian and Pacific countries".[11] In recent years, representatives of Indigenous peoples in Africa have participated actively in sessions of the WGIP.

In the practice of the WGIP, the view has prevailed that definition is the concern of Indigenous peoples and not States. Introducing the draft Universal Declaration on Indigenous Rights in 1988, Chairperson Daes referred to the absence of a definition of beneficiaries as a significant

---

8   UN Doc E/CN 4/Sub 2/1982/33, para 42.

9   *Study of the Problem against Indigenous Populations*, vol 5, *Conclusions, Proposals and Recommendations*, UN Doc E/CN 4/Sub 2/1986/7 Add 4, para 379 and 381.

10 Sub-Commission Resolution 1984/35C, final operative para (d).

11 UN Doc E/CN 4/Sub 2/1991/39 p 2.

feature of the text.[12] Article 8 of the final text adopted by the WGIP in 1993 recognises the right of Indigenous peoples to identify themselves as Indigenous and to be recognised as such.

Questions of definition were again raised in 1995 at the WGIP, and in 1996 and 1997 at the first sessions of the Working Group of the CHR, established to consider the WGIP's Draft Declaration on the Rights of Indigenous Peoples. Governments such as China, Bangladesh, India, and Malaysia are likely to maintain pressure to include a definition of Indigenous peoples in the Draft Declaration on the Rights of Indigenous Peoples.[13]

Review of developments

At its early sessions, the WGIP was primarily concerned with the first element of its mandate, the review of developments.[14] Whilst insisting that it is not a fact-finding tribunal, the WGIP has always considered that the review of "real-life experiences" of Indigenous peoples can assist the clarification of relevant concepts and the formulation of standards.[15] The review of developments contributed to a greater understanding in the WGIP of the historical experiences and contemporary aspirations of Indigenous peoples. This understanding provided the framework for the elaboration of standards on the rights of Indigenous peoples. The review of developments also enables a valuable exchange of information amongst Indigenous peoples' organisations and has become a forum for dialogue on matters of national policy between a number of governments and Indigenous peoples.

The annual reports of the WGIP contain a summary of information received under this agenda item on the situation of Indigenous peoples around the world. The reports include information on general principles, life, integrity and security, culture, religious and linguistic identity, education and public information, economic and social rights, land and resources, Indigenous institutions, and implementation.[16]

---

12 UN Doc E/CN 4/Sub 2/1988/24, para 68.

13 S Pritchard, "The United Nations and the Making of a Declaration on Indigenous Rights" (1997) 3 *Aboriginal Law Bulletin* 4.

14 UN Docs E/CN 4/Sub 2/1982/33; E/CN 4/Sub 2/1983/20; E/CN4/Sub2/1984/20.

15 See, for example, UN Doc E/CN 4/Sub 2/1982/33, para 121.

16 See, for example, *Report of the Working Group on Indigenous Populations on its Twelfth Session*, UN Doc E/CN 4/Sub 2/1994/30.

At its eleventh session in 1993, the WGIP completed its work on a draft declaration on the rights of Indigenous peoples. However, until the question of the WGIP's future is resolved, the review of developments is likely to occupy a central place in its annual discussions.

Evolution of standards

After discussion of various options, the WGIP decided at its fourth session in 1985 that it should aim to produce "a draft declaration on indigenous rights" for eventual adoption and proclamation by the General Assembly.[17] Draft principles prepared at a strategy meeting attended by 90 Indigenous representatives and submitted to the WGIP at its 1985 session left little doubt as to the central aspiration of Indigenous participants:

> All indigenous peoples have the right of self-determination, by virtue of which they have the right of whatever degree of autonomy they choose. This includes the right to freely determine their political status, the right to freely pursue their own economic, social, religious and cultural development and determine their own membership and/or citizenship without external interference.[18]

At the WGIP's sixth session in 1988, the Chairperson tabled a working paper containing a draft Universal Declaration on Indigenous Rights.[19] In 1989 a Revised Draft Universal Declaration on the Rights of Indigenous Peoples was published for discussion.[20] Revision and drafting continued during 1990-1993. In 1993, the *Position of the Indigenous Delegates on Self-Determination* was stated in the following language:

> It is the position of the indigenous delegates . . . that self-determination is the critical and essential element of the Draft Universal Declaration on the Rights of Indigenous Peoples. Discussion on the right of self-determination has been and still is the sine qua non of our participation in the drafting process. The right of self-determination must therefore be explicitly stated in the declaration . . . We believe that the working group should demonstrate consistency and objectivity on this issue because the right of self-

---

17 UN Doc E/CN 4/Sub 2/1985/2, Ann II.

18 UN Doc E/CN 4/Sub 2/AC 4/1985/WP 4; see also draft of the World Council of Indigenous Peoples, UN Doc E/CN 4/Sub 2/AC 4/1985/WP 4/Add 4.

19 UN Doc E/CN 4/Sub 2/1988/25.

20 UN Doc E/CN 4/Sub 2/1989/33.

determination is the heart and soul of the declaration. We will not consent to any language which limits or curtails the right of self-determination. A new article one should state:

Indigenous peoples have the right to self-determination by virtue of which they freely determine their political status and freely pursue their economic, social and cultural development.[21]

At the WGIP's eleventh session in 1993, members of the WGIP agreed upon a final text of the Draft Declaration, including a provision on self-determination in the language of common Article 1 of the Inter-national Covenant on the Civil and Political Rights and the International Covenant on Economic, Social and Cultural Rights.

The WGIP has sought to produce a text which keeps faith with the aspirations of Indigenous peoples, whilst taking into account some of the interests of governments. Disagreement focuses primarily, although by no means exclusively, on the question of self-determination. While Indigenous participants oppose any restriction upon their right of self-determination, most governments continue to call for some qualification.

At the conclusion of its twelfth session in 1994, the WGIP submitted the text of the Draft Declaration to its immediate parent body, the Sub-Commission.[22] The members of the WGIP were of the opinion that the text "was comprehensive and reflected the legitimate aspirations of Indigenous peoples as a whole, as well as a number of suggestions and concerns advanced by observer Governments".[23]

Draft Declaration on the Rights of Indigenous Peoples

The text of the Draft Declaration transmitted by the WGIP to the Sub-Commission session in 1994 contains nine parts. These are:

---

21 Working Grouup on Indigenous Populations, Eleventh Session, 20 July 1993; from the author's notes.

22 See UN Doc E/CN 4/Sub 2/1994/2/Add 1.

23 *Report of the Working Group on Indigenous Populations on its Twelfth Session*, UN Doc E/CN 4/Sub 2/1994/30, para 133.

Part I: Rights to self-determination, participation in the life of the State, freedom from discrimination and nationality

Part I of the Draft Declaration recognises the right of Indigenous peoples to self-determination, as well as to equal rights, freedom from adverse discrimination, participation in the life of the State, and nationality. Article 3 provides:

> Indigenous peoples have the right of self-determination. By virtue of this right, they freely determine their political status and freely pursue their economic, social and cultural development.

Article 4 recognises the right of Indigenous peoples to maintain and develop their distinct characteristics and legal systems, whilst participating fully in the life of the State.

Part II: Threats to the survival of Indigenous peoples as distinct peoples

In Part II, Article 6 proclaims the collective right of Indigenous peoples to live in freedom, peace and security as distinct peoples, and to full guarantees against genocide (including the removal of children).

Articles 7 and 8 proclaim collective and individual rights:

- not to be subjected to ethnocide and cultural genocide (including prevention of and redress for dispossession, imposed assimilation and integration); and
- to maintain and develop distinct identities and characteristics (including the right of self-identification).

Articles 9 to 11 address rights of Indigenous peoples:

- to belong to an Indigenous community or nation;
- not to be forcibly removed from their lands or territories; and
- to special protection and security in periods of armed conflict.

Part III: Cultural, religious and spiritual, and linguistic identity of Indigenous peoples

Articles 12 to 14 proclaim rights connected with the cultural, religious and linguistic identity of Indigenous peoples. These include rights:

- to practise and revitalise cultural traditions and customs (including the right to restitution of cultural, intellectual, religious and spiritual property);

- to practise and develop spiritual and religious traditions (including the rights to religious and cultural sites and to the repatriation of human remains);
- to the revitalisation, use and transmission of histories, languages, oral traditions, writing systems and literature (including the right to designate names for communities, places and persons).

Part IV: Educational, information and labour rights

Article 15 proclaims the right of Indigenous children to all forms and levels of education and recognises the right of Indigenous peoples to establish and control their educational systems and institutions, providing education in their own languages.

Articles 16 to 17 proclaim the rights of Indigenous peoples to have the dignity and diversity of their cultures and aspirations reflected in all forms of education and public information, and to establish their own media in their own languages.

Article 18 refers to international labour law and national labour legislation.

Part V: Participatory rights, development, and other economic and social rights

Article 19 affirms the right of Indigenous peoples to participate fully at all levels of decision-making and implementation in matters affecting their rights, lives and destinies, as well as to maintain their own decision-making institutions.

Article 20 affirms the right of Indigenous peoples to participate fully in devising legislative and administrative measures that may affect them, and requires that States obtain their consent before adopting and implementing such measures.

Article 21 recognises the right of Indigenous peoples to maintain and develop political, economic and social systems, to engage freely in traditional and other economic activities and to compensation where they have been deprived of their means of subsistence and development.

Pursuant to Articles 22 to 24, Indigenous peoples have rights:

- to special measures for the improvement of their economic and social conditions;

- to determine and develop priorities and strategies for exercising their right to development (including the right to administer programs affecting them through their own institutions); and
- to their traditional medicines and health practices.

Part VI: Land and resource rights

Part VI addresses rights connected with the distinctive spiritual and material relationship of Indigenous peoples with their lands, territories, waters and coastal seas and other resources.

Article 26 proclaims the right of Indigenous peoples to own, develop and control the lands and territories, air, water, coastal seas, sea-ice, flora and fauna and other resources they have traditionally occupied or otherwise used. This includes the right to the recognition of their laws, customs, land-tenure systems and institutions for the development and management of resources.

Articles 27 and 28 affirm rights to restitution of or compensation for lands, territories and resources confiscated or used without consent, and to the conservation and protection of the environment and productive capacity of Indigenous lands, territories and resources.

Indigenous peoples are entitled to recognition of the ownership, control and protection of their intellectual and cultural property and to special measures to control, develop and protect their sciences, technologies and cultural manifestations: Article 29.

Article 30 affirms the right of Indigenous peoples to require that States obtain their free and informed consent prior to the approval of projects affecting their lands, territories and other resources, particularly in connection with the development, utilisation or exploitation of mineral and water resources.

Part VII: The exercise of self-determination

As a specific form of exercising their right of self-determination, Indigenous peoples have the right to autonomy or self-government in matters relating to their internal and local affairs: Article 31.

Articles 32 to 36 affirm the rights of Indigenous peoples:

- to determine their citizenship in accordance with their customs and traditions;
- to develop and maintain their institutional structures and juridical customs, procedures and practices;

- to determine the responsibilities of individuals to their communities;
- to maintain and develop relations and cooperation with other peoples across borders; and
- to the recognition and enforcement of treaties, agreements and other constructive arrangements concluded with States or their successors.

Prospects for advancement of the Draft Declaration through the UN system

At its forty-sixth session in August 1994, the Sub-Commission adopted the text of the Draft Declaration transmitted by the WGIP and decided to submit it to the Commission on Human Rights (CHR) at the fifty-first session of that body in 1995.[24]

On 3 March 1995, the CHR adopted a resolution in which it decided:

> to establish an open-ended inter-sessional working group ... with the sole purpose of elaborating a draft declaration, considering the draft contained in the annex to resolution 1994/45 of 26 August 1994 of the Sub-Commission on Prevention of Discrimination and Protection of Minorities, entitled draft "United Nations declaration on the rights of indigenous peoples" for consideration and adoption by the General Assembly within the International Decade of the World's Indigenous People.[25]

Participation of Indigenous representatives

While the WGIP allows a wide representation of Indigenous individuals and organisations to participate in its activities, participation in other UN bodies is more limited. Only NGOs with consultative status have the right to attend public meetings of ECOSOC and its subsidiary bodies, including the CHR and the Sub-Commission, and to make submissions, in written or oral form, on particular agenda items. Article 71 of the UN Charter authorises ECOSOC to make suitable arrangements for consultation with NGOs concerned with matters within its competence. At present, 13 Indigenous peoples' organisations have consultative status with ECOSOC. Of these, only one is from Latin America and two are from the Asia-Pacific region, the National Aboriginal and Islander Legal

---

24 Sub-Commission Resolution 1994/45.
25 Commission on Human Rights Resolution 1995/32.

Services Secretariat (NAILSS) and the Aboriginal and Torres Strait Islander Commission (ATSIC).

Representatives of Indigenous peoples' organisations at the fifty-first session of the CHR lobbied hard to ensure their full and effective participation in the open-ended inter-sessional working group ("the CHR Working Group"), without regard to their status as NGOs in consultation with ECOSOC. At the same time, a number of Asian governments undertook considerable diplomatic efforts to prevent the participation of Asian Indigenous peoples in the CHR Working Group.

In an annex to Resolution 1995/32, the CHR adopted special procedures for authorising the participation of organisations of Indigenous peoples without ECOSOC consultative status in the new working group. These procedures require such organisations to apply to the Coordinator of the International Decade, providing information about, amongst other things, their aims and purposes, programs and activities, and membership. Upon receipt of applications, the Coordinator of the International Decade is required to consult with States concerned, and to forward applications and information received to ECOSOC's Committee on Non-Governmental Organisations for its decision. If authorised to participate, organisations have opportunities to address the CHR Working Group. Their written statements, however, are not issued as official documents.

Whilst the sub-text of Resolution 1995/32 is that States have the power to veto the participation of certain Indigenous groups in the further consideration of the Draft Declaration, this has not succeeded in preventing the participation of these groups under the auspices of NGOs with consultative status. With Resolution 1995/32 the principle of full participation of Indigenous peoples in the work of the UN system was recognised for the first time by a governmental body, in theory at least.

At the first two sessions of the CHR Working Group, significant differences emerged as to the meaning of "participation". Indigenous participants have called for full participation as equal partners in the Working Group's processes, while States maintain a distinction between "Members" of the CHR and "Observers", which include Indigenous participants. At the second session of the CHR Working Group in November 1996, these differences resulted in the withdrawal of all Indigenous participants from the plenary. Their return was predicated on ongoing discussions on the modalities of Indigenous participation and the adoption of working methods which ensure the full and effective participation of Indigenous representatives in all aspects of the CHR

Working Group's work.[26] The real test of Indigenous peoples' standing will come if and when it is necessary to decide whether the consensus of all, including Indigenous, participants is necessary for any changes to the WGIP's text.

A stalemate on definition

The resolution establishing the CHR Working Group encouraged it "to consider all aspects of the Draft Declaration, *including its scope of application*" (emphasis added). At its first session in 1995, the issue of definition was raised by, amongst others, Bangladesh, China, India and Malaysia. An extended debate ensued, with a number of States suggesting that a definition would be useful to distinguish "Indigenous" from "minority" groups, while other States maintained that a definition was unnecessary. A stalemate was reached and discussion turned to substantive provisions of the Draft Declaration. The issue was not discussed at any length at the second session in 1996.

No consensus on the substantive issues

In an address in Sydney on 29 April 1995, the Chairperson/Rapporteur of the WGIP, Erica-Irene Daes, stated that "in a fair and public process, the Draft Declaration should be adoptable without substantive changes". However, at the first two sessions of the CHR Working Group, State delegations identified numerous substantive provisions with which they have difficulties. The CHR is composed of the representatives of 53 States. Some of these are less sympathetically disposed to the aspirations of Indigenous peoples than the independent experts of the WGIP and the Sub-Commission. The rights proclaimed in the WGIP's text address historical experiences and cultural identities unfamiliar to some of the Commission's Member-States. Indigenous peoples' organisations anticipate that a lengthy process of dialogue and education will be necessary to secure the adoption of a text which gives adequate expression to their rights.

Indigenous peoples' organisations are considering strategies to ensure that they are not excluded from the drafting process. Their representatives have begun coordinating their diplomatic efforts and commenced dialogues with Members of the Commission to advance understanding of their aspirations and rights.

---

26 S Pritchard, "The United Nations and the Making of a Declaration on Indigenous Rights" (1997) 3 *Aboriginal Law Bulletin* 4.

The General Assembly

Despite the Commission's widely recognised technical competence, the General Assembly is the final arbiter in standard-setting. Controversial political issues which arise in the course of drafting are often left to the Assembly for resolution.[27] Some Indigenous representatives have affirmed the importance of knowledge of the procedures of the General Assembly that relate to the drafting of human rights instruments. Unlike the CHR, the Assembly's membership extends to all members of the UN. If negotiations on the Draft Declaration are dragging or proceeding too quickly in the CHR, it may be possible to use the Assembly to step up or slow down the momentum. It might also be useful to seek to shape the agenda of the Assembly's Third Committee in preparation for its consideration of the Draft Declaration. For example, if the CHR is hostile to Indigenous peoples' assertions of their right of self-determination, there might be some benefit in seeking to promote a broad debate on the issue in the Third Committee.[28]

---

27 The question as to whether the right of self-determination should be included in the International Covenants on Civil and Political Rights, and on Economic, Social and Cultural Rights, for example, was turned over to the Assembly. The Optional Protocol to the International Covenant on Civil and Political Rights was proposed, debated and adopted in the General Assembly without any consultation with the CHR. See P Alston, "The Commission on Human Rights" in P Alston (ed), *The United Nations and Human Rights*, Oxford University Press, New York, 1992, p 34 ff. In the case of the Declaration on the Right to Development, adopted by the Assembly in 1986, an impasse had been reached in the Commission's Working Group. The Assembly was able to force pace on the issue by adopting the Declaration, although not by consensus. With respect to the Convention against Torture, the Assembly essentially gave its imprimatur to the technical work done by a Working Group of the Commission, but had to resolve a number of outstanding issues, including the shape of implementation machinery. See J Quinn, "The General Assembly into the 1990s" in P Alston (ed), *The United Nations and Human Rights*, Oxford University Press, New York, 1992, p 65 ff.

28 In recent years, statements by various delegations in the Third Committee have reflected greater interest in the theoretical aspects of so-called post-colonial self-determination. See Quinn, The General Assembly into the 1990s, note 25 above, pp 76, 99.

Other items relating to Indigenous rights

Over the years the WGIP has considered a number of other issues relating to Indigenous rights. At its ninth session in 1991, the WGIP considered a separate item on the study of its member Mr Miguel Alfonso Martinez on treaties, agreements and other constructive arrangements between States and Indigenous peoples.[29] At its tenth session in 1992, the WGIP considered as separate items the International Year for the World's Indigenous People (1993)[30], and reports on:

- Indigenous peoples and self-government,[31]
- Indigenous peoples and the environment,[32]
- the ownership and control of the cultural property of Indigenous peoples,[33] and
- the protection of the intellectual property of Indigenous peoples.[34]

Items since added to the WGIP's agenda include:

- the future role of the WGIP,[35]

---

29 *Study on Treaties, Agreements and Other Constructive Arrangements between States and Indigenous Populations*, UN Doc E/CN 4/Sub 2/1992/28.

30 Proclaimed by General Assembly Resolution 45/164 of 18 December 1990. See *Working Paper on Suggestions for United Nations Activities for the International Year for the World's Indigenous People*, UN Doc E/CN 4/Sub 2/1991/39.

31 *Report of the Meeting of Experts to Review the Experience of Countries in the Operation of Schemes of Internal Self-government for Indigenous Peoples* (Nuuk, Greenland, 24 to 28 September 1991), UN Doc E/CN 4/1992/42.

32 *Report of the United Nations Technical Conference on Practical Experience in the Realization of Environmentally Sound Self-Development of Indigenous Peoples* (Santiago, Chile, 18 to 22 May 1992), UN Doc E/CN 4/Sub 2/1992/31 and Add 1.

33 *Working Paper on the Question of the Ownership and Control of the Cultural Property of Indigenous Peoples*, UN Doc E/CN 4/Sub 2/1991/34.

34 *Intellectual Property of Indigenous Peoples: Concise Report of the Secretary-General*, UN Doc E/CN 4/Sub 2/1992/30; see also *Study on the Protection of the Cultural and Intellectual Property of Indigenous Peoples, by Ms Erica-Irene A Daes, Special Rapporteur of the Sub-Commission*, UN Doc E/CN 4/Sub 2/1993/28.

35 *Working Paper by Mr Alfonso Martinez on the Future of the Working Group*, UN Doc E/CN 4/Sub 2/AC 4/1994/10; *Note by the Chairperson-Rapporteur of the Working Group on Indigenous Populations on the Future Role of the Working Group*, UN Doc E/CN 4/Sub 2/AC 4/1993/8.

- consideration of a permanent forum for Indigenous peoples,[36] and
- the International Decade of the World's Indigenous People.

International Decade

In 1987, the WGIP called for an International Year of the World's Indigenous Peoples, and in 1990, the General Assembly proclaimed 1993 as the International Year of the World's Indigenous People.[37] The International Year was based on the theme "A New Partnership". Indigenous peoples were involved in planning and evaluating activities through the appointment of Indigenous associate experts to the UN and the participation of Indigenous representatives in technical meetings.

The Vienna World Conference on Human Rights (1993), recommended, amongst other things, that the General Assembly proclaim an International Decade of the World's Indigenous People.[38] The World Conference recommended that the International Decade include action-oriented programs to be decided upon in partnership with Indigenous peoples and that the establishment of a permanent forum for Indigenous peoples in the UN system be considered within the framework of the Decade.[39]

In 1993, General Assembly proclaimed the International Decade of the World's Indigenous People, commencing on 10 December 1994.[40] The resolution's preamble refers to the importance of considering the establishment of a permanent forum. Its text invites governments to ensure the planning and implementation of the Decade on the basis of full consultation and collaboration with Indigenous peoples.

---

36 *Report by the Secretariat on a Permanent Forum in the United Nations for Indigenous People*, UN Doc E/CN 4/Sub 2/AC 4/1994/11; *Note by the Chairperson-Rapporteur, Ms Erica-Irene Daes, on the Consideration of a Permanent Forum for Indigenous Peoples*, UN Doc E/CN 4/Sub 2/AC 4/1994/13; *Guidelines for the Establishment of a Permanent Forum of the World's Indigenous Peoples Prepared by the Chairperson-Rapporteur, Ms Erica-Irene A Daes*, UN Doc E/CN 4/Sub 2/AC 4/1994/11.

37 General Assembly Resolution 45/164, 18 December 1990.

38 *Report of the World Conference on Human Rights, Vienna, 14-25 June 1993*, UN Doc A/CONF/157/22, sect II, para 29.

39 UN Doc A/CONF/157/22, sect II, para 32.

40 General Assembly Resolution 48/163, 21 December 1993.

Future UN involvement with Indigenous issues

As the Draft Declaration begins its ascent to the General Assembly, Indigenous peoples' organisations have begun considering options for future UN action in relation to Indigenous rights. The adoption of international standards will signify merely the beginning of the empowerment of Indigenous peoples through international law. Much work will be necessary to secure the implementation of the Draft Declaration and to bring about changes in the lives of Indigenous peoples.

Future of the WGIP

Despite increasing recognition of the need for international cooperation in addressing the rights of the world's Indigenous peoples, the WGIP is the only forum within the UN system in which Indigenous peoples can raise issues of concern to them. The conclusion of a Draft Declaration on the Rights of Indigenous Peoples does not mean that the WGIP has exhausted its raison d'être. Some Indigenous peoples have argued that the WGIP has a permanent role to play in securing recognition and protection of Indigenous rights.[41] Others view the WGIP as a valuable medium-term forum, to be replaced in time by a new body within the UN system.

These are questions which Indigenous peoples' organisations will consider during the International Decade. In the absence of an alternative, the WGIP must, for the short term at least, continue its efforts to promote the rights of Indigenous peoples. To ensure that the agenda item "review of developments" can contribute in a meaningful and measurable way to improving the situation of Indigenous peoples, Aboriginal and Torres Strait Islander Social Justice Commissioner, Mick Dodson, has suggested that the WGIP call on ECOSOC and the General Assembly to adopt resolutions:

---

41 Amongst the goals for the International Decade proposed in the B'okob' (Chimaltenango) Declaration of the First World Summit of Indigenous Peoples of 27 May 1993 is that the UN "continue and strengthen the Working Group on Indigenous Peoples as a permanent institution working to monitor and ensure the fulfilment of the rights stated in the [UN draft] declaration [on the rights of Indigenous peoples]". See also *Future Role of the Working Group: Working Paper Submitted by Mr Miguel Alfonso Martinez, Member of the Working Group*, UN Doc E/CN 4/Sub 2/AC 4/1993/10, p 11.

- enabling it to receive communications from Indigenous individuals and communities concerning violations of their rights;
- reviewing the mandate of the Voluntary Fund for Indigenous Populations[42] to enable Indigenous peoples to attend meetings of specialised agencies and bodies of the UN system when matters of concern to Indigenous peoples are being considered, and to negotiate activities and projects of relevance to them. [43]

During the fifteen years of its existence, the WGIP has gained a genuine understanding of the diversity and aspirations of Indigenous peoples. The WGIP has become a repository of considerable expertise on Indigenous peoples' rights, and has an important role to play in contributing to the further elaboration of the Draft Declaration and ensuring its passage through the UN system to the General Assembly. It has been suggested that the WGIP could make its expertise available to its parent bodies in their consideration of the Draft Declaration.[44] The WGIP might also contribute to the elaboration of draft international instruments and guidelines in other areas, such as intellectual and cultural property rights, sustainable development affecting Indigenous territories, and the negotiation of modern-day treaties and agreements between Indigenous peoples and States.

Permanent forum

The Vienna World Conference on Human Rights (1993) recommended consideration of the establishment of a permanent forum for Indigenous people in the UN system. The proposal was endorsed by the General Assembly.[45] The CHR has called on the WGIP to give priority consideration to institutional issues in connection with the establishment of a permanent forum and has requested the preparation of a technical note on the question.[46] Lively discussion of the future role of the WGIP

---

42 Contained in General Assembly Resolution 40/13 (1985).

43 See *A Permanent Forum in the United Nations for Indigenous People: Information Received from Governments and Indigenous Organizations*, UN Doc E/CN 4/Sub 2/AC 4/1994/11/Add 2.

44 See *Future Role of the Working Group: Note by the Chairperson-Rapporteur of the Working Group on Indigenous Populations*, UN Doc E/CN 4/Sub 2/AC 4/1993/8, para 6.

45 Resolution 48/163 of 21 December 1993.

46 Resolution 1994/28 of 4 March 1994.

and consideration of a permanent forum for Indigenous peoples began during its 1994 session.

Issues being considered in the establishment of a permanent forum include:

- What should be the mandate of the permanent forum – the protection and promotion of the rights of Indigenous peoples? Or should it address environment and development issues as well?
- What functions should a permanent forum exercise – analytical, advisory, conciliatory, investigatory, decision-making?
- What should its institutional status be within the UN system – an expert committee, a functional commission of ECOSOC?
- To whom should it submit its reports – the Secretary-General, the General Assembly, ECOSOC, CHR?
- How should its membership be composed – Independent experts, Indigenous peoples only, States and Indigenous peoples, a tripartite model including non-Indigenous NGOs?
- How should its membership be selected – election by governments, by governments and/or regional groups of Indigenous peoples, appointment by the UN Secretary-General?
- To whom should participation in its meetings be open – governments, non-Indigenous NGOs, all Indigenous peoples?

Whilst many details remain to be resolved, Aboriginal and Torres Strait Islander Social Justice Commissioner Mick Dodson has suggested that increasing consensus is emerging on a number of points:

- that the permanent forum should be given a mandate to supervise implementation of the Draft Declaration on the Rights of Indigenous Peoples, and to assist in the resolution of disputes and the enforcement of treaties and other agreements. Increasingly, a role for the forum in coordinating UN activities and programs for Indigenous peoples, including operational activities for development, has been identified.
- that the forum must have transparent, user-friendly procedures. This includes adequate benchmarks or indicators to evaluate implementation of the Draft Declaration, as well as clear guidelines on reporting by States.

- that the composition of the forum must incorporate independent elements and/or the membership of Indigenous peoples.[47]

In discussions surrounding the permanent forum, a number of models have been suggested.

Indigenous peoples have expressed interest in a model based on the Commission on Sustainable Development (CSD). The idea for a CSD emerged during the fourth session of the Preparatory Committee for the UN Conference on Environment and Development (UNCED). During UNCED, governments agreed to establish the CSD as a functional commission of ECOSOC, to be supported by a secretariat unit and a high-level advisory body. In 1992, the forty-seventh session of the General Assembly adopted a resolution establishing a high-level CSD to enhance cooperation for the integration of environment and development issues, and to examine progress in the implementation of Agenda 21, adopted in Rio.[48]

The Secretary-General, CSD, ECOSOC and the General Assembly receive expert advice on the implementation of Agenda 21 from a high-level Advisory Board. The Advisory Board consists of persons with relevant expertise drawn from scientific disciplines, industry, finance and other non-governmental constituencies, as well as disciplines related to environment and development. The CSD has adopted a multi-year thematic program of work as a framework for assessing progress in the implementation of Agenda 21. This is intended to ensure an integrated approach to environment and development components, and to linkages between sectoral and cross-sectoral issues. Within this framework, the Secretary-General is required to prepare reports on urgent and major emerging issues to be addressed at high-level meetings.

Aboriginal and Torres Strait Islander Social Justice Commissioner Mick Dodson has suggested that the establishment of a permanent forum as a functional commission of ECOSOC would recognise that Indigenous peoples' issues extend beyond the sectoral framework of human rights. An appropriate institutional response might be the establishment of a forum in which there is an integrated approach to the environmental, developmental, and other economic and social aspects of Indigenous peoples' rights, as well as a long-term, cross-sectoral approach to implementation. Mick Dodson has suggested that a permanent forum

---

47 *A Permanent Forum in the United Nations for Indigenous People: Information Received from Governments and Indigenous Organization*, UN Doc E/CN 4/Sub 2/AC 4/1994/11/Add 2, p 5.

48 General Assembly Resolution 47/191.

based on this model might adopt a multi-year program of work, supported by inter-sessional technical working groups. It might examine progress by States towards implementation of the Draft Declaration on the rights of Indigenous peoples, in accordance with guidelines on State reporting requiring discussion of sectoral and cross-sectoral issues, and drawing on the assistance of specialised agencies within the UN system, as well as scientific and other non-governmental constituencies. Such a body might promote scientific research, the development of composite indicators and the elaboration of protocols and guidelines. It might also be authorised to receive communications from Indigenous individuals and peoples, and to activate an emergency mechanism to take action to protect the rights of Indigenous peoples in crisis situations.

Another model sometimes canvassed is that of the Trusteeship Council. The status of the Trusteeship Council as one of six principal organs of the UN signifies the importance attached at the time of the adoption of the UN Charter to the development of the peoples of trust territories towards self-government or independence (Article 76, UN Charter). Although membership of the Trusteeship Council was restricted to members of the UN, the Council made effective use of a petitions procedure and regularly dispatched missions to trust territories. On the basis of the Council's reports, the General Assembly made detailed recommendations for each administering authority. The establishment of an Indigenous Peoples' Council as a new principal organ of the UN, or the reconstitution of the Trusteeship Council as such a Council, would require an amendment of the UN Charter pursuant to the procedure under Chapter XVIII.

Specialised agencies and Indigenous peoples

Indigenous peoples' organisations have argued that within the framework of the International Decade, specialised agencies and related UN bodies must develop comprehensive, coordinated and adequately funded programs to address the development needs of Indigenous peoples. The emphasis of such programs should be on the improvement of economic and social infrastructure in Indigenous communities and the enhancement of self-reliance.

Mick Dodson has suggested that to ensure maximum control by Indigenous peoples of the development process, advisory services and technical and other development assistance must be provided directly to

Indigenous peoples and communities.[49] It is interesting to note some of the areas in which specialised agencies have provided development assistance to the peoples of non-self-governing territories. These include early childhood development, maternal and child health, primary school education (UNICEF); agricultural development, human resources development, hydrogeology, civil aviation, building technology, electrical engineering, export promotion, livestock development, tourism, telecommunications upgrading (UNDP); management of land resources, forestry and fisheries, crop development, agricultural statistics (FAO); training of teachers, literacy programs, development of technical/ vocational curricula, provision of documentation and books, upgrading of information facilities, provision of fellowships and scholarships, cultural heritage inventories and protection and restoration of cultural and historical sites (UNESCO); management of health-care programs, fellowships for medical personnel and public health administrators, provision of human resources for hospitals, health equipment maintenance, improvement in laboratory facilities (WHO); human settlements, biodiversity and transboundary pollution (UNEP).[50]

UN Office of Indigenous Peoples

For the mid-term at least, the WGIP and the Centre for Human Rights have a central role to play in advancing the rights of Indigenous peoples within the UN system. The WGIP is the focal point for the consideration of future UN activities concerning Indigenous peoples and can contribute to ensuring the progress of the Draft Declaration through to the General Assembly. The Centre for Human Rights has onerous responsibilities in relation to the International Decade and in coordinating relevant activities of the specialised agencies and other bodies within the UN system.

---

49 *A Permanent Forum in the United Nations for Indigenous People: Information Received from Governments and Indigenous Organization*, UN Doc E/CN 4/Sub 2/AC 4/1994/11/Add 2 p 10. See Chapter 26 of Agenda 21, adopted by the UN Conference on Environment and Development, which calls on UN operational programs and specialised agencies to support programs of technical assistance and exchanges of information amongst Indigenous peoples, UN Doc A/CONF/151/26, vol III.

50 See "Role of the Specialised Agencies and the International Institutions Associated with the United Nations in the Implementation of the Declaration on the Granting of Independence to Colonial Countries and Peoples" (January 1993) 43 *Decolonisation Bulletin* (UNDPA Doc 93-19530), 19.

Concerted efforts will be necessary to ensure that secretariat services in support of these activities are adequately resourced. Until the question of a permanent forum for Indigenous peoples is resolved, the Office of Indigenous Peoples appears best located within the Centre for Human Rights in Geneva.

Comment: *Mick Dodson*

Aboriginal and Torres Strait Islander
Social Justice Commissioner

The Working Group on Indigenous Populations (WGIP) is not called the Working Group on Indigenous Peoples. That is deliberate, because in international law it is peoples who have a right to self-determination, not populations.

The Working Group is the one platform on the international stage where Indigenous peoples from all around the world have been able to come together to articulate our rights as peoples. It is the place where we have been able to put to the international community the rights which we believe the international community is obliged to protect. It is the place where we have created a description of the status we wish to ensure for the future of our peoples.

The aspirational quality of the Working Group has been a source of criticism. Some people say that the Working Group operates at such a peripheral level of the UN that its deliberations are virtually meaningless, that it has no status in the UN system, and that its work will simply be undone by governments which must ultimately endorse any UN declaration of our rights. While the WGIP may not have any independent status in the UN system, it cannot be so easily dismissed.

It has already had a tremendous impact, not just on Indigenous peoples ourselves. It is no exaggeration to say that the WGIP has been a small revolution in the UN system. A lot of people forget that before 1970, as far as the UN was concerned, Indigenous people were virtually invisible. The common wisdom was that we were one of the minorities whose grievances were supposed to be resolved through the meagre protective mechanisms that minorities were offered. The UN is made up of 185 governments, and rapid and radical transformation is unlikely. What has been achieved in a little over 12 years is remarkable by any standard.

The Working Group itself comprises five non Indigenous experts, elected from the Sub-Commission on the Prevention of Discrimination and Protection of Minorities. What is particularly unusual about this Working Group is that it has gone outside normal UN practices and opened its sessions to participation by interested parties. That means that Indigenous peoples and their organisations have been able to send along representatives, irrespective of whether they have any formal standing in the UN. Indigenous involvement has received practical support from the UN General Assembly, which in 1985 created a voluntary fund to assist Indigenous peoples who would otherwise be unable to attend sessions due to lack of resources.[51]

Perhaps even more remarkable has been the quality of our participation. We have not just been observers or bystanders. Australian Indigenous representatives, together with Indigenous representatives from around the globe, have been actively involved in the work of the Working Group. The involvement of people who are the subject of UN deliberations is quite unprecedented. As you know, what we say about ourselves, our problems and our aspirations, is very different to what government officials and government representatives are likely to say about us.

The Working Group has come to play a far more extensive role than its mandate would suggest. It is a fine example of how we can use existing structures and transform them to meet our needs and aspirations. As the meeting place between the world's Indigenous peoples and key international organisations, the Working Group has provided many of us with a unique opportunity to interact with a world that would be otherwise impenetrable. We have made sure that it has functioned as a highly visible platform where we can draw attention to our grievances.

It has also been more than that. The Working Group has become the focal point of our coming together as the world's Indigenous peoples. In a sense, the Working Group is all about what international law and the UN have neglected. It is about bringing Indigenous people into the UN system where we have been marginalised and unnoticed. It is about forcing the UN system to face its responsibility as the body charged with protecting the rights of all peoples. It is about transforming the UN from a club serving the interests of its members, namely nation States and their well-suited diplomats, to a body of all peoples.

The presence of Indigenous peoples at the UN has some very direct effects. In the first years of the Working Group, Indigenous peoples argued that any declaration of Indigenous peoples' rights must include the

---

51 In April 1997, Mick Dodson was elected Chairperson of the UN Voluntary Fund for Indigenous Populations. *Editor's note.*

recognition of the right to self-determination. The members of the Working Group thought that we were crazy. The Chairperson made it clear that there was no way that the Working Group could support recognition of such a politically contentious right. An examination of the drafts from one year to the next reveals that our perspectives were gradually accepted. Last year, when the final draft left the Working Group it contained the unqualified right to self-determination as one of its articles.

The process is far from over, and in some ways the hardest part is still to come. The Draft Declaration is now in the Commission on Human Rights, which is primarily a governmental place. However we have already seen some progress in terms of gaining acceptance for Indigenous participation in the new Working Group of the CHR. We must go there and keep insisting that our rights are not watered down and that our interests are accommodated.

The Working Group's influence on the UN goes well beyond the production of the Draft Declaration. Indigenous issues were prominent at the Vienna World Conference on Human Rights, they were on the agenda for the Social Development Summit in Copenhagen and the Women's Conference in Beijing. The International Year of the World's Indigenous Peoples has become an International Decade. In July 1995, a seminar was held in Copenhagen to discuss a permanent forum for Indigenous peoples in the UN. Indigenous peoples are now on the agenda whenever human rights issues are discussed.

Perhaps just as important as the impact the Working Group has had on the UN system is the impact it has had on us. The feeling that we are not alone has transformed the way many of us approach the whole struggle. We now see that it is a global struggle, not just between a single Indigenous people and a government, but between the world's Indigenous peoples and the world's colonial governments. While our version of the struggle has its local variants, all our struggles tell essentially the same story. We are still all dealing with the legacy of colonialism. Indigenous people speak about the gross violations of their peoples' rights and put up innovative, substantial proposals for change. And governments come back with all the reasons why it can't possibly happen, and usually with some cosmetic alternative.

To be fair, I must say that the Australian government has been by far the most cooperative and supportive of any government represented at the Working Group. It is a pity that they don't bring that attitude back on the plane from Geneva.

Part III

The UN treaty-based human rights system and individual complaints

5

The UN treaty-based
human rights system: an overview

Hilary Charlesworth

Introduction

The system for monitoring international human rights treaties is often
regarded as a model. Environmental lawyers sometimes look with envy at
the human rights monitoring system: there has been talk in environmental
circles about trying to create a similar system for implementing environmental treaties. But, although there is a fairly well developed system in
practice it is in many ways deeply flawed, and in need of significant
reform.

Composition of the human rights treaty bodies

Six of the major human rights treaties have an independent monitoring
body: the Committee on the Elimination of Racial Discrimination (CERD
Committee), the Human Rights Committee (which monitors the International Covenant on Civil and Political Rights (ICCPR)), the Committee
on Economic Social and Cultural Rights (CESCR Committee), the
Committee on the Elimination of Discrimination against Women
(CEDAW Committee), the Committee against Torture (CAT Committee)
and the Committee on the Rights of the Child (CROC Committee). There
is also a committee which monitors the International Convention on the
Suppression and Punishment of the Crime of Apartheid, to which
Australia is not a party. The latest human rights treaty, the Convention on
the Rights of Migrant Workers and the Members of their Families, also
foreshadows the creation of a specialised committee. That Convention
has not yet entered into force.

The committees that I am going to focus on are the first six, because Australia is a party to all those treaties. There are three committees in which Australians should take a particular interest, because Australians have served on them: the Human Rights Committee, on which Elizabeth Evatt serves with great distinction; Philip Alston has been a leading light of the Committee on Economic, Social and Cultural Rights; and Elizabeth Evatt was a member and later chaired the CEDAW Committee, before she was appointed to the Human Rights Committee.

The members of the committees are so-called independent experts. They are elected by meetings of the countries that have accepted those particular treaties. Sometimes it is questionable whether in the end you get people of the highest calibre, as there is a fair amount of politicking in ensuring that particular candidates are elected. Although I have been very critical of the Australian Government in its human rights performance, in the people it has put up for these expert committees it has chosen people of enormous calibre. Their performance has significantly increased Australia's human rights profile abroad.

The gender balance of these committees should also be noted. There are very few women serving on these committees. For example, the Human Rights Committee, the central monitoring body in the human rights system, has three women out of eighteen members. The CAT Committee has no women as members. The CROC Committee has six women out of ten members. Interestingly, all twenty-three members of the CEDAW Committee are currently women. That is the only committee that has been criticised by the Economic and Social Council for its gender imbalance. Thus, as with issues involving Indigenous rights at the UN, there are significant issues concerning who is actually creating the law that is implemented.

All of these committees have different memberships and meet for different periods of time. The longest and most frequent meetings are those of the Human Rights Committee – a total of nine weeks a year. The CEDAW Committee's annual meeting was extended in 1994 to three weeks. It continues to be one of the committees which meets for the least time.

There is certainly an issue about the productivity of these committees. The amount of work that they have to perform is so massive that it is almost setting the system up for failure to demand that they do it in such a brief period of time.

Functions

The functions of these bodies are defined in the particular treaties. Their first function is to consider the periodic reports of States parties on how they are implementing their treaty obligations. The second major function is to receive individual communications. The Optional Protocol to the ICCPR, the Convention the Elimination of All Forms of Racial Discrimination (Article 14) and the Convention against Torture (Article 22) provide individuals with the right to make special communications directly to these committees. A third function set out in the same treaties is to consider communications received from States parties concerning the failure of other States parties to fulfil their obligations. It is striking that this procedure has never been used in the UN system, essentially because it is an issue of international politics. It would be seen as exceptionally serious to take a country before one of the committees. The only international case in which one nation formally complained about another's human rights practices came before the European Court of Human Rights. In this case, Ireland took Great Britain before the European Court to complain about its treatment of those suspected of terrorism offences in Northern Ireland.

The fourth function of these committees is to make policy recommendations. Depending on the committee, these are sometimes called general recommendations or general comments. The Human Rights Committee, for example, has put out a series of some 30 comments on areas of human rights. Of particular relevance is their general comment on Article 27 of the ICCPR which deals with minority rights, and which covers Indigenous rights. This provides a three-page distillation of all the international jurisprudence about minority rights, including Indigenous rights. Another function of these committees which has to my knowledge never been used, is the capacity for treaty monitoring bodies to be used to settle disputes about the interpretation of a treaty between States parties. This does not involve a formal settlement of disputes, just an informal conciliation process.

Finally, all of the committees report to the UN General Assembly on their activities, either once a year or once every two years. Sometimes these reports are rather bland documents, indicating only that the committee has received the States parties' reports and all is terrific in the world. However, some of the committees do provide a frank discussion of problems in particular countries.

In addition, one of the committees, the CAT Committee, has the power to make confidential inquiries about well-founded allegations of torture in a particular country.

How is the treaty-based system working? A Canadian jurist, Ann Bayefsky, has recently argued that the system is at crisis point and breaking down under the strains.[1] It has been referred to as the UN's own Third World. There is an increasing number of treaty parties. According to December 1996 figures, the number of countries that have accepted these treaties ranges from 150 for the Convention on the Elimination of All Forms of Racial Discrimination, the ICCPR 132, the International Covenant on Economic, Social and Cultural Rights 134, the Convention on the Elimination of All Forms of Discrimination against Women 154, the Convention against Torture 97 and the Convention on the Rights of the Child with the largest number of ratifications and accessions, 195. Treaty bodies meet for a maximum of nine weeks each year. Even if the treaty body receives reports from countries only every four years, the backlog cannot be eliminated, and the system remains in a state of crisis.

Participation of NGOs

There is a fair amount of corridor diplomacy each time these committees meet in New York or Geneva. Outside each meeting room are lobbyists from NGOs who seek to discuss particular issues with committee members. Generally, these committees have a good relationship with the NGO community. To a significant extent they depend on the NGO community for independent information. Both NGOs from a particular country, and those such as Amnesty International with a global coverage, are essential to keep the human rights treaty system honest. That is why groups such as the National Aboriginal and Islander Legal Services Secretariat, although it has focused on the Working Group on Indigenous Populations, potentially have an extremely valuable role to play. NGOs in Australia have not been active enough with respect to Australia's reports to these various monitoring bodies.

---

1   See A Bayefsky, "Making the Human Rights Treaties Work" in L Henkin and JL Hargrave (eds), *Human Rights: An Agenda for the Next Century*, Studies in Transnational Legal Policy, No 26, American Society of International Law, 1994, pp 229-297.

Again, generally, Australia's reports are much more honest than the norm. Whereas some countries that are otherwise regarded as good international citizens sometimes take their reporting obligations in a very dilatory way, Australia doesn't. However, even though our reports are of quite good standard, they tend to provide very positive spins on particular fact situations. Australia has developed a technique which I call "confess and avoid". For example, the report will admit that a particular Indigenous community has shocking rates of illness, and then detail all the measures that have been put into place to solve the problem.

More "hard" information should be given to these committees so that when the representatives of Australia present Australia's reports, they can be questioned more closely. Generally speaking, the exchanges between the Australians and the committees have been exceptionally polite. The Australian representatives are thanked for being honest, and it becomes a very self-congratulatory exchange. Australian NGOs should make sure that the treaty monitoring bodies have the information to question the Australian Government representatives, to make it a more testing and more meaningful exchange. One of the committees, the Committee on Economic, Social and Cultural Rights chaired by Philip Alston, has now begun to allow NGOs to make oral presentations to it. That committee has very good, productive relationships with NGOs. This is why it is one of the most effective committees in the system.

With respect to individual complaints, again NGOs have a valuable role with respect to the treaty-monitoring bodies. In particular, NGOs can help in providing support to people making communications.

Reform initiatives

I have suggested that the system is in crisis, and that the crisis is not just financial. Certainly, the human rights area within the UN is suffering from the same financial crisis as the whole of the UN system. However, the crisis is also a result of a tendency in the UN system to respond to a problem by drafting a new treaty, without considering how it will impact on the system as a whole. With the increasing number of treaties and treaty parties, the system is grinding to a halt.

The system was set up in a totally different era. The idea was that these committees would perform two different functions. First, they would require countries to engage in internal self-analysis. By putting together country reports, there would be soul searching at the governmental level. A second hope was that with the creation of independent monitoring bodies, the so-called "Dracula effect" would apply. The "sunlight" of publicity would prevent human rights abuses (Dracula always operated in the dark). Neither of these hopes for the system has actually worked. The reports are often essentially bureaucratic governmental documents, drafted without any real consultation with the NGO community, and are also extremely hard to obtain.

The second reason that these functions are not being performed is the issue of resources and backlog. The fault lies on both the States parties to the treaties and also on the treaty monitoring bodies themselves. States parties are very dilatory about their reports. Even Australia, which devotes significant resources to human rights, is considerably behind on its reports under a number of important treaties, most particularly the ICCPR.[2]

States are also undermining the system by making reservations to these treaties. There are significant numbers of reservations to all the treaties. In some cases, particularly CEDAW, the reservations are quite extraordinary. For example, the Republic of Mali has made a reservation to CEDAW which in essence says that it will make no change to its domestic laws. Other countries have reservations to CEDAW saying that the definition of 'non-discrimination' must be consistent with religious law, Islamic law and other laws.

Another way that States are letting down the system is by nominating government officers for expert positions on the treaty bodies. Ann Bayefsky has concluded that over half of the so-called independent experts in the treaty monitoring system are employed in some capacity by their nominating government. The treaty bodies are also letting down the system by failing to challenge countries when they make their reports, or to follow up deficiencies in a considered way.

What can be done to change this fairly depressing picture? What are some areas for reform? Suggestions for reform from observers such as Ann Bayefsky include the creation of a single treaty body. Michael Lavarch, the former Federal Attorney-General, endorsed this suggestion in a speech to the UN Commission on Human Rights in Geneva in 1995. A full-time, single-treaty body would make reporting much less of a burden for States parties and would be more efficient. It would also highlight the universal applicability of all human rights and stop that

---

2   As at June 1997, Australia's third report to the Human Rights Committee on implementation of the ICCPR was more than five years overdue. Australia's fourth periodic report is also now overdue. *Editor's note.*

compartmentalisation of human rights treaties that has tended to occur, especially with women.

A second suggestion for reform is the need for more pressure on countries to remove their reservations to these treaties. Australia has a number of unjustifiable reservations to our acceptance of several of these treaties. We have a reservation to Article 4 of CERD, and a series of reservations to CEDAW and to the ICCPR. Other countries also have significant reservations and we should encourage our government to put pressure on those countries to withdraw them.

On 11 November 1994, the Human Rights Committee adopted a General Comment on Reservations to the Covenant.[3] It is a fascinating and bold statement. It says that reservations to human rights treaties must be seen in a different way to reservations to other treaties. It provides that there should not be reservations to articles in human rights treaties that are customary international law principles. The Human Rights Committee is saying that human rights treaties are not simply agreements between States that they can withdraw from at will. There are some norms that are binding even on States that are not parties, such as the norm of non-discrimination. Therefore States should not be allowed to derogate from that obligation in reservations. Whether other countries object to a particular reservation should not be relevant.

The system could also be strengthened if the General Assembly were to start identifying recalcitrant States, by naming in resolutions those countries that are not fulfilling their reporting obligations and their other human rights duties. Yet another way to secure the integrity of the system is by being tougher on countries that accept human rights treaties and then do not fulfil their obligations. Focusing on universal ratification as an independent good is really not focusing on the main issue. There should be a mechanism for actually expelling countries from the human rights treaty regime if they do not adhere to minimum human rights standards.

It could also be valuable to consider discontinuing the reporting obligation. At the moment, it does not work particularly well. The committees could then put more effort into fact finding, rather than the time-consuming job of listening to what is often government propaganda on human rights.

---

3   General Comment 24(52), UN Doc CCPR/C/21/ Rev 1/Add 6.

A final important reform would be to ensure the impartiality of committee members. We should be putting pressure on our government to ensure that people who are nominated and elected to the treaty bodies are genuinely impartial and independent.

Comment: *Michael O'Flaherty*
Secretary of the Committee on the Elimination of Racial Discrimination

I have to react to the analysis of the treaty system as being in total crisis and chaos. It has its problems, but we should acknowledge considerable improvements in the last few years. I found Ann Bayefsky's comments on the treaty system rather unfair and damaging. Many groups will lose faith in the treaty system if we are overly critical and fail to acknowledge the small improvements and the potential for change that exists within the system.

The first of these improvements is that the committees are becoming more innovative with the procedures they are developing outside of their traditional work of dealing with States' reports and individual petitions. For example, the Committee on the Elimination of Racial Discrimination is developing a radical procedure for responding to crisis situations around the world. The chairpersons of the treaty bodies have met with the Secretary-General of the UN to discuss the development of urgent reaction procedures. They discussed the coordination of these procedures with other UN human rights operations, including methods for notifying the Security Council of crisis situations.

Another important development is with regard to the annual reports. I agree that the annual reports are poor documents, but they are changing. Nearly all human rights treaty body annual reports now include observations and criticism with regard to specific countries.

Finally, I would note the developing role of NGOs at the treaty bodies. Whilst this role remains an unofficial one in most of the committees, it is a role of increasing importance and status.

6

Individual complaints: an overview and admissibility requirements

Hilary Charlesworth

Introduction

The right of individual communication to a treaty body is available under three treaties: the Optional Protocol to the International Covenant on Civil and Political Rights (ICCPR), the Convention on the Elimination of All Forms of Racial Discrimination (CERD), and the Convention against Torture (CAT). Australia has accepted all three rights of individual communication. We ratified the Optional Protocol in 1991 and accepted the other two procedures in 1993. The right of individual complaint is currently available to all within Australian jurisdiction; that is, you do not have to be a national of Australia to complain.

A two-stage approach

The complaints are processed in a two-stage procedure. Each committee deals first with admissibility. If the committee decides that a complaint is admissible, it then considers the merits of the case. Even if a committee accepts the admissibility of a complaint, it can reconsider admissibility at the merits stage. Sometimes the country concerned asks for reconsideration of admissibility at the merits stage.

Admissibility is a very important hurdle. Of all the communications received by the Human Rights Committee under the Optional Protocol to the ICCPR, 45 percent have been found inadmissible. Thus it is essential to prove that a case is admissible, and considerable work needs to go into the admissibility aspect of complaints. There is a high success rate once a case is admissible, with a violation found in 75 percent of cases.

One also needs to be realistic about the time lines involved. A decision on admissibility typically takes two years. Interim measures such as injunctions are available, but these are also very slow.

Admissibility requirements

The admissibility requirements are as follows. First, the communication must be with respect to a State party to the Optional Protocol. Second, the complaint must be made by the victim of an alleged violation. Third, the complaint must be in writing. The procedure is sometimes called a postcard procedure, as there are no other formal requirements for the written complaint. There is no possibility of oral procedures, and it is therefore important to have careful documentation of all elements of the complaint.

Fourth, the complaint must not be anonymous. Fifth, according to Article 3 of the Optional Protocol there must not be an abuse of the right to submit a complaint. For example, the Human Rights Committee has considered that resubmitting a rejected complaint is an abuse of the right to submit a complaint.

The sixth requirement is that the complaint not be incompatible with the ICCPR. Effectively, there are two ways that a complaint can be incompatible with the ICCPR. The first concerns time limits. If the alleged breach occurred before Australia accepted the Optional Protocol, the Human Rights Committee will not accept it, because at the time of the breach Australia had not accepted the right of individual complaint. That is known to lawyers as *ratione temporis*. It is possible, however, to complain about something that started in the past as long as it continues in the present. The second basis for incompatibility is one of substance; for example, a complaint about the breach of a right not in the ICCPR.

The seventh admissibility requirement is that at the time the complaint is made to the Human Rights Committee, the same subject matter is not being considered under any other international procedure. The same matter can not be the subject of simultaneous complaints to the Human Rights Committee, the Committee on the Elimination of Racial Discrimination, and the Committee against Torture.

Finally, complainants must establish that they have exhausted all domestic remedies unless those remedies are unduly prolonged.

Against whom can complaints be made?

The Human Rights Committee only hears complaints against parties to the ICCPR. These are all governments. There is, however, a question as to whether governments are ever responsible for the actions of groups or corporations within their jurisdiction. This area of law is at a very early stage. It is arguable that if, for example, a government knew about a corporate practice of race discrimination over many years, gave the corporation money and support, and never criticised or otherwise pressured the corporation, then that country should be held liable for a human rights violation. In the case of *Velasquez*[1] in the Inter-American Court of Human Rights, the brother of a person killed by terrorists established that the Honduran Government not only knew of the actions of these terrorist groups, but positively encouraged them to engage in terrorist activity. The Inter-American Court of Human Rights held that Honduras was responsible for the activities of these otherwise "private groups" because it had positively tolerated the activities. Thus, in order to address the actions of so-called "private groups" it is necessary to establish a link between the government's tolerance and the actions.

Who can complain?

Article 1 of the Optional Protocol to the ICCPR provides that only a victim of a breach or their personal representative can make a communication to a treaty body. An organisation such as the National Aboriginal and Islander Legal Services Secretariat, an Aboriginal Legal Service, or a Land Council cannot be the author of a communication. In a number of cases from Uruguay, people in jail have authorised a relative or a friend to act as their personal representative. Where another person is to be authorised to bring the complaint, the authority must be in writing.

The complainant must be personally affected by the violation. A decision by the Human Rights Committee, *Poongavanam v Mauritius*,[2] concerned a complaint by a male Mauritian who had been convicted on a murder charge by an all-male jury. At that time in Mauritius there could by law only be all-male juries. The complainant complained that this was a violation of the ICCPR because all-male juries violated the principle of

1   *Rodriguez Velasquez v Honduras*, Inter-American Court of Human Rights, Judgment of 29 July 1988, (1988) 9 HRLJ 212.

2   *Poongavanam v Mauritius*, Human Rights Committee, *Report of the Human Rights Committee*, UN Doc A/49/40 (1994) p 362.

women's equality with men. The Committee gave this argument very short shrift. Because the man was not personally hurt by the denial of equality to women in Mauritius, he could not use that violation of equality rights in his own case. The Human Rights Committee is not interested in abstract challenges. In another case,[3] a group of Mauritian women submitted a communication to the Human Rights Committee in relation to a Mauritian law that provided that if a Mauritian woman married a non-Mauritian she lost her citizenship, and her children were not Mauritian citizens. Under the same law, if a Mauritian man married a non-Mauritian, his spouse and children were Mauritian citizens. Of the 20 women who made the complaint, only three were actually married to non-Mauritians. The rest were unmarried women. The Human Rights Committee refused to consider the claim of the unmarried women. The case proceeded to the merits phase only in relation to the three women who were married to non-Mauritians and actually affected by the law.

In the case of *Lansmann v Finland*,[4] 23 Saami reindeer herdsmen complained to the Human Rights Committee of a violation of Article 27 through the actions of the Finnish Government in giving a quarrying licence in land used by them for reindeer herding. There was no problem with 23 people submitting the communication because all could show that they were individually affected.

Clearly, the choice of a complainant in these cases is extremely important.

Exhaustion of domestic legal remedies

A particularly critical issue of admissibility is the requirement of exhaustion of domestic remedies, unless they are unduly prolonged.

The requirement that domestic remedies must be exhausted ensures that international procedures are used as a last resort, and prevents international committees from being overwhelmed with complaints. It also embodies the principle that problems are best solved at home. In Australia this means that a case involving, for example, race discrimination would have to be taken through all stages of either the Federal or State laws, including all appeal mechanisms. This is a fairly demanding requirement. In some cases,

---

3 *Aumeeruddy-Cziffra et al v Mauritius*, Human Rights Committee, *Report of the Human Rights Committee*, UN Doc A/36/40 (1981) (The Mauritian Women case).

4 Communication No 511/1992, UN Doc CCPR/C/52/D/511/1992 (8 November 1994).

however, there are no laws in place. Where Australia's laws are not comprehensive, international possibilities are particularly important. Moreover, complainants only have to pursue avenues provided by law and not political avenues. In a number of cases, States parties have argued that complainants have not used all domestic remedies because they did not complain, for example, to an Ombudsman. This is essentially an administrative, not a legal remedy. The Human Rights Committee has decided that it is not necessary to employ every administrative remedy, only to pursue remedies provided by law.

Sometimes it is argued by complainants that there is no point in pursuing legal remedies because the legal system is entirely corrupt or unsympathetic to them. In a case involving Senegal, *Kone v Senegal*,[5] a Senegalese Opposition politician said that he had not complained to Senegalese courts about torture because of the corrupt judiciary. The Human Rights Committee rejected that argument. It held that although there are cases in which the legal system is not working or incapable of delivering a remedy, it would not assume this. The Committee required actual evidence to this effect.

Where there is a precedent directly against a complainant, it is not necessary to go all the way to the ultimate court of appeal. In the case of *Pratt and Morgan v Jamaica*,[6] the Human Rights Committee made it clear that the legal remedies rule does not require resort to appeals that objectively have no prospect of success. At times, the Committee has to make quite fine decisions on what amounts to a firm precedent against a particular point.

In Australian law, the domestic remedies requirement is often not onerous, because there is no bill of rights, and therefore many violations have no remedy at all. In general, the author of a communication has to tell the Human Rights Committee what measures have been taken. The onus is then on the country involved to indicate that other remedies exist. A number of cases involving Uruguay have concerned the exhaustion of domestic remedies. In *Rodriguez v Uruguay*,[7] it was argued that there

---

5   *Kone v Senegal*, Communication No 386, UN Doc CCPR/C/52/D/386/1989 (27 October 1994)

6   *Pratt and Morgan v Jamaica*, Communications Nos 210/1986 and 225/1987, Human Rights Committee, *Report of the Human Rights Committee*, UN Doc A/44/40 (1989), p 222.

7   *Rodriguez v Uruguay*, Communication No 322/1988, UN DocCCPR/C/51/D/322/1988 (9 August 1994).

were no domestic remedies to pursue against an alleged torturer because of a sweeping general amnesty. The Human Rights Committee held that the amnesty laws prevented any effective domestic remedies.

In a number of cases the Human Rights Committee has considered situations in which there are legal remedies, but the complainant lacks the money to pursue them. In the case of *Hylton v Jamaica*,[8] the Human Rights Committee held that if the person can establish that they themselves lacked the funds and that legal aid was not available, domestic remedies need not be pursued to their conclusion.

Finally, the Optional Protocol provides that all domestic remedies must be exhausted, unless they are "unreasonably prolonged". The Human Rights Committee has said that it will look at the circumstances of each case. In a case involving Madagascar,[9] a person had initiated a court action to obtain redress for a violation of human rights and, four years later, the action had not yet got on the court lists. In that case, the Human Rights Committee was prepared to say that four years was unreasonably prolonged.

Postscript: the ICCPR and Indigenous peoples

The right that is most critical for Indigenous peoples under the ICCPR is the right set out in Article 1, the right to self-determination. In a decision in 1992, the *Lubicon Lake Band* case,[10] the Human Rights Committee said that the right to self-determination is a collective right that cannot be claimed by an individual. Their reasoning was that the Optional Protocol allows individuals to make claims, and that therefore the Optional Protocol cannot extend to Article 1 because individuals cannot claim collective rights. The Committee did not allow the argument based on Article 1 to proceed. It did, however, hear the case under Article 27, concerning the rights of ethnic minorities, and find that the rights of the Lubicon Lake Band had been violated.

Because the Human Rights Committee has a blind spot about the right to self-determination, Indigenous groups need to think creatively about

---

8 *Hylton v Jamaica*, Communication No 407/1990, UN Doc CCPR/C/51/D/ 407/1990 (15 July 1994).

9 *Hammel v Madagascar*, Communication No 155/1983, *Selected Decisions of the Human Rights Committee under the Optional Protocol*, UN Doc CCPR/C/OP/2, p 179 (3 April 1987).

10 *Ominayak v Canada*, Communication No 167/1984, Human Rights Committee, *Report of the Human Rights Committee*, UN Doc A/45/50 (1990).

other provisions in the ICCPR which might be useful. Useful provisions include non-discrimination on the basis of race, which is in Article 26, and the right to preservation of one's culture, which is Article 27.

A central issue for human rights law is the conflict between individual rights and collective rights. A very common clash occurs between religious or cultural rights and women's rights. In the *Lovelace* case,[11] Canada argued that a provision of the *Indian Act* pursuant to which women lost their status as Indians upon marrying non-Indians was merely seeking to preserve the traditions of First Nations. The Human Rights Committee rejected the argument and held that the right to non-discrimination was more important in that case. Moreover, the Canadian Government did not produce substantial evidence to demonstrate a deep cultural practice. While there could be an argument that many Indigenous peoples consider collective rights to be more important than individual rights, one would need to hear from Indigenous women on the issue. A conflict might arise if most Indigenous women in a community were in favour of a practice that seemed, on superficial examination, to be a violation of women's rights. Such a case would raise issues relating to the definition of "culture" that have not yet been clarified.

Finally, some comments on the requirement of exhausting domestic remedies. By way of example, it has been said that only some expressions of Aboriginal cultural and intellectual property are protected by Acts of parliament, and that the courts are unable to adequately protect all expressions of Indigenous cultural and intellectual property. An artist whose intellectual property has been exploited without redress could assert that domestic remedies have been exhausted. It would be up to the Australian Government to argue that the author of the communication had forgotten a particular legislative scheme and that, accordingly, a domestic remedy exists. Thus, the onus would be on the Australian Government to prove that there is a remedy. Moreover, it is possible that a domestic remedy will not be culturally appropriate. For example, it is questionable whether the Human Rights Committee would require people to break their sacred laws in order to pursue all available domestic remedies. I make this observation in light of the General Comment on Article 27[12] and the increasing sensitivity of the Committee to women's issues.

---

11 *Lovelace v Canada*, Communication No 24/1977, *Selected Decisions of the Human Rights Committee under the Optional Protocol*, UN Doc CCPR/C/OP/1 (1988) pp 86-90.

12 General Comment No 23(50) (Art 27); see S Pritchard, "The International Covenant on Civil and Political Rights and Indigenous Peoples", below.

7

Individual complaints:
historical perspectives and the
International Covenant on Economic,
Social and Cultural Rights

Philip Alston

My task is twofold: to provide an account of the historical development of international human rights complaints procedures and to talk about the relevance of complaints procedures for economic, social and cultural rights.

Historical perspectives

The right to petition, or in other words, the right to complain, has been central to most systems for the promotion of human rights since the eighteenth century. In 1950, a particularly distinguished and influential British international lawyer by the name of Hersch Lauterpacht wrote that any international arrangement to promote or protect human rights which did not make provision for a universal complaints procedure would be neither serious nor meaningful. Lauterpacht recognised that a meaningful international human rights system had to be based primarily upon a petition system which allowed for individuals to submit complaints.

But the history of approaches to this issue by governments within the UN system shows considerable reluctance to accept that proposition. In order to understand the present situation it is important to have a sense of the evolution of governmental attitudes. One version of this history is reflected in *Human Rights Fact Sheet No 7*, published by the UN Centre for Human Rights and dealing with "Communications Procedures". It says that:

When it met for the first time in 1947 the United Nations Commission on Human Rights [it actually met for the first time in 1946, but that is another matter] saw that procedures for handling communications would be needed. The procedures established since then have been improved and widened in scope over the years.

This is, in reality, a fundamental distortion of the truth. While a few Western countries saw the need for communications procedures, the main proponents were developing countries that had only recently been liberated from their colonial relationships. Despite, or perhaps because of, their efforts the Commission on Human Rights decided very rapidly, indeed as early as 1947, that it had "no power" whatsoever to deal with complaints. Instead, it set up a bureaucratic procedure which led to a formal listing of complaints from which the key details of names and all but the skeletal details of the allegations were removed. The first head of the UN Human Rights Secretariat, a Canadian named John Humphrey, later described the system he had helped to set up as "the world's most elaborate waste paper basket". The listed complaints were summarised so as to be virtually meaningless and were then circulated confidentially to governments. This indicates that governments are very concerned about the potential of complaints procedures for actually making a difference. Complaints procedures do empower individuals to compel governments to respond, and they are therefore of considerable significance.

The UN did not have a change of heart about responding to complaints until there was growing disillusionment with its inability to do anything about apartheid in South Africa. This was linked with a major campaign by Third World States, African in particular, to compel the UN to be more effective and active in its campaign against racial discrimination. What is now known as the "1503 procedure" began to emerge in 1967, when a major push within the UN context by Third World countries for a response to racism resulted in a very generally formulated UN resolution. This paved the way for the Commission on Human Rights to break with its longstanding refusal to discuss specific violations of human rights.

The 1503 procedure was reluctantly accepted by some governments because it provided that complaints would not be discussed in the public sessions of the Commission on Human Rights. Rather, the procedure would be entirely confidential. If those governments which were still not prepared to have a proper violations procedure in place had prevailed, the procedure would involve little more than a group of governments in the Commission meeting privately and saying to the Idi Amins of the world:

"Could you just give us a few more details about the measures that you are taking to try to address the alleged violations. If we can get some details of that nature, we will be much happier." In practice, then, the procedure was set up subject to a wide range of procedural limitations which were designed to limit access to it and to limit its potential effectiveness. It had very few of the characteristics which an objective observer would suggest might be necessary to facilitate a reasonable response to allegations of gross violations. While the procedure was an important breakthrough in principle, by 1995 the 1503 procedure is an almost total waste of time.

In most cases the Commission on Human Rights does little more than decide to keep a situation under review. In some cases, a special representative of the Commission might visit the country concerned, sometimes over a period of years. Eventually the matter is either dropped altogether, or if a major political push is successful, the case might be transferred to the public sessions of the Commission for consideration under a more effective, public, procedure.

There are innumerable cases which are already the subject of one or other of the public procedures and, as a result, I believe that the 1503 procedure is no longer justified. The Commission's public debate is potentially effective and a wide variety of other international procedures now exists. The 1503 procedure serves a negative function in so far as it takes the pressure off governments acting within the UN context to set up a serious, global violations procedure. Moreover, while the 1503 procedure purports to address all human rights issues, it has virtually never addressed economic, social and cultural rights issues in any depth.

One final word from a historical perspective is in order. When governments were adopting the various human rights treaties at which we are looking now, there was no great desire to include complaints procedures. Indeed the opposite was the case: governments did not want to add petition procedures to the treaty-based arrangements that were being negotiated. However, the 1503 procedure paved the way for the inclusion of a petition procedure in the Convention on the Elimination of All Forms of Racial Discrimination (CERD), which was adopted in 1965. Until that time, there was no agreement to include an Optional Protocol to the International Covenant on Civil and Political Rights (ICCPR). It was in fact due to the precedent set by CERD in relation to this supposedly narrow area of racial discrimination which strengthened the hands of those who wanted a more generalised complaints procedure in connection with the ICCPR. As a result the Optional Protocol was drafted in great haste in 1966, the final year of the 18-year process of drafting the ICCPR. Had it not been for the CERD precedent, created because racial discrimination was seen as a reasonably safe area by the majority of UN members, we would not have had the complaints procedure under the Human Rights Committee.

Subsequently, NGOs and some of the treaty bodies have started to call for the development of more complaints procedures. A major proposal was put to the 1996 Beijing Women's Conference to endorse the need for an Optional Protocol to the Convention on the Elimination of All Forms of Discrimination against Women (CEDAW). Various academic commentators have advocated the adoption of complaints procedures under the Convention on the Rights of the Child.

The International Covenant on Economic, Social and Cultural Rights

The Committee on Economic, Social and Cultural Rights has also called for an optional protocol procedure under that covenant. The call has been supported by both the 1993 Vienna World Conference on Human Rights and the Commission on Human Rights. Such support does not of course bring with it any assurance of governmental support when the moment eventually comes.

Perhaps the main question in this connection is why do we need an optional protocol in relation to economic and social rights? The answer is that there is no substitute for a complaints procedure to enable both policy-makers and practitioners to come to grips with the essence of any given human right. If one is dealing with the right to a fair trial or the right to freedom of the press, there are many details which need to be filled in to give content to those rights. For example, in relation to the right to a fair trial, when is government-paid counsel required, when is interpretation necessary, what procedural safeguards are indispensable, how long can pre-trial proceedings reasonably last? The answers to those sorts of questions have always had to be worked out at the international level primarily through coming to grips with very concrete situations, most often in the context of communications procedures.

In relation to the International Covenant on Economic, Social and Cultural Rights (ICESCR), the single most neglected right is the right to take part in cultural life. There has been no serious international reflection on what that means. There are virtually no guidelines which indicate how this right plays out in any given context. That situation is not so different to the one that prevailed several decades ago in relation to some of the key civil and political rights. Until there is a complaints procedure, the Committee on Economic, Social and Cultural Rights will always find it extremely difficult to come to grips with the specificities of, for example, the cultural rights of Aboriginal groups.

At present, there are many developments going directly contrary to acceptance of the notion of economic and social rights and its implementation in practice. Most observers and governments assume that the trend towards deregulation, privatisation and reliance upon the free market is in some way incompatible with respect for economic, social and cultural rights. The more appropriate response, of course, is that those very trends make it all the more imperative to ensure that basic minimum protection is provided to all persons in relation to their rights to food, education, health care and so on. But instead of such a recognition, there is all too often a superficial assumption that these are outdated types of rights, the validity of which was undermined by the demise of Eastern European socialism.

8

Individual communications under the Optional Protocol to the International Covenant on Civil and Political Rights

Elizabeth Evatt

Preliminary

The Human Rights Committee is based in Geneva, halfway around the world. Its Optional Protocol procedure is studded with technical requirements. Its procedures may take more than two years to reach finality. Its decisions are often densely written and inscrutable. And yet, despite this, it can turn out to be a surprisingly accessible process. It can be effective, not just for the individual whose case is decided, but for many others affected by the same kinds of violations. The Committee has found violations of rights on the basis of a handwritten letter from a prisoner on death row. Formality for its own sake has no place in the procedure, though the basic rules of natural justice and equality between the parties are observed.

Prisoners have been released, laws have been changed, compensation has been granted as a result of communications to the Human Rights Committee. It is a means of recourse for individuals to seek redress for grievances, and it is an essential element in making the International Covenant on Civil and Political Rights an effective instrument in promoting and protecting human rights. It gives immediacy and sharpness of definition to the general principles of the Covenant. This said, I emphasise that the Human Rights Committee is not a court. It does not sit in appeal from national courts and its decisions are not legally binding, unlike those of the European Court of Human Rights, or the International Court of Justice.

The Human Rights Committee does not have power to investigate, or to arbitrate or mediate. It decides cases on the basis of the written material submitted to it by the parties. It does not make findings of fact as such, but expresses its views as to whether the material put to it by the parties establishes a violation of the Covenant. It is an independent body, and it values its independence of governments. Between 1976 and July 1994, the Human Rights Committee received 578 communications. Of these, 201 were found inadmissible and views on the merits had been adopted in 193 cases. In 147, violations of the Covenant were found to have occurred. Most of the cases involved questions such as fair trial, arbitrary detention, torture and cruel, inhuman and degrading treatment. One commentator described the range of cases in these terms:

> Complaints about political imprisonment, torture and disappearances in Uruguay, political kidnapping in Zaire, sex discrimination in Mauritius and the Netherlands, political killings in Suriname, problems of Indian tribes in Canada, allegations of political discrimination in Nicaragua, and oppressive treatment of aliens and politicians in Madagascar.[1]

There are infinite opportunities to use the Optional Protocol to the Covenant, but it does require familiarity with the jurisprudence and procedures of the Human Rights Committee. This chapter aims to throw light on some of the mysteries and to present the Optional Protocol procedure as user friendly.

The Protocol

The individual complaints procedure under the International Covenant on Civil and Political Rights is established by the First Optional Protocol. The Protocol is a separate treaty, connected to the Covenant. It is "Optional" in the sense that States who ratify the Covenant can elect whether or not to ratify the Protocol and thereby recognise the competence of the Human Rights Committee to deal with claims by individuals that their rights under the Covenant have been violated by a State. Eighty-nine States out of 134 parties to the Covenant have now done so. Australia ratified the Protocol in 1991. This means that Australian citizens and other persons in Australia can use the procedure if they meet the requirements.

---

1   T Opsahl, Ottawa, 1990.

Outline of the procedure

An individual in Australia whose rights under the Covenant are said to have been violated may commence proceedings under the Optional Protocol by sending a written communication setting out the details of the alleged violation to the Human Rights Centre at Geneva. No particular form is required, but the model form issued by the Centre for Human Rights is useful, since it will ensure that all points are covered.

Communications should be in written form and signed. When submitted by a representative the authorisation should be attached. A two-part procedure is then set in motion. The first stage deals with the question of admissibility. The Committee cannot deal with a communication unless it is admissible in terms of the Protocol. Both parties, the author of the communication and the State, may make submissions on the question of admissibility before it is determined. The Committee can find that a communication is inadmissible without asking the State for any submissions, but it cannot proceed to find it admissible until the State has been asked for its submissions on that question (Rule 80).This could take up to a year. The Committee can review its decision on admissibility.[2] A review would arise if the situation changed, for example where the State had remedied the violation,[3] or where a pending case in the State was later decided against the author.

If the communication is found to be admissible by the Committee, both the author and the State are asked to make submissions on the merits of the case. This could take another year, or perhaps longer. There are no oral hearings. Cases are determined by the Committee on the basis of the written submissions from the parties. Procedural rules ensure that the parties receive and have an opportunity to reply to each others' submissions. After the Committee has considered the matter, it adopts its views as to whether the author's rights under the Covenant have been violated. If so, it may also express its view as to the remedies which should be provided.

---

2   Rule 93(4).

3   For example, *CF et al v Canada*, Communication No 113/1981, *Selected Decisions of the Human Rights Committee under the Optional Protocol* vol 2 p 1, UN Doc CCPR/C/OP/2 (12 April 1985). See also *JM v Jamaica*, Communication No 165/1984, *Selected Decisions of the Human Rights Committee under the Optional Protocol* vol 2 p 17, UN Doc CCPR/C/OP/2 (26 March 1986).

Admissibility

Looking more closely at the procedure, step by step, there are many technical hurdles to jump at the admissibility stage. The focus here is on those issues likely to be relevant in the context of claims by Australian Indigenous people.

What is a victim?

The claim must be brought by or on behalf of an individual who claims to be a victim of a violation of a right set out in the Covenant (Article 1). The individual must be identified. Anonymous communications are inadmissible (Article 3). There is no age limit, and cases have been brought by and for children.

Individual must be personally affected

To be a victim, the individual must be personally affected. There are several components of this. First, claims cannot be made on an abstract basis to challenge policies or laws, independently of their actual effect on a particular individual (this type of claim is known as an *actio popularis*). For example, to challenge the failure of the government to deliver health services without discrimination, there must be an identified individual who can be shown to be actually affected by the alleged violation.

Second, the adverse effect on the individual must have occurred or be imminent. In a Netherlands case decided in 1993,[4] many citizens claimed that their right to life under Article 6 had been violated because there had been an agreement to deploy cruise missiles fitted with nuclear warheads on the territory of the State. The missiles would be a target for the enemy and the authors could be an accessory to the crime against humanity.

The Committee's view was that for a person to claim to be a victim of a violation of a right protected by the Covenant, he or she must show either that an act or an omission of a State party has already adversely affected his or her enjoyment of such a right, or that such an effect is imminent. The deployment did not at the relevant period of time place the authors in the position of victims whose right to life was violated or was put under imminent prospect of violation. The authors were found not to be victims.

---

4   *EW et al v Netherlands*, Communication No 429/1990, UN Doc CCPR/C/47/ D/429/1990 (29 April 1993).

Organisations or companies are not victims

Under the decisions of the Committee, companies cannot claim to be victims;[5] nor can organisations or associations as such.[6] However, members of an organisation may individually rank as victims. Several individuals can claim to be victims in the sense of Article 1 of the Optional Protocol if they are actually affected. In the case of a claim brought by a group of individuals, the Committee's view is that provided each of the authors is a victim within the meaning of Article 1 of the Optional Protocol, nothing precludes large numbers of persons from bringing a case. The mere fact of large numbers of petitioners does not render their communication an *actio popularis*.

These rules may not sit well with the values of Indigenous communities, since they preclude claims being brought on behalf of a named community or tribal group as such. When Chief Bernard Ominayak, Chief of the Lubicon Lake Band, brought a case on behalf of his Band, the Committee said that there was no objection to groups of individuals who claim to be similarly affected collectively to submit a communication about alleged breaches of their rights.[7] However, under later decisions it appears that only named members of a group can be victims. It would have to be shown that a violation affected named individuals. This is not necessarily an insuperable obstacle, though it is rather unrealistic for communities.

In a case from Finland, the authors were 48 named individuals who were members of the Muotkatunturi Herdsmen's Committee and

---

5   *A Newspaper Publishing Company v Trinidad and Tobago*, Communication No 360/1989, Human Rights Committee, *Report of the Human Rights Committee*, UN Doc A/44/40 (1989).

6   *Hartikainen v Finland*, Communication No 40/1978, *Selected Decisions under the Optional Protocol*, UN Doc CCPR/C/OP/1 p 74 (9 April 1981). *JRT and the WG Party*, Communication No 104/1981, *Selected Decisions under the Optional Protocol*, UN Doc CCPR/C/OP/1 p 25 (6 April 1983). This has been criticised, see Manfred Nowak, *Commentary on the United Nations Covenant on Civil and Political Rights*, N P Engel, Kehl am Rhein, 1993, p 658, especially with regard to Articles 1, 18, 21, 22, 23, 25 and 27.

7   *Ominayak v Canada*, Communication No 167/1984, Human Rights Committee, *Report of the Human Rights Committee*, UN Doc A/45/40 (1990), vol 2, para 32.1.

members of the Angeli local community.[8] The Committee was satisfied that each ranked as a victim for the purposes of the claim and that each had exhausted local remedies.

Victim must be within the jurisdiction of the State party

Individual victims need not be citizens of the State party provided that they are present in the State or within the jurisdiction of the State. This is an expansion of meaning, as Article 26 of the Covenant says that persons must be within the territory *and* subject to the jurisdiction of the State. The Committee has admitted claims where the victim is outside the State party's boundaries, provided that he or she remain subject to the jurisdiction of the State, for example, where a passport is refused to a citizen who is overseas.

What type of harm can be considered?

Future harm

In *Lansmann v Finland*,[9] the authors (Indigenous Saami) sought to prevent quarrying under a mining lease which they said would cause serious harm to their reindeer herding, a cultural right protected under Article 27 of the Covenant. While no violation was found to have occurred in the circumstances, the State was put on notice that if mining were significantly expanded, this might constitute a violation of the authors' rights. It was implicit in this case that the Committee could deal with the case if the projected quarrying could be shown to pose a real threat to the authors' rights under Article 27. It could not only find a violation but it could propose measures to prevent the harm. The question of interim measures is considered below.

Indirect harm

A person may be adversely affected in his or her enjoyment of a right by laws even if the laws in question had not been directly applied to that person. In two cases involving Article 17, which protects privacy and family life, the Committee has found that the prospect of the application of the law had interfered with the author's privacy or family life, thus making the author a victim.

---

8   *Lansmann v Finland*, Communication No 511/1992, UN Doc CCPR/C/52/D/ 511/1992 (8 November 1994), para 9.3.

9   Note 8 above.

In the *Mauritian Women* case,[10] the law did not accord the same rights of permanent residence in Mauritius to the husband of a Mauritian woman as it did to the wife of a Mauritian man. The law had not been enforced against the authors or their alien husbands. Nevertheless the Committee found that the future possibility of deportation and the existing precarious residence situation represented an interference with the family life of the Mauritian wives and their husbands (Article 17). In *Toonen v Australia*,[11] the author had shown that the threat of enforcement of laws making homosexual conduct criminal had affected him personally (Article 17).

Another example of an indirect effect arose where the mother of a victim of torture was found also to be a victim under Article 7, because of the distress and anguish caused to her by the disappearance of her daughter and the uncertainty over her fate.[12] Individuals affected indirectly are, nevertheless, victims.

Who can initiate proceedings?

Acting for oneself, or through counsel

An individual can act for himself/herself. In this case the victim is also the "author" of the communication. Alternatively, individuals can act through counsel. It is not necessary, though it might be helpful, to consult a lawyer or to act through a lawyer. As there are no oral hearings the cost of a hearing would not be incurred.

Acting through an authorised representative

A third person can make a communication on behalf of the alleged victim, but the victim must give written authority. The Canadian *Mikmaq* case failed partly because the author did not prove that he was authorised to act for the Mikmaq or that he personally was a victim of violation of

---

10 *Aumeeruddy-Cziffra et al v Mauritius*, Human Rights Committee, *Report of the Human Rights Committee*, UN Doc A/36/40 (1981) (the *Mauritian Women* case).

11 *Toonen v Australia*, Communication No 488/1992, UN Doc CCPR/C/50/D/488/1992 (8 April 1994).

12 *Almeida de Quinteros v Uruguay*, Communication No 107/1981, *Selected Decisions of the Human Rights Committee under the Optional Protocol*, UN Doc CCPR/C/OP/2 (21 July 1983).

rights.[13] Non-governmental organisations may also act, with the authority of the victim. In *Hertzberg v Finland*,[14] an organisation for sexual equality acted for the alleged victim.

Assumed authority

Even without proof of express authority a person can act on behalf of another person if the Committee is satisfied that the other person cannot act for himself or herself, for example where that person has disappeared or is in prison, and there is reason to believe, because of a close family relationship or otherwise, that the victim would approve the author acting on his or her behalf. Rule 90(1)(b) provides that while normally the victim or his representative act, in exceptional cases a communication may be submitted by other persons on behalf of the victim.

What kind of claim can found a communication?

Claim must concern a violation of the Covenant

A communication by an individual must claim a violation of one or more of the rights set out in the Covenant (Optional Protocol, Articles 1 and 2). Only certain provisions of the Covenant, Articles 6-27, can found claims.[15] In the *Lubicon Lake Band* case in 1990,[16] the author alleged that the Government of Canada had violated the Lubicon Lake Band's right of self-determination, which arises under Article 1. The Band claimed violation of the right to determine freely its political status and pursue its economic, social and cultural development, as well as the right to dispose freely of its natural wealth and resources and not to be deprived of its own means of subsistence. The circumstances were that despite laws and treaties, the Canadian Government had allowed the provincial government of Alberta to expropriate the territory of the Band for the

---

13 *AD v Canada*, Communication No 78/1980, *Selected Decisions of the Human Rights Committee under the Optional Protocol*, UN Doc CCPR/C/OP/2 (29 July 1984).

14 *Hertzberg v Finland*, Communication No 61/1979, *Selected Decisions of the Human Rights Committee under the Optional Protocol*, CCPR/C/OP/1 (2 April 1982) concerning the Finnish broadcasting company.

15 *Ominayak v Canada*, Communication No 167/1984, Human Rights Committee, *Report of the Human Rights Committee*, UN Doc A/45/40 (1990).

16 Note 15 above.

benefit of private corporate interests, including leases for oil and gas exploration.

The Committee decided that it could not deal with the question whether the Lubicon Lake Band is a "people" under the Optional Protocol, and could not consider whether their right to self-determination under Article 1 of the Covenant had been violated. The Committee could deal only with claims that individual rights set out in Articles 6 to 27 had been violated.

There is, of course, no power to deal with complaints about property rights or other rights not covered by the Covenant. However, interference with land rights, or failure to recognise land rights, might be considered as a denial of cultural rights under Article 27.

Claim must be compatible with the Covenant

A communication will be considered inadmissible if the Committee considers it to be incompatible with the provisions of the Covenant.[17] In practice, the claim must reveal how it is said that a particular article of the Covenant has been violated in respect of the author. If the circumstances do not accord with the Committee's interpretation of the Covenant, the communication may be found inadmissible. Some claims are rejected as manifestly ill-founded on the basis of a substantive legal interpretation of the Covenant. This can lead to some very lengthy debates on the meaning of the Covenant at the admissibility stage, which some consider inappropriate.

While the issue need not be considered in this context, there are questions as to whether the Committee should look behind a claim that a particular right has been violated, when the circumstances which constitute the violation have been adequately set out. It is arguable that the Committee should not embark on a legal analysis of the claim at the admissibility stage.

Not an abuse of the right to submit

Communications are to be considered inadmissible if the Committee considers that they are an abuse of the right of submission (Optional Protocol, Article 3). An example is a Netherlands case where the author complained that his right to presumption of innocence was violated by the requirement that he show his car registration on the windscreen of his

---

17 Optional Protocol to the International Covenant on Civil and Political Rights, Articles 1 and 3.

car.[18] Excessive delay in commencing proceedings could also be an abuse of the right of submission.[19]

Sufficient substantiation

The claim has to be "sufficiently substantiated".[20] It is not enough for an author to complain about violation of his or her rights in very general terms, without documenting or otherwise substantiating the claim. There is no clear guidance as to what is sufficient to substantiate a claim. It can be compared to establishing a prima facie case. The test has been described in these terms:

> Although at the stage of admissibility an author need not prove an alleged violation, he must submit sufficient evidence in substantiation to constitute a prima facie case.[21]

A "claim" is therefore not just any allegation, but an allegation supported by a certain amount of substantiating evidence. Where the Committee finds that the author has failed to make at least a prima facie case justifying further examination, it holds the communication inadmissible on the ground that the author has no claim under Article 2.

Who is the complaint about?

Violation must be by a State party

The alleged violation must be by a State party that has ratified the first Optional Protocol.

Extent of State responsibility

The State party may be responsible for a violation of rights by an independent agency to which it has delegated functions.[22] It may, for example, be held responsible for violations by companies which it wholly

---

18 *HJH v Netherlands*, Communication No 448/1991, UN Doc CCPR/C/43/D/448/ 1991 (8 November 1991); *JJC v Canada*, Communication No 367/1989, UN Doc CCPR/C/43/D/367/1989 (13 November 1991).

19 Optional Protocol to the International Covenant on Civil and Political Rights, Article 3.

20 Rule 90(b).

21 J Moller, Ottawa, 1990.

22 *B d B et al v Netherlands*, Communication No 27/1988, Human Rights Committee, *Report of the Human Rights Committee*, UN Doc A/44/40 (1989) p 286.

or substantially owns, such as a broadcasting corporation.[23] The trend to privatisation could limit the potential scope of the communications procedure. The State should continue to be responsible for private prisons, as this is a direct responsibility under Article 10.

In some circumstances, the State could be held responsible for violations of rights by private persons, for example, where the State has failed to implement a clear obligation to prohibit or penalise certain conduct: Articles 8 and 20, and possibly Articles 7 and 26. The Committee has said that the State must protect minorities (including Indigenous minorities) against acts of other persons in the State.

Time limits

Violation prior to entry into force of the Optional Protocol: ratione temporis

The jurisprudence of the Committee is that:

> The Committee cannot consider alleged violations of the Covenant which occurred before the entry into force of the Optional Protocol for the State party, unless the events complained of have continuing effects which in themselves constitute a violation of the Covenant.

Thus where acts of torture had occurred before the State had ratified the Optional Protocol, the Committee could not consider the case.[24] This decision remains controversial.[25] The prohibition on "retrospectivity" is not absolute, however.

Continuing effects

In the case of *Lovelace v Canada*,[26] the author had been excluded by the *Indian Act* from participation as a member of her tribe because she had married an outsider. Her individual right to enjoy her culture in

---

23 *Hertzberg v Finland*, Communication No 61/1979, *Selected Decisions of the Human Rights Committee under the Optional Protocol*, CCPR/C/OP/1 (2 April 1982).

24 *MT v Spain*, Communication No 310/1988, Human Rights Committee, *Report of the Human Rights Committee*, UN Doc A/46/40 (1991).

25 M Nowak, "The Activities of the UN-Human Rights Committee: Developments from 1 August 1989 through 31 July 1992" (1993) 14 *Human Rights Law Journal* 1, 18-19.

26 Communication No 24/1977, *Selected Decisions of the Human Rights Committee under the Optional Protocol*, UN Doc CCPR/C/OP/1 p 83 (30 July 1981).

community with other members of the tribe was thus denied to her by the law. The Act had applied to her before the entry into force of the Protocol. However, she claimed that the violation continued, because she was still affected by the law, in particular because she still could not claim a legal right to reside where she wished. This continuing effect was considered by the Committee to be a violation of her rights under Article 27. Essentially, it is the violation itself which continues.

Implications for Australian cases

The Optional Protocol came into effect for Australia on 25 December 1991. Some Australian cases have already been found to be inadmissible, on the basis that the events, acts and omissions occurred before the entry into force of the Optional Protocol, and there was no evidence to show that they had effects after that time.

Recently, attention has focused on the violation of human rights involved in the forced removal of Aboriginal children from their families. These violations occurred before December 1991, and only the effects of those violations that continue after that date could give rise to claims. A recent Argentinian case may be relevant to such cases. It concerned a child of "disappeared" parents who herself disappeared as a baby.[27] After 7 years, her grandmother had traced the child, who was then 7 years old. She had been adopted as a result of the action of the government. There was considerable delay in the legal proceedings in sorting out the identity and guardianship of the child. The Committee found that some of the alleged violations of the child's rights had occurred before the Covenant and the Optional Protocol came into force for Argentina. However, the proceedings to establish the identity and guardianship of the child had extended over 10 years, during which time the child had reached 18. Her identity was legally recognised only when she was 17. The Committee found that the failure to give her prompt and effective relief from her predicament was a violation of Article 24, under which children have a right to special measures of protection. The Committee stated:

> Bearing in mind the suffering already endured by the author, who lost both of her parents under tragic circumstances imputable to the State party, the Committee finds that the special measures required under article 24(1) were not expeditiously applied by Argentina, and that the delay in legally

---

27 *De Gallicchio v Argentina*, Communication No 400/1990, UN Doc CCPR/C/ 53/D/400/1990 (27 April 1995).

establishing her real name and issuing identity papers also entailed a violation of article 24(2), which is designed to promote recognition of the child's legal personality.

This decision may relate to the particular provisions of Article 24, so that its principle would apply only where the rights of children were at issue. Even so, it establishes an important principle in cases where there is delay in investigating and putting right an earlier violation of the rights of a child.

Time limits on claims

There is no actual time limit for the submission of claims, though excessive delay in commencing proceedings might make a case hard to prove, or lead to it being considered an abuse of the right of submission.[28]

Exhaustion of local remedies

The remedies available under national law to vindicate rights must be used before taking the case to the Committee. In other words, "domestic" remedies must be exhausted. This diminishes the interference by international bodies in local affairs. Remedies given by national courts are also more effective as they are easier to enforce.

The actual provisions of the Optional Protocol are as follows. Under Article 2 of the Optional Protocol, individuals who have exhausted local remedies may submit a written communication to the Committee for consideration. Article 5(2) of the Protocol precludes the Committee from considering communications unless it has ascertained that the individual has exhausted all available domestic remedies. However, this shall not be the rule where the application of domestic remedies is unreasonably prolonged. There are some other qualifications on this rule.

One problem for Australia, with its myriad of jurisdictions, is to ascertain which particular remedies are available. In cases like *Toonen*[29] there may be no domestic remedies available.[30]

Author must act with due diligence

The basic principle is that a complainant must display reasonable diligence in the pursuit of available domestic remedies. Mere doubts

---

28 Optional Protocol to the International Covenant on Civil and Political Rights, Article 3.

29 Note 11 above.

30 The issue was not contested by the Australian Government.

about the effectiveness (or the cost) of available remedies do not absolve the author from the requirement to pursue such remedies.

Authors cannot usually claim exemption from acting with due diligence on the basis that their pursuit of domestic remedies would be too time-consuming or too costly. In one case, the authors had failed to initiate any proceedings in Norway, arguing that remedies would not have been effective because the practice they were challenging was legal in Norway and because the Covenant could not be directly applied by Norwegian courts. They said that exhaustion of domestic remedies would be prolonged and "a waste of time and money". The Committee said that the pursuit of the authors' case could not be deemed a priori futile and that the authors' doubts about the effectiveness of domestic remedies did not absolve them from exhausting them.[31]

Remedies must be available and effective

The Committee has decided that a claim cannot be rejected as inadmissible on the ground of failure to exhaust domestic remedies unless the remedies are not only available but also effective, that is, offer a reasonable prospect of success. Remedies which have no or only hypothetical prospect of success need not be resorted to for purposes of the Optional Protocol (Article 5(2)(b)). For example, the *Lubicon Lake Band* case made it clear that the authors were not obliged to pursue remedies through litigation unless they were likely to be effective in restoring the traditional or cultural livelihood of the Lubicon Lake Band in Canada, which was at the time allegedly at the brink of collapse.[32]

Another example of this rule is where the same issue has been determined against the interests of the author by a recent decision of the highest court. In *Lansmann*,[33] the Committee said that:

> wherever the jurisprudence of the highest domestic tribunal has decided the matter at issue, thereby eliminating any prospect of success of an appeal to the domestic courts, authors are not required to exhaust domestic remedies, for purposes of the Optional Protocol.

---

31 *A and SN v Norway*, Communication No 224/1987, Human Rights Committee, *Report of the Human Rights Committee*, UN Doc A/43/40 (1988), p 246 (exposure of child to religious values at nursery school). See also *RT v France*, Communication No 262/1987, Human Rights Committee, *Report of the Human Rights Committee*, UN Doc A/44/40 (1989) p 277.

32 *Ominayak v Canada*, Communication No 167/1984; Human Rights Committee, *Report of the Human Rights Committee*, UN Doc A/45/40 (1990).

33 Note 8 above.

This principle could enable individuals who did not take part in unsuccessful national litigation by other members of their group to join them as parties to a communication to the Human Rights Committee.

In practice, a State is expected to indicate what remedies ought to have been pursued, and their potential effectiveness. The absence of legal aid to pursue a constitutional remedy may lead the Committee to determine that the remedy is not available.

No other international procedure

Article 5(2)(a) precludes the Committee from considering communications unless it has ascertained that the same matter is not being examined under another procedure of international investigation or settlement. This would seldom be an issue for Australia unless a case had been taken to one of the other UN committees, such as the Committee on the Elimination of Racial Discrimination, raising substantially the same issues.

Procedure for determining admissibility

After receiving a communication, the Human Rights Committee invites the State which is alleged to have violated rights to make written submissions on the question of admissibility. It then makes a preliminary decision on admissibility, that is, whether the complaint meets the conditions outlined above and other requirements. If necessary, the Committee can request additional information from the parties before it makes its decision.

How the Committee makes its determinations

This part of the chapter discusses how the Committee goes about its work under the Optional Protocol. Points to bear in mind are these:

- The Committee works in several languages. All documents have to be translated and the discussions interpreted.
- The members of the Committee come from diverse backgrounds and legal systems.
- The Committee is not a permanent body; it comes together only three times each year, for three to four weeks, and it must complete its work in that period.
- Independence.

The case load has been growing steadily, and the Committee constantly reviews its methods of dealing with communications to increase its efficiency. Some of the Committee's functions are delegated to working groups or to special rapporteurs.

From the point of view of the author or representative, the matter is dealt with by way of correspondence with the Centre for Human Rights in Geneva. Attendance or oral hearings are not provided for. The main primary submissions are the original submission and any further submission on the merits by the author, and the submissions on admissibility and the merits by the State. There could also be submissions by the author in reply to the State, and there may be a request for further information.

Preliminary work: the Secretariat

Communications are first dealt with by the Secretariat staff, who are responsible for registering communications and allocating file numbers. The Communications Secretariat are lawyers at the Centre for Human Rights at Geneva, and they work for the Human Rights Committee and for other bodies. Communications may be lodged in any language, but the working languages of the Centre for Human Rights are English and French. If communications are in languages other than these there could be delays in getting translation.

The Secretariat has limited discretion to decide whether a communication should be registered. Many letters and documents are received at the Centre, and it is not always clear whether an author wants the matter to be considered under the Optional Protocol. If the communication concerns a State that is a party to the Optional Protocol, and it seems to be the desire of the author to rely on the Covenant and Protocol, it can be registered. Otherwise further information may be sought. The Secretariat works in close cooperation with the Special Rapporteur on New Communications.

The Secretariat staff prepare summaries and drafts for the Committee to use as the basis for its work, and these are translated into the necessary languages. Members of the Committee may, if they wish, consult the original file of the case. This is practicable only for those who are familiar with the relevant language.

The Special Rapporteur on New Communications

A Special Rapporteur on New Communications considers all new communications and may act between sessions as follows:

1. The Special Rapporteur may request a State party or an author to submit further information on the issue of admissibility prior to a decision of the Committee on this issue (Rule 91).

2. The Special Rapporteur can also bring a case directly to the full Committee to recommend that it be found inadmissible without even calling on the State party to make a submission on admissibility. This would be done if the case clearly did not raise any issue which the Committee could consider. However, only the full Committee can reach a decision that a communication is inadmissible, and the Committee cannot find a case admissible until the State party has had the opportunity to make a submission (Rule 80).

3. Where a communication raises an urgent question, the Special Rapporteur is authorised to request a State to take interim measures to prevent irreparable damage to the victim of the alleged violation (Rule 86). This power has been used sparingly, usually in cases where a person is under imminent sentence of execution or is due to be extradited. These requests have been respected in nearly every case, though there was one notorious exception concerning a prisoner executed in Trinidad and Tobago.

The Special Rapporteur reports to the Committee on action taken on new communications at each session.

Procedural justice issues

The Committee is required to bring communications to the attention of the State party alleged to be violating any provisions of the Covenant (Optional Protocol, Article 4(1)). The State must submit within six months its written explanations or statements clarifying the matter and the remedy (if any) that has been provided by that State (Article 4(2)). The six-month period is applied to the State at the admissibility stage and to both parties at the merits stage (Rule 93(2)(3)) and is one reason for the prolonged nature of the proceedings.

Admissibility: the pre-session Working Group on Communications

After submissions are made on the question of admissibility, a pre-session Working Group on Communications consisting of five members of the Committee can decide on its own account that a communication is admissible, without reference to the full Committee, provided that it is unanimous (Rule 87). If the Working Group is not unanimous in the view that the communication is admissible, the question of admissibility is referred to the Committee to decide. Any cases that the Working Group considers inadmissible are referred to the full Committee for decision.

Cases found inadmissible by the full Committee, whether on the recommendation of the Working Group or the Rapporteur on New Communications, are concluded. They can be revived in limited circumstances, for example, if domestic remedies previously not exhausted are exhausted later.

From admissibility to the merits

Once the Working Group or the whole Committee has decided that a case is admissible, the Committee requests further submissions from the parties in respect of the issues that are to be determined on the merits. When the submissions are received, and there has been an opportunity for each party to reply, the matter is referred to another pre-session Working Group with further draft material from the Secretariat. This could be two years after the date of the original communication, and sometimes longer.

Working Group

The Working Group then considers the merits of the case and sends a revised draft decision to the full Committee.

The Committee

Each member has an opportunity to speak and to express agreement or disagreement with the draft and to make suggestions for amendments. A member generally takes responsibility to see that the final text prepared by the Secretariat represents the consensus view of the Committee. This could be the presenter, or the person whose suggestions were found acceptable by the Committee. Sometimes members whose views are in conflict are asked to try to find a compromise. The need to reach agreement means that the texts of the Committee's decisions are at times truncated and hard to understand.

Burden of proof

The Committee does not follow rules of evidence and proof. These are not appropriate to procedures which rely entirely on written submissions, and the Committee is not a court to make findings of fact. The author has to establish at least a prima facie case of violation. But the burden of proof cannot rest solely on the author, especially considering that the author and the State party do not always have equal access to the evidence and that frequently only the State party has access to relevant information.

The State's obligation to submit written explanations or statements clarifying the matter means that a State party has a duty to investigate in good faith all allegations of violation of the Covenant made against it and its authorities, especially when such allegations are corroborated by evidence submitted by the author of the communication. It has a duty to furnish to the Committee the information available to it.[34] If it does not do so, and if it fails to provide any answers or explanations and simply denies the allegations, the Committee can attach appropriate weight to the author's complaint and the material in support, provided that it is sufficient to substantiate the allegations.

It is implicit in the Optional Protocol that a State party provides the Committee, in good faith and within the imparted deadline, with all the information at its disposal. In the circumstances, due weight must be given to the author's allegations, to the extent that they have been substantiated. The extent to which corroboration is required is contentious. On one view, in communications involving torture or disappearances, findings could not be based on uncorroborated allegations, especially when such corroboration could have been obtained.[35] However, where it is impossible to provide corroboration, then it would not necessarily be insisted on.

Consensus and individual opinions

Technically, under Rule 51 a quorum is 12 and decisions are made by a majority. However, voting is rare as normally an attempt is made to reach decisions by consensus.

Views fluctuate concerning the value of consensus. One former member, Torkel Opsahl,[36] considers it on the whole a wise rule. In his

---

34 *Bleier v Uruguay*, Communication No 30/1978 *Selected Decisions of the Human Rights Committee under the Optional Protocol*, UN Doc CCPR/C/OP/1 p 109 (29 March 1982).

35 See individual opinions in *Valcalda v Uruguay*, Communication No 9/1977 *Selected Decisions of the Human Rights Committee under the Optional Protoco*, UN Doc CCPR/C/OP/1 p 43 (26 October 1979).

36 T Opsahl, Ottawa, 1990. Opsahl commented that because the UN system is based on the coexistence of different civilisations and legal systems, the idea of majority voting has not really worked.

view, efforts to reach consensus together with the spirit of understanding and cooperation of the members have contributed to the reputation of the Committee as a body that has not been torn by political and ideological divisions and has refused to be involved in any kind of manoeuvring. Opsahl also concedes the drawbacks of consensus. An insignificant minority, or one person, can prevent effective decision-making. Some decisions, in order to accommodate divergent views, are watered down, phrased ambiguously or reduced to the lowest common denominator. People may suppress their views to avoid disturbing the apparent agreement.

Another Committee member, Andreas Mavrommatis, has argued that consensus is not so suitable for judicial or quasi-judicial mechanisms. It can lead to delays, frustration and to a tendency not to declare obviously inadmissible communications as such if, after a long discussion, one or two members were still of a different opinion.[37]

Dissenting views are uncommon in the work of the Committee. They are useful when the discussion has been protracted and no agreement has been reached. They also allow individuals to add further observations to the decision. I consider it worthwhile to aim for consensus, since this gives a decision the force of opinion of the whole Committee. However I accept the criticisms of the consensus process, in particular the excessive time taken with debates on admissibility.

Remedies

When the Committee finds that a State has violated rights under the Covenant, it generally adds to its views observations about the remedies to which the victim is entitled under the Covenant (Article 2(3)). These remedies could include:

- commutation of sentence;
- release from custody;
- compensation or other reparation;
- investigation of violations;
- prosecution of violators;
- cessation of violation;
- prevention of further violations;
- amendment of laws.

---

37 Ottawa, 1990.

States are asked to inform the Committee, within 90 days, of the measures taken to give effect to the Committee's views.

Publication

Communications are dealt with by the Committee in closed session, and there is no publicity permitted until the final determination (except where interim measures are requested). When the Committee has adopted its views on the merits, these are forwarded to the State and to the author of the communication (Article 5(4)). This is usually the first point at which publicity can be given to the fact of the communication. This means that, in theory, no one may know of the case until it is finally decided. I personally would not take such a restrictive view of the Optional Protocol as to preclude parties from publishing the fact of the submission of a communication.

Recently the Committee has adopted the practice of issuing a public statement at the end of its session about the communications dealt with in that session.[38] All decisions are published in full in the annual report of the Committee to the General Assembly. This does not appear for many months.

What has been the effect of the Committee's views?

The benefits of the procedure include the political as well as the legal effects. Even if a case does not succeed, it requires a reasoned approach to the application of a particular provision to particular facts and individuals. The very process of requiring a State to respond to a well argued case of violation may highlight inadequacies in law and policy, and even if an actual violation of Covenant rights is not found, this exercise could lead to policy review. However the Optional Protocol procedure is not a substitute for a bill of rights.

The views of the Human Rights Committee under the Optional Protocol are not legally binding or enforceable. Nevertheless, States ratifying the Covenant have undertaken to provide effective and enforceable remedies to persons whose rights have been violated. As parties to the Optional Protocol, they recognise the competence of the Human Rights Committee to establish whether there has been such a

---

38 This follows Rule 83, under which the Committee may issue communiqués regarding the activities of the Committee at its closed meetings.

violation. When a violation is established, a remedy should be provided, either that recommended or another that is equally appropriate.

Special Rapporteur for Follow-Up

Whatever the legal effect of the Committee's views, in practice the effectiveness of the communications procedure depends on the willingness of States to implement the views and recommendations of the Committee in cases where they are found to have violated rights. While many States take their obligations under the Covenant seriously, it should not be assumed that all act promptly and conscientiously. In fact, not a great deal was known until recently about whether States had in fact carried out the Committee's recommendations. The Human Rights Committee is now seeking information on a systematic basis from States and from authors about follow-up action. A Special Rapporteur for Follow-Up was appointed in 1990, and procedures have been devised to deal with States who fail to cooperate. The results of the Committee's inquiries are publicly available.[39]

Up to July 1994 the Committee had found violations in 142 cases. Information had been sought for all these cases but had been received in only 65. (In a few cases the date for providing information had not been reached.) In about one-quarter of the 65 cases in which information had been provided, the replies showed that the State was willing to implement the Committee's views or to provide a remedy of some kind. In one third of the cases, the replies were not satisfactory. The State challenged the Committee's decision, or suggested that the recommended remedy would not be provided. There were, however, some good results:

- Some victims had been released from custody. For example, in *Bolanos v Ecuador*,[40] the author had been kept in pre-trial custody for six years. Upon the Committee finding a violation, he was released from custody and the State assisted him to find employment.

---

39 Rule 99, see Human Rights Committee, *Report of the Human Rights Committee*, UN Doc A/49/40 (1994).

40 Communication No 238/1987, Human Rights Committee, *Report of the Human Rights Committee*, UN Doc A/44/40, p 246 (1989). See also *Vasilskis v Uruguay*, Communication No 80/1980, *Selected Decisions of the Human Rights Committee under the Optional Protoco*, UN Doc CCPR/C/OP/2 p 105 (31 March 1983); *Marais v Madagascar*, Communication No 49/1979, *Selected Decisions of the Human Rights Committee under the Optional Protoco*, UN Doc CCPR/C/OP/2 p 82 (24 March 1983).

- Some victims had received compensation.[41] For example, in *Torres v Finland* an alien who had been arrested and was subject to extradition was unable to challenge the legality of his detention before a court. This was found to violate his rights under Article 9(4) of the Covenant.[42] He was paid compensation, and the *Aliens Act* was revised in order to make the provisions governing detention compatible with the Covenant.[43]

- Legislation incompatible with the Covenant had been amended, or new local remedies introduced.[44] The Australian Government responded to the *Toonen*[45] decision by enacting the *Human Rights (Sexual Conduct) Act* 1994 (Cth). In another well-known case, *Lovelace v Canada*,[46] Canada took substantial steps to amend section 12(1)(b) of the *Indian Act* to overcome the exclusion of the author from the enjoyment of her cultural rights. Canada also considered that the Canadian Charter of Rights and Freedoms was a response to the findings of a violation of the Covenant, since section 15 would provide an effective remedy for

---

41 *Van Alphen v Netherlands*, Communication No 305/1988, Human Rights Committee, *Report of the Human Rights Committee*, UN Doc A/46/40 (1991) para 705. Ex gratia compensation was provided for keeping the author, a lawyer, in detention for nine weeks for refusal to cooperate in an investigation against his clients, violating Article 9(1).

42 *Torres v Finland*, Communication No 291/1988, Human Rights Committee, *Report of the Human Rights Committee*, UN Doc A/38/40 (1983).

43 Human Rights Committee, *Report of the Human Rights Committee*, UN Doc A/46/40 (1991) para 705.

44 In *Vuolanne v Finland*, a new law was passed to allow conscripts to have the decision of confinement reviewed by a court: Communication No 265/1987, Human Rights Committee, *Report of the Human Rights Committee*, UN Doc A/44/40 (1989) p 249. In *Zwaan-de Vries v Netherlands*, the authors who had been discriminatorily excluded by the law from a pension available to men were provided with a pension by law: Communication No 182/1984, Human Rights Committee, *Report of the Human Rights Committee*, UN Doc A/42/40 (1987), p 160. See also *Broeks v Netherlands*, Communication No 172/1984, Human Rights Committee, *Report of the Human Rights Committee*, UN Doc A/42/40 (1987) p 139. In *Aumeeruddy-Cziffra et al v Mauritius*, legislation was amended to remove the discriminatory effects of those laws on the ground of sex: Communication No 35/1978, *Selected Decisions under the Optional Protocol*, UN Doc CCPR/C/OP/1 p 67 (9 April 1981).

45 Note 11 above.

46 Note 26 above.

anyone who alleges that their rights to equality before the law and the equal protection of the law have been violated.

In some well-known cases the outcome is still uncertain. For example, in the *Lubicon Lake* case,[47] the negotiations are not completed. In 77 cases in the follow-up survey, no information had been provided. Forty-three of these had come from four States, and these States had failed to reply to at least four requests for information. They are Jamaica, Madagascar, Suriname and Zaire.

More needs to be done to persuade States to cooperate with the Committee and to give proper weight to its views under the communications procedure. The new steps being taken by the Committee are expected to result in far more information being available about implementation and about difficulties which may be faced by States in carrying out their obligations under international human rights instruments.

Request for information on measures taken

The Committee has introduced two practices to bring home to States their responsibilities under the Optional Protocol procedures. First, it has added a request at the end of each of its views finding violation, as follows:

> Bearing in mind that, by becoming a State party to the Optional Protocol, the State party has recognised the competence of the Committee to determine whether there has been a violation of the Covenant or not and that, pursuant to article 2 of the Covenant, the State party has undertaken to ensure to all individuals within its territory and subject to its jurisdiction the right recognised in the Covenant, and to provide an effective and enforceable remedy, in case a violation has been established, the Committee wishes to receive from the State party, within 90 days, information about the measures taken to give effect to its views.

Second, when the Committee considers reports from States which are parties to the Optional Protocol it will, in appropriate cases, recommend that the State party review and include information in its next report on the procedures established to ensure compliance with the views and recommendations adopted by the Committee under the First Optional Protocol, also bearing in mind its obligations under Article 2 of the Covenant. The Guidelines for Reports require that, where relevant, State reports should

---

47 *Ominayak v Canada*, Note 7 above.

explain what action has been taken relating to communications, including what remedies have been afforded the authors of communications whose rights the Committee has found to have been violated.

Recent developments on follow-up

Before the Committee's fifty-third session, the Special Rapporteur for Follow-Up, Mr Mavrommatis, met with representatives of several States that had not provided information about action taken pursuant to the Committee's views concerning a violation of the Covenant, or had failed to take any appropriate action to implement those views. The States that had failed to cooperate in the follow-up procedure were Zambia, Colombia and Suriname. Before the fifty-fourth session, the Special Rapporteur visited Jamaica, which had been named for failing to reply to at least four requests for information. Information about the Committee's follow-up procedures is included in its annual report for 1994.

Other issues concerning effectiveness

The Committee has gone a long way to develop procedures that make it harder for States to avoid their obligations under the Covenant. If public opinion, that is, the opinion of the body of States and the world community, stood behind the Committee, its work would be more effective. Regrettably, there is little publicity given to the Committee's work and little active support at the political level in the form of condemnation of States who fail to cooperate.

Some problems and issues

No oral hearing

The absence of any provision for oral hearings by the Human Rights Committee has caused some concern to commentators in Australia.[48] An oral hearing, if required in every case, would certainly make the procedure less accessible and more expensive.[49] However there may be

---

48 Senator Rod Kemp, quoted in Joint Standing Committee on Foreign Affairs, Defence and Trade, *A Review of Australia's Efforts to Promote and Protect Human Rights*, AGPS, Canberra, 1994, para 2.28 ff.

49 V Dimitrijevic, Ottowa, 1990.

some cases where an oral hearing could help to clear up misunderstandings or help to unravel complex facts. Ultimately, however, the Committee is not a court and its views do not create enforceable rights and obligations. Nor is it an appellate tribunal to pronounce on the correctness or otherwise of national court decisions. Its role is to reach a view as to whether a Covenant right has been violated.

While the Optional Protocol does not provide for an oral hearing, it is not necessarily excluded. The Committee has to consider communications "in the light of all *written* information made available to it by the individual and by the State party concerned."[50] The Committee is required to hold closed meetings while considering communications.[51] No doubt these provisions were included in the Protocol by States to protect themselves from adverse publicity. Confidentiality can also protect complainants whose personal security is at issue. In the case of one country, the only complaint ever received was from a person already in exile. The need for further changes in procedure might be explored if it were shown that the current methods could result in injustice.

Confidentiality of proceedings

The Committee requires both the State and the author of a complaint to maintain confidentiality about the complaint, and to refrain from publishing their submissions until the matter is concluded and the State and the author have been notified of the result.[52] Up to the point of admissibility, the need for confidentiality may have some justification. The requirement of confidentiality after that point, however, seems inconsistent with the principle of freedom of expression. There seems no reason why the author of a complaint may not make that fact known publicly if they so wish. Maintaining confidentiality about the nature of a complaint until the process is complete makes it even harder for people to be informed about the Committee's work under the Protocol.

Balance of membership

The members of the Committee are elected by all the States that have ratified the Covenant. The result is that some members of the Committee

---

50 Optional Protocol to the International Covenant on Civil and Political Rights, Article 5(1).

51 Optional Protocol to the International Covenant on Civil and Political Rights, Article 5(3).

52 See Rules of Procedure, 96 to 98.

come from States that have not ratified the Protocol.[53] The Joint Standing Committee on Foreign Affairs, Defence and Trade has recommended that the Australian Government urge the UN to confine the membership of the Human Rights Committee to nationals of those countries which have ratified the Optional Protocol.[54]

I doubt whether this proposal is soundly based. The Committee deals with periodic reports from States as well as with communications. All 132 States which are parties to the Covenant have an obligation to submit reports to the Committee, and all are entitled to nominate a candidate for election to the Committee to take part in that process. In June 1996, 89 States had ratified the Protocol, and the number is increasing slowly each year.[55]

Another factor to consider is that the members of the Committee act independently of their States. There is a strong collegiate bond between the members; they see their allegiance as being to the Covenant and to the rights it protects. There are several highly experienced experts from States who have not ratified the Protocol. They have made significant contributions to the jurisprudence of the Committee. One has recently been nominated to the International Court of Justice. Nothing would be gained by excluding these experts from membership of the Committee because their countries had not ratified the Protocol. It has also been suggested that some of these members come from States which are not democratic. The six States who have nationals on the Committee and who have not ratified the Protocol are the United States, the United Kingdom, Israel, India, Egypt and Japan.

Observations on time pressure

The procedures adopted by the Committee mean that cases can come to the full Committee for the first time at the point when a decision on the merits has to be made, perhaps a year or more after a working group has found it to be admissible in respect of certain articles of the Covenant. The full Committee may take a different view on admissibility, perhaps

---

53 See Joint Standing Committee on Foreign Affairs, Defence and Trade, *A Review of Australia's Efforts to Promote and Protect Human Rights*, AGPS, Canberra, 1994, para 2.27 ff.

54 Note 53 above, para 2.33.

55 See United Nations, *Human Rights International Instruments: Chart of Ratifications as at 30 June 1996*, UN Doc ST/HR/4/Rev 14.

considering that other issues ought to have been taken into account. The time pressure on the Committee means that members may not have the time they would like to consider the issues. Also, they may not be able to read the original file if it is in another language.

The right of minorities to their own culture, religion and language

Article 27

Article 27 of the Covenant provides as follows:

> In those States in which ethnic, religious or linguistic minorities exist, persons belonging to these minorities shall not be denied the right, in community with the other members of their group, to enjoy their own culture, to profess and practice their own religion, or to use their own language.

This provision protects the right of individuals to maintain the culture, language and religion of their own group where it differs from that of the majority. It is separate from the right to equality and the right to be free from discrimination on grounds of ethnicity, language or religion.[56] It is also a restraint on majority power, in the interests of minorities. To understand the approach of the Human Rights Committee to Article 27, it is necessary to look at three principal sources:

- the decisions of the Committee under the communications procedure;
- the Committee's General Comment, which sets out its general views on the application of Article 27;
- the recommendations and observations made by the Committee as a whole in the reporting procedure.

In general terms, the Committee has seen Article 27 as being counter to integrationist or assimilationist policies. It has emphasised the obligation of States to take positive measures to protect the language, religious and cultural rights of members of minority groups.[57] Article 27 is, in the Committee's view, directed to ensure the survival and continued development of the cultural, religious and social identity of the minorities

---

56 See General Comment No 23, *Compilation of General Comments and General Recommendations adopted by Human Rights Treaty Bodies*, UN Doc HRI/GEN/1/Rev 2 (29 March 1996) para 4, p 38.

57 General Comment No 23, note 56 above.

concerned, thus enriching the fabric of society as a whole.[58] A proviso is that the rights protected may not be used in a manner inconsistent with other provisions of the Covenant, for example, to undermine or violate the rights of others.[59]

Application to Indigenous people

The rights protected by Article 27 apply to Indigenous people. Most decisions under Article 27 have been in relation to Indigenous peoples in Canada, Sweden and Finland. No cases under this provision from Australia have been considered on their merits. Some issues which have arisen in the decisions and comment of the Committee are these:

Does a minority exist, and who belongs to it?

The question whether a minority exists in a particular State is to be established by objective criteria.[60] It is for the Committee to say whether a particular minority exists and whether an individual belongs to such a minority. An individual may not be excluded from membership of a minority group by laws or policies of the State except on reasonable and objective grounds.[61]

Must the State protect against private acts?

States must not only refrain from any action that may have the effect of denying or violating the rights in question, they must also protect those rights against the acts of other persons within the State party.[62]

Is the right claimed a group right?

The rights under Article 27 are individual rights, not group rights. However, members of a group can act together in bringing proceedings, if their rights are affected in the same way. The individual rights protected under Article 27 depend on the ability of the minority group to which the individual belongs to maintain its culture, language or religion.

---

58 General Comment No 23, para 9, note 56 above.

59 General Comment No 23, para 8, note 56 above; M Nowak, note 5 above, p 505.

60 General Comment No 23, para 5.2, note 56 above.

61 *Lovelace v Canada*, note 26 above; *Kitok v Sweden*, Communication No 197/1985, UN Doc CCPR/C/33/D (27 July 1988) p 221.

62 General Comment No 23, para 6.1, note 56 above; also M Nowak, note 6 above, p 503.

Positive measures may be necessary to protect the identity of a minority and the rights of its members to maintain their culture, to enjoy and develop it and to practice their religion.[63]

To what extent does Article 27 protect economic activities?

The Committee has taken the view that Article 27 protects economic activities of members of minorities which are part of their culture.[64] The enjoyment by Indigenous peoples of traditional activities such as hunting and fishing, particular uses of land and the rights to live in reserves protected by law,[65] may require positive legal measures of protection and measures to ensure the effective participation of members of minority communities in decisions which affect them.[66]

---

63 General Comment No 23, para 6.2, note 56 above; M Nowak, note 6 above, p 504 queries this.

64 General Comment No 23, para 9.2, note 56 above; *Lansmann v Finland*, note 8 above.

65 *Ominayak v Canada*, note 7 above: "The rights protected by article 27 include the right of persons in community with others, to engage in economic and social activities which are part of the culture of the community to which they belong" (para 32.2). The Committee recognised that historical inequities and more recent developments threaten the way of life and culture of the Lubicon Lake Band and constitute a violation of Article 27 so long as they continue (State party proposed to rectify the situation by a remedy deemed appropriate). In *Kitok v Sweden*, note 61 above at 221, the author had been denied membership of the Saami community and the right to carry out reindeer husbandry, by the Saami community. The reason for allowing limitations was to restrict the number of reindeer breeders for economic and ecological reasons and to secure the preservation and wellbeing of the Saami minority. This was reasonable and consistent with Article 27.

66 General Comment No 23(50), para 7; *Lansmann v Finland*, note 8 above.

9

Individual communications: the Convention against Torture and the Convention on the Elimination of All Forms of Racial Discrimination

Michael O'Flaherty

The Convention against Torture

Introduction

The Convention against Torture and Other Cruel, Inhuman or Degrading Treatment or Punishment is one of the range of preventative and investigatory devices set up by the international community in response to the unremitting reports from around the world of suffering inflicted on persons by or with the connivance of governments. The Convention is distinguished from other devices in that it contains legally binding obligations and is open for ratification by all States of the world. It also contains an array of investigatory procedures.[1]

---

* The views in this chapter are the author's own and he does not purport to represent those of treaty bodies, their members or the UN Secretariat.

1 There is an extensive literature on the Convention and the work of the Committee. See, for instance, M Nowak, "The Implementation Functions of the UN Committee against Torture", in *Fortschritt im Bewusstsein der Grund- und Menschenrechte: Festschrift fuer Felix Ermacora*, Kehl am Rhein, Strasbourg, Arlington, 1988; A Dormenval, "UN Committee against Torture: Practice and Perspectives" (1990) 8 *Netherlands Q Hum Rts* 26; H Burgers and H Danelius,

Article 1 defines torture as:

> any act by which severe pain or suffering, whether physical or mental, is intentionally inflicted on a person for such purpose as obtaining from him or a third person information or a confession, punishing him for an act he or a third person has committed or is suspected of having committed, or intimidating or coercing him or a third person, or for any reason based on discrimination of any kind, when such pain or suffering is inflicted by or at the instigation of or with the consent or acquiescence of a public official or other person acting in an official capacity. It does not include pain or suffering arising only from, inherent in or incidental to lawful sanctions.

States parties are obliged to take effective action to prevent such acts in their jurisdictions (Article 2) and not to return ("refoule") persons to States where there are substantial grounds to believe that they would be subject to torture (Article 3). By Article 4 States undertake to criminalise torture, attempted torture and complicity therein. Articles 5, 6, 7, 8 and 9 concern the establishment of international jurisdiction for cases of alleged torture and address issues of extradition and international cooperation. Article 10 contains an obligation on States to provide education on the prohibition of torture for all relevant public officials, whereas Article 11 addresses the obligation to ensure that the prohibition is adequately reflected in rule books and guidelines. The requirements to promptly investigate allegations or evidence of torture and to duly compensate victims are contained in Articles 12, 13 and 14. The invalidity of statements or confessions made under torture is ensured by Article 15.

Article 16 contains an undertaking to prevent:

> acts of cruel, inhuman or degrading treatment or punishment which do not amount to torture . . . when such acts are committed by or at the instigation of or with the consent or acquiescence of a public official or other person acting in an official capacity.

It is further stipulated that the obligations contained in Articles 10, 11, 12 and 13 "shall apply with the substitution for references to torture of references to other forms of cruel, inhuman or degrading treatment or punishment".

(*cont*)

The United Nations Convention against Torture, M Nijhoff, Dordrecht, 1988; N Lerner, "The UN Convention on Torture" (1986) 16 *Israel YB Hum Rts* 126; ME Tardu, "The United Nations Convention against Torture and other Cruel, Inhuman or Degrading Treatment or Punishment" (1987) 4 *Nordic JIL* 303; A Byrnes, "The Committee against Torture" in P Alston (ed), *The United Nations and Human Rights: A Critical Appraisal*, Clarendon Press, Oxford, 1992.

The Convention provides for the establishment of a Committee against Torture with ten members to be elected by the States parties but to serve in their individual capacities.[2] The Committee was established in 1987 and commenced its work in 1988. The Committee, which usually meets for two two-week sessions each year, is charged with responsibility for the examination of reports submitted at regular intervals by the States parties (Article 19), the implementation of an inter-State complaints procedure (Article 21), the operation of a unique investigatory device (Article 20) and the receipt and examination of individual complaints (Article 22). States must declare that they recognise the competence of the Committee with regard to the inter-State and the individual complaints procedures. A State which does not wish to be bound by the Article 20 investigatory procedure must expressly so declare (Article 28 (1)).

As of 30 June 1996 the Convention had been ratified or otherwise acceded to by 97 States. Australia became a party on 8 August 1989 and made the declaration concerning Article 22 on 28 January 1993 without appending any reservations.

An overview of the individual complaints procedure

The procedure[3] permits individuals to complain directly or through representatives to the Committee about a State party in circumstances where they are the alleged victims of violations of the Convention and the State party has made the necessary declaration under Article 22. The function of the Committee is to gather all necessary information, primarily by means of written exchanges with the parties (the State and the complainant), to consider the admissibility and merits of complaints and to issue its "views" accordingly.

Though not ineffective in having its views respected by States parties it should be noted that the Committee is not a court, does not issue

---

2 Articles 17 and 18.

3 An examination of the analogous procedure under the terms of the Optional Protocol of the International Covenant on Civil and Political Rights will yield a number of insights as to the effectiveness of the individual communication mechanisms in general and the likely direction to be taken by the Committee against Torture in the years ahead. See M O'Flaherty and L Heffernan, *The International Covenant on Civil and Political Rights – International Human Rights Law in Ireland*, Brehon, Dublin, 1995, at chapter 4, together with the references cited therein.

"judgments" and has no means to enforce any views which it might adopt. Furthermore all exchanges with the Committee currently take only written form. The length of proceedings can vary from case to case. On average a period of two years may be envisaged, although in urgent situations the Committee can dispose of a matter in a matter of months. It can be assumed that as the workload increases there will be a corresponding delay in the processing of cases. There is no provision for the awarding of any financial assistance to needy applicants to assist them in taking a case to the Committee.[4]

All steps of the procedure under Article 22 are confidential until the point where the Committee adopts its views or otherwise concludes a case. As a matter of practice, views are reported in the Committee's annual report together with a summary of the information made available to the Committee. Decisions on non-admissibility are also reported.[5]

By 13 December 1995 the Committee had received 38 communications. Of these, 10 are at the pre-admissibility stage, 18 were deemed inadmissible, 4 were discontinued, and, of 4 considered on the merits, 3 were found to indicate a violation of the Convention.

The admissibility requirement

Before a case can be considered on its merits it is necessary for it to have been found admissible.[6] The conditions for admissibility are as follows:

1. A case may only be taken against a State and never an individual. The State must be a party to the Convention and must have accepted the individual communication jurisdiction of Article 22. Further-more, the alleged violation of the Convention must have occurred since the date when Article 22 came into force for that State.[7] For Australia the operative date is 28 January 1993.

2. Anonymous communications will not accepted. However the wish of the communicant to have his or her name withheld will be respected where the circumstances so warrant.

---

4   It should be noted however that the procedure itself is free and there is no requirement that communicants have legal representation.

5   See Rule 111, Rules of Procedure, UN Doc CAT/C/3/Rev 1.

6   Rule 107, Rules of Procedure, note 5 above.

7   See Communications No 1, 2, 3 /1988, reported in Committee against Torture, *Report of the Committee against Torture*, UN Doc A/45/44 (1990).

3. Article 22 states that communications may be submitted by or on behalf of alleged victims. This provision has been translated into the Rules of Procedure as follows:

> [The] communication should be submitted by the individual himself or by his relatives or designated representatives or by others on behalf of an alleged victim when it appears that the victim is unable to submit the communication himself, and the author of the communication justifies his acting on the victim's behalf.

This formulation leaves unclear the extent to which a case might be brought without the consent of an alleged victim, for instance by a well meaning NGO in a situation where the victim is not in a position to give his or her consent.[8] In the case of *B M'B v Tunisia*,[9] a communication from a person on behalf of a dead victim of torture was deemed inadmissible because the communicant was unable to provide "sufficient proof to establish his authority to act on behalf of the victim".

4. Communications will be considered inadmissible if they are deemed to be an abuse of the right of petition or to be incompatible with the provisions of the Convention. These provisions are sufficiently unclear to allow for an overlapping of concern with other admissibility requirements. It is clear that they may cover a wide range of fact situations and would certainly preclude communications designed to subvert the work of the Committee, containing allegations of a frivolous nature or abusive of the Committee or the Convention. Cases will also be deemed inadmissible if the communicant fails to provide a minimum amount of information indicating a possible violation of the Convention.[10] Cases

---

8 The Secretariat in an informal fact-sheet for communicants (the sheet appears not to have a reference number) states that an NGO may be entitled to take a case in circumstances where they can "justify their acting on the victim's behalf".

9 Communication No 14/1994, Committee against Torture, *Report of the Committee against Torture*, UN Doc A/50/44 (1995) at annex V.

10 The Committee in 1994 declared inadmissible two cases on the basis that the accounts provided by the communicants "lacked the minimum substantiation that would render (them) compatible with article 22 of the convention". X v Switzerland, Communication No 17/1994, Committee against Torture, *Report of the Committee against Torture*, UN Doc A/50/44 (1995) at annex V, and Y v Switzerland, Communication No 18/1994, Committee against Torture, *Report of the Committee against Torture*, UN Doc A/50/44 (1995) at annex V. In both cases the Committee formed the view that the communicants had failed to indicate that they personally were endangered by a general situation of instability and human rights abuse in a third State (Zaire) to which they were at risk of being refouled.

brought after an excessively long delay following exhaustion of local remedies (see below) might also fall foul of these provisions.[11]

5. A communication will be considered inadmissible if the matter has been or is being considered under another procedure of international investigation or settlement. This provision clearly covers international redress procedures under the terms of regional human rights instruments. However it is not clear to what extent it refers to non-conventional procedures such as those under Economic and Social Council Resolution 1503 and the mandate of the Special Rapporteur on Torture and other mechanisms of the UN Commission on Human Rights, such as its Sub-Commission's Working Group on Indigenous Populations. One may however presume that the Committee will follow the Human Rights Committee which has held that such procedures do not fall foul of the analogous provisions of the Optional Protocol to the International Covenant on Civil and Political Rights. It may indeed be noted that in at least two sets of cases to date the States involved declined to argue that cases were inadmissible on the grounds that they arose within general situations which had already or were currently receiving the attention of Special Rapporteurs of the Commission on Human Rights.[12]

6. Before a case can be taken to the Committee, all domestic remedies should have been exhausted. However, this rule does not apply where the application of domestic remedies is unreasonably prolonged or is unlikely to bring effective relief to the victim. In the case of *Halimi-Nedzibi v Austria*,[13] the Committee indicated that a delay of some three years in processing a case before the national court constituted unreasonable delay. In *REG v Turkey*,[14] the alleged victim had taken no action to seek redress domestically and it was argued that he had no hope of justice in Turkey. The Committee was reluctant to accept such a sweeping generalisation and deemed the communication

---

11 There is no time limit within which a case must be brought following exhaustion of local remedies.

12 Communications No 1, 2, 3/1988, note 7 above, and *Mutombo v Switzerland*, Communication No 13/1993, Committee against Torture, *Report of the Committee against Torture*, UN Doc A/49/44 (1994) at annex v.

13 Communication No 8/1991, Committee against Torture, *Report of the Committee against Torture*, UN Doc A/49/44 (1994) at annex v.

14 Communication No 4/1990, Committee against Torture, *Report of the Committee against Torture*, UN Doc A/46/44 (1991).

inadmissible. In *MA v Canada*,[15] an inadmissibility decision, the Committee further developed this point and stated that:

> In principle, it is not within the scope of the Committee's competence to evaluate the prospects of success of domestic remedies, but only whether they are proper remedies for determination of the author's claims.

In the case of *Parot v Spain*,[16] the Committee, in declaring the case admissible, noted that a genuine if misguided attempt to exhaust local remedies was sufficient "even if these attempts to engage available local remedies may not have complied with procedural formalities prescribed by law", in that the attempts made "left no doubt as to Mr Parot's wish to have the allegations investigated".

If the State chooses to argue that local remedies have not been exhausted it must offer substantiating evidence in support of this assertion.

If a communication is deemed inadmissible on the grounds of non-exhaustion of local remedies the option remains of re-submitting the matter subsequently when the remedies can be shown to be exhausted, unreasonably prolonged or ineffective.[17] To date the Committee has allowed the re-opening of one case which it had previously deemed inadmissible, *IUP v Spain*.[18]

The procedure

The first step in taking a case to the Committee is to address a communication to its Secretariat at the UN Centre for Human Rights in Geneva, Switzerland.[19] This first communication should include as much information as possible indicating both the satisfaction of the admissibility requirements and the applicability of the terms of the Convention to the specific matter being alleged. Once the materials have arrived in Geneva a staff member there will open a dossier and make contact with

---

15 Communication No 24/1995, Committee against Torture, *Report of the Committee against Torture*, UN Doc A/50/44 (1995) at annex V.

16 Communication No 6/1990, Committee against Torture, *Report of the Committee against Torture*, UN Doc A/50/44 (1995) at annex V.

17 Rule 109, Rules of Procedure, note 5 above.

18 Communication No 6/1990, Committee against Torture, *Report of the Committee against Torture*, UN Doc A/48/44 (1993).

19 Committee against Torture, Communications Branch, Centre for Human Rights, United Nations, Palais des Nations, CH-1211, Geneva, Switzerland.

the communicant to elicit in greater detail as much relevant information as possible. All information transmitted can be in the communicant's own language, but the matter will be dealt with more speedily if information is given in a language such as English, Spanish or French.

Once the Secretariat is of the view that it has sufficient information the case is given a reference number and listed in the register of cases. The Secretariat is obliged to duly register all cases where the communicants insist that they so do and where the impugned State party has made a necessary declaration under Article 22.[20]

At this stage the file will probably be allocated to a member of the Committee known as a Special Rapporteur, whose task is to elicit as much information as possible in order to bring the case to the attention of the Committee, to refer the case for comment to the State party as appropriate, and to decide on any interim decisions or actions which may be required.[21] In practice the Special Rapporteur will from the outset seek information on both admissibility issues and the merits of the case. The view of the State party will be sought and the communication brought to its attention. The identity of the communicant will not be disclosed if he or she has requested confidentiality. Both the State party and the communicant must provide requested information within stated time limits of normally two months. Where information on the merits of the case is requested from the State party there is a time limit for replying of six months.[22] Failure to abide by these time limits may result in the case proceeding without the requested information.[23]

If the circumstances so warrant, the Special Rapporteur (and of course the Committee itself) are empowered to request the State party to take certain actions to protect the alleged victim.[24] Such requests are made without any prejudice to the eventual decision of the Committee on

---

20 Rule 98, Rules of Procedure, note 5 above.

21 The Rules of Procedure also allow for the establishment of a working group of the Committee which may meet inter-sessionally if it so chooses. However no such group has yet been convened and the Committee has instead made use of special rapporteurs who, at the thirteenth session of the Committee (1995) were endowed with equal authority to working groups. See Decision of the Committee, "Working Methods of the Committee Relating to its Function under Article 22 of the Convention", UN Doc A/50/44 at annex v.

22 Rule 110, Rules of Procedure, note 5 above.

23 Rules 108 and 110, Rules of Procedure, note 5 above.

24 Id.

admissibility or the merits of a case. Urgent requests of this nature have been made to the governments of Switzerland and Canada where the communicants indicated that they were likely to be deported to a State in circumstances where they believed that their lives would be endangered. The governments honoured the request.[25]

When the Special Rapporteur is of the view that sufficient information has been gathered to form a view on admissibility, the case is put to the Committee for its consideration. The Committee has indicated that it is not constrained to address only the arguments made by the parties, but may address other matters which it considers of relevance. Thus in its first three cases, considered together, it examined questions arising under the provisions of an Article (14), which had not been raised by the parties.[26] Should the Committee take a decision that a case is admissible it is free to revoke that decision subsequently in the light of further information provided by the State party. Before a decision of revocation is made the communicant is afforded an opportunity to comment on the information provided by the State party.[27] As noted above, a decision of inadmissibility may also be reviewed subsequently by the Committee in the light of new information made available to it and upon written request from the complainant.

The Committee may choose to make its decision on the merits of a case simultaneously with its decision on admissibility.[28] Such a circumstance might arise where the State does not dispute admissibility and all relevant information has already been gathered. It will also occur in especially urgent cases, such as *Mutombo v Switzerland*.[29] In that case the State party did not dispute admissibility and the entire case was disposed of within five months.

Decisions on admissibility are communicated immediately to the State party and the communicant. If the matter has been found admissible the State party is forwarded any new material which may have been provided by the communicant and is requested to offer its views on the merits of the case. As already noted, the State party is subject to a time limit for its reply of six months.

---

25 *Mutombo v Switzerland*, note 12 above; *Khan v Canada*, Communication No 15/1994, Committee against Torture, *Report of the Committee against Torture*, UN Doc A/50/44 (1995) at annex V.

26 Communications No 1, 2, 3 /1988, note 7 above.

27 Rule 110, Rules of Procedure, note 5 above.

28 Rule 105, Rules of Procedure, note 5 above.

29 Note 12 above.

In its consideration of the merits, the Committee may defer its decision pending receipt of further information. In all cases where further information is requested the State party and the communicant are kept fully informed. All requests for further information are subject to a time limit in which to reply.[30]

The Rules of Procedure of the Committee allow the Committee to hold confidential oral hearings in cases where it is of the view that hearings would be of assistance in gathering necessary information concerning the merits of a case.[31] There is no such provision with regard to cases which are only at the admissibility stage. No hearings have as yet occurred. The Committee is also empowered to make reference to information made available to it by UN bodies or specialised agencies which have a bearing on the determination of the merits of a case.[32]

When the Committee is of the view that it has gathered sufficient information it proceeds to a consideration of the merits and the adoption of its views.

The practice of the Committee is to adopt views by consensus.[33] Members are free however to append individual views to those of the Committee[34] – a right which has not yet been exercised. Though the Committee has no power to make awards, pecuniary or otherwise, it is free to make recommendations to the State party regarding such matters.

The views of the Committee are communicated to the State party and the communicant. Further to the Rules of Procedure the State party is invited to inform the Committee in due course of the action it takes in conformity with the Committee's views.[35] In the case *Halimi-Nedzibi v Austria*,[36] "due course of time" was deemed by the Committee to be to 90 days.

The Committee has not as yet developed a procedure for the follow-up of cases subsequent to the adoption of its views.

---

30 Rule 110, Rules of Procedure, note 5 above.

31 Id.

32 Rule 111, Rules of Procedure, note 5 above.

33 On this practice see M Schmidt, "Individual Human Rights Complaints Procedures Based on United Nations Treaties and the Need For Reform" (1992) 41 *ICLQ* 645.

34 Rule 111, Rules of Procedure, note 5 above.

35 Id.

36 Note 13 above.

The International Convention on the Elimination of All Forms of Racial Discrimination

Introduction

The communication right under the Convention is contained in Article 14. Communications may only be considered from persons or groups (see below) subject to the jurisdiction of States parties which have made the necessary declaration recognising the competence of the Committee to receive such communications. Australia made this declaration on 28 January 1993 and did not append any reservations.

The admissibility requirements and the procedure for the processing of communications is largely the same as that under the Convention against Torture. What follows therefore is a presentation only of the points of difference.[37]

Admissibility requirements

1. Article 14 makes provision for the establishment of national bodies to consider petitions concerning allegations of racial discrimination and for the subsequent submission of such petitions to the Committee in given circumstances. This provision, which has not been implemented by States parties, is probably not an obligatory one and the absence of such bodies may not be seen as an impediment to the exercise of the right of petition to the Committee. Certainly the Committee in its jurisprudence and its Rules of Procedure[38] has not understood the provision in an obstructive manner.

2. Both individuals and groups of individuals may make communications under Article 14.[39] Unless they are acting in a representative capacity (the regulations in this regard are as with the Torture Convention) they must present themselves as victims of a violation of the Convention by the State party.[40]

---

37 For a select bibliography, see chapter 13 in the present volume: "Substantive Provisions of the International Convention on the Elimination of All Forms of Racial Discrimination".

38 Committee on the Elimination of Racial Discrimination, Rules of Procedure, UN Doc CERD/C/35/Rev 3 as amended.

39 Article 14(1).

40 See N Lerner, "Curbing Racial Discrimination – Fifteen Years CERD" (1983) 13 *Israel YB Hum Rts* 170 at 180.

3. The Rules of Procedure indicate that communications must be submitted within six months after available domestic remedies have been exhausted, "except in the case of duly verified exceptional circumstances".[41] This time restriction is not stipulated in Article 14. The rule instead has its origins[42] in the Committee's desire to adequately acknowledge the provisions of Article 14 concerning national bodies while at the same time not allowing them to obstruct the right of petition. However a reformulation of the Rules of Procedure could continue to achieve this purpose while at the same time removing the six month time limit for those petitions emanating from the jurisdiction of States parties which have not established such bodies.

4. The Committee is not disbarred from considering communications concerning matters which are or have been considered by other international investigation or redress procedures.

5. Concerning exhaustion of local remedies, both the Convention and the Rules of Procedure are worded more restrictively than the relevant provisions under the Torture Convention, in that it is not stated that remedies which are unlikely to bring effective relief need not be pursued. However this difference is probably of no practical significance.[43]

6. The Rules of Procedure do not make provision for the inadmissibility of communications which are manifestly ill-founded. Communications must however be compatible with the provisions of the Convention and not be abusive of the right of petition.

The procedure

7. The address for communications is The Committee on the Elimination of Racial Discrimination, United Nations Centre for Human Rights, Communications Branch, Palais des Nations, CH-1211 Geneva, Switzerland.

8. The Rules of Procedure of the Committee on the Elimination of Racial Discrimination make provision for the appointment of working groups and special rapporteurs with similar functions to those under the

---

41 Rule 91(f), Rules of Procedure, note 38 above.

42 E Schwelb, "The International Convention on the Elimination of All Forms of Racial Discrimination" (1966) 15 *ICLQ* 1043.

43 A Byrnes, "The Committee against Torture", note 1 above at 536.

provisions of the Rules of Procedure of the Committee against Torture. However there is no provision for taking actions between sessions, such as requesting a State to take immediate steps to protect a victim. Any initiatives of this sort must await a meeting of the Committee.

9. The Convention[44] ensures absolute confidentiality for communicants and their identities may only be revealed to States parties on receipt of express permission. Oddly, however, the provision of the rules permitting for the holding of oral hearings on the merits[45] (as yet unemployed) does not, unlike its Torture Convention counterpart, stipulate that the sessions be closed.

10. Once a matter has been declared admissible the time limit on the State party for submission of its comments on the merits is three months.[46]

11. Whereas the Committee against Torture formulates its "views" on the merits, the Committee on the Elimination of Racial Discrimination formulates an "opinion". Article 14, paragraph 7(b) also permits the Committee to make "suggestions and recommendations". To date, the "opinions" of the Committee do not differ in substance from the Torture Committee's "views" though they may well diverge in the future to reflect the different scope and content of the two respective instruments.

---

44 Article 14(6)a.

45 Rule 94(5) "The Committee may invite the presence of the petitioner or his representative and the presence of representatives of the State party concerned in order to provide additional information or to answer questions on the merits of the communication".

46 Rule 94(2), Rules of Procedure, note 5 above.

Part IV

The UN treaty-based human rights system and periodic reporting

10

Periodic reporting: the International Covenant on Economic, Social and Cultural Rights and the Convention on the Rights of the Child

Philip Alston

In the following comments, I would first like to provide some background in relation to reporting systems and then to examine how they might best be used in a practical way.

Background

In terms of background, the first reporting system was established at the insistence of the United States, not because of a wish to develop an effective reporting system, but because it wanted to undermine the drafting of two Covenants by demonstrating that all of the aims to be promoted by the Covenants could be achieved through other means. Accordingly, in 1953 the United States Government proposed a system of voluntary reporting by all States, to be based upon the provisions of the Universal Declaration of Human Rights. That system began in 1955 and was not wound up until 1981. It had generated large amounts of paper but no effective scrutiny of States' compliance with human rights norms.

Beginning with the establishment of reporting procedures in the International Convention on the Elimination of All Forms of Racial Discrimination (CERD), in 1965, a big change occurred in relation to the formal monitoring role played by international bodies. This Convention, which was followed by several other major treaties, set up a separate entity charged specifically with monitoring. Governments agreed to these reporting systems on the basis of various assumptions, the most important of all being that the whole exercise would be essentially formalistic in nature and diplomatic in character. To reinforce these assumptions they made sure that only governmentally sourced information would be taken into account by the international committees, or "treaty bodies" as they came to be called. Second, these supervisory bodies were expected to perform their functions without any input from NGOs. These groups were neither expected to provide alternative sources of information nor to follow-up in any way on the work of the committees. Third, the only outcome of reporting was to be the adoption of what the International Covenant on Civil and Political Rights (ICCPR) calls General Comments, and what the International Covenant on Economic, Social and Cultural Rights (ICESCR) calls General Recommendations.

Happily, as we now know, all that has changed radically. Indeed the key characteristic of the human rights chess game is that once governments have agreed to do something, the procedure or mechanism that they have created rapidly escapes from their control and has a good chance of evolving into something quite useful. In relation to reporting, this has happened in a fairly dramatic way. The scope and reach of reporting procedures developed steadily throughout the 1980s but they were given a particularly significant fillip by the termination of the Cold War. This was mainly because the Communist countries had played an especially negative role in trying to prevent the development of any sort of effective international scrutiny.

In terms of the major developments that have taken place, it is of particular importance to note that all sources of information are now drawn upon and taken fully into account by the committees. This applies as much to reports by NGOs and media reports as it does to information with an official imprimatur (from either a government or an international organisation such as UNICEF or the World Bank). Another significant although rather gradual change has seen the direct involvement of NGOs. It used to be the case that they might slip a brown paper envelope containing information about alleged violations to one of the members of the treaty bodies during an informal rendezvous in a UN coffee lounge. The member might then pretend that the relevant information had come from some other source, in order to ensure that its relevance and veracity would not automatically be challenged by other members. Today such charades have finished. Members can say to a government: "Amnesty International says the following. What is your response?" The government is forced to reply not by attacking the NGO, but rather by focusing on the substance of the allegations made.

Finally, the committees are now prepared to arrive at clear and sometimes strong conclusions. Up until only about three or four years ago, the committees insisted on leaving their conclusions very much up in the air by simply recording the random observations of a number of different members, with all their inconsistencies and contradictions. Governments could then say: "Well, yes it is true that member X claimed that prison conditions in our country are inhumane, but member Y pointed out that we have made enormous progress and that the government is clearly doing everything it reasonably can". These more or less "non-conclusions" meant that NGOs and others received very little reward for all their efforts, and governments were not compelled to focus on any specific issues in terms of the conclusions they drew from the supervisory exercise. Today the committees adopt what most of them call "Concluding Observations". These are generally straightforward and identify the major problems and criticisms which the Committee considers need to be addressed by the government concerned.

Practical use of reporting procedures

How can these procedures be used in a practical way? The two committees with which I am dealing – the Committee on Economic, Social and Cultural Rights, and the Committee on the Rights of the Child – are probably the most innovative and progressive of the six major committees. Let us consider first the process of drawing up the national report, as required by the terms of the Covenant or Convention. In most countries, including Australia, it is unclear who ultimately is responsible for drawing up reports. The process remains largely a bureaucratic exercise and the political responsibility for reports is very muted. The challenge is for NGOs to change this from a bureaucratic, not particularly well coordinated chore, into a major political priority. Only where there is sufficient scrutiny of the procedure and of the content of reports by interested groups at the domestic level will governments start taking reporting more seriously. It should not be assumed that making a difference through reporting requires NGOs to go to Geneva or even to know how the process in Geneva (or, in a few cases, New York) works in any detail. The real focus should be on the content of the report in the context of domestic policy-making and political processes.

Effective use and lobbying of these committees involves consideration of what it is that the committee can actually do for you. An organisation should start with an assessment of its ideal bottom line: "What would we like the Human Rights Committee to say about the situation of, for example, Indigenous people in Australia?" That issue is only going to take up, at the most, one page in the Committee's overall Concluding Observations on its consideration of the relevant country's report. The Committee will not wish to get into details which it is in no position to verify effectively. Rather, groups should seek to identify major issues of concern, while at the same time using language which is sufficiently measured and restrained, even if not diplomatic. Thus, for example, criticism of a government as being callous, uncaring, hypocritical, and racist for its continuing oppression and impoverishment of Indigenous peoples in Northern Australia is not going to get very far in terms of leading to concrete conclusions being adopted by the Committee. Instead, the challenge for a group or its representative is to formulate its submission in a way that enables a Committee member to say: "You have provided enough evidence to convince me that it is true, so we will draw attention to the problem in the report".

In the Committee on Economic, Social and Cultural Rights and the Committee on the Rights of the Child, as in each of the other committees, it helps greatly if the information and the desired conclusions are drafted in a way that enables them to be fed directly into the drafting process through a committee member or the Secretariat. If the formulation is sufficiently accurate, nuanced and tailored to the style of the committee, its chances of being adopted are infinitely greater. For that reason, very long reports and lobbying in relation to complex micro issues are of limited use compared to the skilled, careful drafting of a single page which can be provided in an appropriately confidential and careful manner to a key member.

Finally, it should be noted that the Committee on the Rights of the Child and the Committee on Economic, Social and Cultural Rights demonstrate an approach which is very open to NGOs. The Committee on Economic and Social Rights devotes the first afternoon of its sessions to hearing oral submissions by NGOs on the situations in particular countries. Such NGOs do not need to have consultative status with the Economic and Social Council. Indeed, experience shows that small but credible NGOs operating only in the domestic context of the country concerned will often be the best informed and most persuasive sources of information with which to compel a government to address specific issues in detail.

The Committee on the Rights of the Child has a similar, rather more informal procedure. For NGOs who can go to, or be represented in, Geneva, there are very direct opportunities to feed information in and to compel responses by governments. This applies particularly in the context of the work of the working group which draws up the initial list of written questions put to the government in response to the formal report. NGOs should also consider framing strategic questions to be put to the government representatives, and providing selected committee members with information sufficient to pursue these questions. Experience shows that governments generally seek to keep their answers at a level of generality which enables the key concerns to remain obscure. It is only when a committee member is in possession of much more precise and detailed information that an official representative can be obliged to respond to the allegations with any precision. Failure to do so leaves the government in the position of failing to discharge a burden of proof which has thus been imposed upon it.

11

Periodic reporting: the International Covenant on Civil and Political Rights and the Convention on the Elimination of All Forms of Discrimination against Women

Elizabeth Evatt

Introduction

This chapter aims to explain briefly how the reporting process works, why it is important, and how individuals and groups can use it. The focus is on the use of the International Covenant on Civil and Political Rights (ICCPR) by Indigenous Australians. Some references are made to the Convention on the Elimination of All Forms of Discrimination against Women (CEDAW). The procedures under both instruments are similar.

Reporting procedures: a summary

States parties are obliged to submit written reports to the Human Rights Committee (HRC) every five years, explaining what they have done to give effect to ICCPR rights and the progress made in the enjoyment of those rights. The HRC studies the reports in the presence of representatives of the government, and raises its concerns about laws and practices and about the actual state of human rights in that country. Non-governmental organisations, such as Amnesty International and Human Rights Watch, assist in this process by providing the HRC with written information about laws and practices from their own point of view, drawing attention to violations and abuses. The HRC then puts its conclusions about the State into a formal concluding comment which then stands as a benchmark for the development of human rights in that State. Points to note:

- the reporting process is an open and public process;
- the HRC can raise any questions relevant to the State's compliance with its obligations under the ICCPR;
- the HRC can draw conclusions and make recommendations for future action by the State;
- there is a real possibility for the community to be actively involved, before, during and after the process.

Obligations under the Covenant

States must report every five years

Under Article 40, States parties ratifying the ICCPR undertake to submit reports within one year of the entry into force of the ICCPR and thereafter whenever the HRC so requests. In practice States are requested to report every five years, unless there are special factors indicating the need for more frequent reports (such as situations where massive violations of rights are occurring or are threatened). Under CEDAW, reports are due every four years.

Australia: a late report

The HRC has not considered a report from Australia since 1988, seven years ago. Our third report under the ICCPR should have been submitted in December 1991. It is now five-and-a-half years late. Other States have done better, for example, the United Kingdom and Russia have presented their fourth reports. Australia's third report under the ICCPR may not come up for consideration until 1998 or later unless something happens quickly. This highlights the fact that the reporting process, while it is a legal obligation, is not directly enforceable. It depends on States fulfilling their obligations.

Australia's third report under CEDAW was considered by the CEDAW Committee in July 1997.

Reports have to follow guidelines

Under Article 40(1) of the ICCPR, reports should set out the measures that States have adopted to give effect to the rights recognised in the ICCPR and should describe the progress made in the enjoyment of those rights. State reports are to indicate factors and difficulties affecting the implementation of the ICCPR (Article 40(2)). Guidelines prepared by the HRC indicate what material States should include in their initial and periodic reports. The initial report should describe the general legal framework within which civil and political rights are protected, measures in law and practice to give effect to the ICCPR, whether there is specific provision to enable the rights to be enforced in courts, and the remedies available. It should also explain the extent to which each of the rights protected under the ICCPR, including Article 27, are enjoyed in actual practice. Reports should explain the legal measures taken by the State party to allow the implementation of the views of the HRC under the Optional Protocol, and should reflect the General Comments adopted by the HRC.

Later reports should take into account concerns expressed by the HRC during the consideration of the earlier report, highlight measures taken to follow up on the HRC's suggestions and recommendations, and show what progress has been made in the realisation of ICCPR rights. Periodic reports should provide information on any measures taken during the reporting period to further implement the ICCPR and in respect of matters which, owing to time constraints, remained unanswered.

Similar guidelines apply to reports under Article 18 of CEDAW.

How the reporting process works

The examination of reports: procedure

The HRC meets three times a year, in March, July and October. About five or six reports are considered at each session. When a written report is submitted to the HRC, representatives of the State are invited to attend a meeting of the HRC to discuss the contents of their report. In the dialogue with the representatives of the States, each member can ask questions to clarify issues, raise concerns and ascertain whether ICCPR standards are being met. The procedure under CEDAW is similar; the CEDAW Committee meets once each year.

Do the laws comply?

The HRC has to assess whether the laws of a State are fully compatible with the principles of the ICCPR. It examines the Constitution and basic laws of the State, and decisions of national courts or tribunals. The material for this analysis is usually provided by the State party, and the HRC may ask for supplementary material.

Are remedies available for violation of rights?

The HRC is concerned to ensure that effective and enforceable remedies are available to individuals claiming that their rights under the ICCPR have been violated. The ICCPR requires that provision be made for individuals to take effective enforcement action or to recover compensation for any violation of rights (Articles 2(3), 9(5)). Similar provisions are contained in Article 2 of CEDAW.

Is the Covenant known to law-enforcement agencies?

Another question is whether all relevant judicial officers, government officials and police have a proper understanding of and respect for human rights, and whether any steps have been taken to provide those officers with education and training in human rights or to inform the public of their rights. Education of judges and law enforcement officers helps to ensure that the ICCPR principles are known, understood and respected.

De facto enjoyment of rights

The HRC also needs to assess how far the rights under the ICCPR are actually enjoyed. More is needed than the texts of laws and court decisions. The HRC has to assess the actual situation for the individual and whether people know about their rights and how to use them.

Constructive dialogue

The HRC is an independent body; it carries out the functions assigned to it by the ICCPR. Its aim in the examination of State reports is to encourage States to take a positive view of their obligations. The procedure is sometimes called a constructive dialogue, though it seldom achieves a real dialogue. At its best it allows for a genuine exchange of views, information and ideas. Some States, and Australia is one of these, send high-level competent delegations and provide accurate and detailed information. The HRC uses its own knowledge of the situation in its examination of a State report. In some cases the process itself does affect the attitudes of State representatives. In other cases it is difficult to believe that the HRC's message has been understood.

Procedure for periodic reports

The procedure for first reports and for periodic reports differs. As Australia is now into its third reporting cycle, this chapter deals only with periodic reports. The observations are generally valid for CEDAW as well as for the HRC.

Once a State's first report has been considered, there is considerable material on the record. When later reports are submitted, the HRC may want to review the earlier dialogue and follow up its concerns. For these and other reasons, there is a more elaborate procedure for periodic reports.

Pre-sessional working group

A pre-sessional working group, consisting of five members of the HRC, meets during the week before the session to prepare written questions for States presenting periodic reports. These questions are based on the material already before the HRC from the earlier consideration of that State, including its reports and the summary record of discussions. The list of questions is sent to the State representatives some days before the session.

Presenting the report

The actual presentation of the report can take at least three meetings for second and later reports – a meeting of three hours occupies half a day. The State representatives answer the written questions. Each member of the HRC may intervene with follow-up questions. The State representative replies to these oral questions. When all questions have been answered, the members of the HRC make their observations and comments, and then the public proceedings for that State are finished. As in the case of first reports, the HRC, in closed session, adopts a Concluding Comment about the State (see below).

Record of proceedings

A summary record is kept of the whole proceedings, including the closed sessions. The HRC sends an annual report on its activities to the General Assembly. This used to include a summary of the discussions. Under recent decisions, the only record of the presentation of State reports to the HRC which appears in the annual report is the Concluding Comment on that State.

Getting to the truth

What is the actual situation in a State?

HRC members prepare for the examination of a State report by studying the material submitted by the State, and the record of earlier discussions with that country. The ICCPR does not make provision for the HRC to receive any information apart from that supplied by the States parties to assist it in its examination of that State. States may provide information about their laws and constitution, but they seldom provide useful information about the current human rights situation. Reports by the State to other human rights treaty bodies, and records of their comments, are also available to the HRC. The reports are of course prepared by the State itself. To test whether rights are actually enjoyed, the HRC needs information about the actual situation in the State and about any alleged violations of rights in that State.

Preparation for examination of reports by members

Members can do their own research and make use of sources other than the State report in the dialogue with that State. They can approach NGOs in the countries concerned. But the time for such activities is necessarily limited, especially in the case of members who are engaged in other duties between the sessions of the HRC.

Specialised agencies of the UN

The HRC receives information from the specialised agencies of the UN. The pre-sessional working group on reporting meets with representatives of specialised agencies, such as the International Labour Organisation, the UN High Commissioner for Refugees (UNHCR), and the Food and

Agriculture Organization (FAO).[1] The discussions enable the HRC to be informed about issues such as freedom of association and the treatment of refugees in the States whose reports are due to be considered at the session.

Assistance by NGOs

The most useful information comes from NGOs who provide the HRC with written information about the actual situation in States whose reports are being considered, or about particular laws which may raise concerns. Organisations such as Amnesty International and Human Rights Watch have proved to be reliable sources of information for the HRC about human rights violations and other problems which might not otherwise come to its attention. Sometimes the picture this alternative material presents is considerably less flattering to the State than their own report. It may include specific information about individuals who are alleged to have been tortured in police custody, or give details of other abuses. The State will be confronted with this information and expected to respond.

Informal role for NGOs

NGOs in some respects represent a voice which otherwise would be absent from the dialogue: that of the persons most vitally affected. However, it is a restricted voice. The ICCPR does not provide for NGOs to take part directly in the consideration of State reports to the HRC. They cannot speak or ask questions, though they can and do attend to observe meetings. On the other hand, it is relatively easy for organisations to arrange for information they have prepared to be delivered to members of the HRC personally. In some cases they can organise informal discussions during the time the HRC is in session, at lunch time, or even at breakfast.

Other treaty bodies, such as the Committee on Economic, Social and Cultural Rights, have better arrangements for the involvement of NGOs than the HRC and the CEDAW Committee. The main body assisting the CEDAW Committee is the International Women's Rights Action Watch (IWRAW).

---

1   Acting on the decision taken at the fifty-second session (July 1994).

National NGOs

Another development in recent years has been the arrival of NGOs and individuals from the States whose reports are under consideration. NGOs from Ireland, Japan and the United States have supported the HRC in recent times by providing information and arranging informal discussions. The NGOs from Japan and the United States included Indigenous organisations raising issues under Articles 26 and 27 of the ICCPR.

Concluding comments

Basic information

After the dialogue, the HRC prepares a written assessment, or "Concluding Comment", about the State, which includes recommendations to the State to revise those aspects of law and practice which fall short of ICCPR standards. This provides a benchmark for the next report, which should, in theory, come five years later.

Concluding Comments identify areas of potential violation

The Concluding Comment enables the HRC to identify and express views on situations where it appears that States have failed to respect and ensure rights or where ICCPR rights may have been violated, whether or not the State has accepted the HRC's jurisdiction under the Optional Protocol procedure. As the comments are adopted by consensus, they could become an influential source of opinion about the scope of particular ICCPR rights. The HRC has, for example, stated clearly that very long periods of detention without charge during which interrogation may take place are incompatible with Article 9(3). Examples are Bulgaria, Dominican Republic, Egypt, Japan,[2] Hungary, Iran, Italy, Korea,[3] Niger, Slovenia, Uruguay and Venezuela.

---

2   Human Rights Committee, *Report of the Human Rights Committee*, UN Doc A/49/40 (1994), paras 98, 110.

3   Human Rights Committee, *Report of the Human Rights Committee*, UN Doc A/47/40 (1992), paras 511 ff, 516.

Using these comments in national action

Concluding Comments can be used by individuals and groups within a State working to bring about improvements in human rights. Although not legally binding, they are reached by consensus and should be given weight as a view of the whole HRC about the State's level of compliance with ICCPR obligations.

How does Australia rate?

The HRC had not adopted the practice of framing a Concluding Comment when Australia's second report was considered in 1988. Individual members of the HRC expressed appreciation for the vigour with which the Human Rights and Equal Opportunity Commission (HREOC) was carrying out its mandate. Some members drew attention to the plight of Aboriginal people and welcomed the fact that the government had frankly acknowledged the problems and was endeavouring to deal with them.[4] The human rights situation of Indigenous people will undoubtedly be raised when Australia's third report is presented.

There is in fact no institution other than the HREOC with a mandate to ensure that Australian laws and policies remain consistent with our obligations under the ICCPR. Nor can ICCPR rights be enforced directly in the courts.

How to use the procedure

How can individuals or groups contribute to the process?

Individuals or organisations can contribute:

- by taking part in any consultations which may be held by the government before a country report is prepared;
- by providing written information to the HRC;
- by attending the session at which the report is presented to observe and to "lobby" members informally;
- by building on the work of the HRC by using it in advocacy for change at home.

---

4   Human Rights Committee, *Report of the Human Rights Committee*, UN Doc A/43/40 (1988), para 458.

Pre-report consultations

The ICCPR does not require national governments to consult the community before reports are prepared and submitted. The report is a statement by the government about the situation as the government sees it. But governments which are sensitive to public opinion may well consider it proper to consult the community before deciding which issues to raise in the report.

The Australian Government held community consultations in regard to the second report under CEDAW. The Department of Foreign Affairs has regular discussions with human rights organisations and the agenda includes the current report under the ICCPR.

How to find out when the report will be considered?

There is no obvious way to find out when Australia's reports to any of the committees will be considered. As soon as a report is submitted to a committee, this information ought to be made public. When the date is set for the presentation, this should also be made public. As things stand, one can ask the relevant department. In the case of the ICCPR, that is the Attorney-General's Department. Alternatively, one can ask the Human Rights Centre in Geneva.[5] For CEDAW, the Office of the Status of Women would be the main source of information in Australia. CEDAW is serviced by the Division for the Advancement of Women in New York.[6]

In practice, information about new reports which have been received is publicly available at each session of the HRC. In the final days of the session, agreement is reached on the reports to be considered at the following session. That information is publicly available from the Human Rights Centre, but it is a poor substitute for having ready access to the information in Australia.

How to get a copy of Australia's report

There is no established way to get a copy of Australia's report to the human rights committees. The Office of the Status of Women has

---

5   Secretary, Human Rights Committee, Centre for Human Rights, Ave de la Paix, CH-1211, Geneva 10, Tel 41-22-9173965, Fax 41-22-9170099.

6   Department for Policy Co-ordination and Sustainable Development, United Nations Headquarters, New York, New York, 10017, USA, Tel 212-9631151, Fax 212-9633463.

distributed Australia's reports under CEDAW, but other reports are not distributed. I believe that it is intended to table future reports in parliament. In the meantime, copies of reports to the HRC could be obtained from the Attorney General's Department in Canberra, or from the Human Rights Centre in Geneva.

What should be in your submission?

This depends on what message you want to convey. Perhaps the goal is to draw to the attention of the HRC one specific situation, say health problems leading to diminished life expectancy of Aboriginal people. Factual data should be provided, including statistics and extracts from official and other reports. This material should, ideally, be tied in with a reference to the relevant provisions of the ICCPR. It could be the right to life, Article 6, or Article 24, which requires measures to protect children, or Article 26, because of discrimination in the provision of health services, or Article 27, because failing health standards may contribute to an erosion of culture. If the complaint is about prison conditions, then Articles 7 and 10 should be covered.

Another approach is to comment on the government's report, article by article, identifying issues that are not dealt with adequately or which you want to raise with the HRC. This approach would take the form of an alternative report. It is more useful for the HRC if submissions are tied in to specific provisions of the ICCPR. That may seem rather daunting, as it requires a study of the ICCPR itself, and the interpretative material. However, it should be emphasised that the ICCPR imposes on Australia, as on other countries, obligations which are legally binding. This work of analysis is essential if we want to use the ICCPR effectively to enhance rights. The main sources for such a study are the reports of the HRC, and in particular, the General Comments, decisions of the HRC and Concluding Comments.

General Comments

The General Comments of the HRC[7] on particular articles of the ICCPR draw on its experience under the communications procedure and the reporting procedure. These indicate how the HRC approaches each article and what it expects of States in implementing their obligations. The General Comments are intended to give a broader understanding of the

---

7   UN Doc CCPR/C/21/Rev 1; UN Doc CCPR/C/21/Add 1 and Add 2.

interpretation and application of the ICCPR, and to guide States as to the kind of measures which are needed to protect ICCPR rights and freedoms. The HRC adopts its General Comments by consensus, sometimes after prolonged discussions. As a result, they have the authority of the HRC as a whole.

Twenty-four General Comments have been adopted to date. The most recent include those on religious freedom, rights of members of minorities (which include Indigenous peoples) and reservations to the ICCPR. A General Comment is now being prepared on Article 25 – participation in the conduct of public affairs and democratic rights. The General Comments can be found in the annual reports of the HRC, and are published in other collections.

Decisions

Decisions of the HRC under the communications procedure could also be studied, but the reporting process can range more widely than the communications procedure. In the reporting process, the HRC is not constrained by the narrow basis of its jurisdiction under the Optional Protocol. It can point to violations of ICCPR rights even in cases where it may not be able to receive and deal with a communication.

Concluding Comments

The HRC's Concluding Comments are a useful source of views about the issues which can be raised in the reporting procedure. They touch on subjects which may not be covered by a General Comment, or which cannot be dealt with effectively in the communications procedure. For example, the HRC has made observations concerning Article 1 and the right of self-determination in its comment on the initial report of Azerbaijan. The HRC regretted the position taken by Azerbaijan in the report regarding the principle of self-determination. It recalled that under Article 1 of the ICCPR, that principle applies to all peoples and not merely to colonised peoples.[8]

Some examples of Concluding Comments: Article 27

Numerous Concluding Comments of the HRC refer to Article 27 and Indigenous people. For example:

---

8   Human Rights Committee, *Report of the Human Rights Committee*, UN Doc A/49/40 (1994), paras 291 ff, 296.

- The HRC has commended Norway for the devolution of responsibility to the Saami assembly (Sametinget) with regard to matters affecting the life and culture of members of the Saami community and noted with satisfaction that the Saami language may be used in contacts with public bodies and before the courts. [9]

- In regard to Mexico, the HRC has expressed concern about the situation of Indigenous people in the following language:[10]

  Article 27 of the Constitution concerning agrarian reform is often implemented to the detriment of persons belonging to indigenous groups. The delay in resolving problems relating to the distribution of land has weakened the confidence of these populations in both local and federal authorities. Moreover, these persons are subject to special laws, particularly in Chiapas, which could create a situation of discrimination within the meaning of Article 26 of the Covenant.

  The Committee recommended that the government give consideration to more equitable land distribution within the framework of agrarian reform and that it take into account the rights and aspirations of indigenous populations in that connection. Indigenous populations should have the opportunity to participate in decision-making on matters that concern them.[11]

- The HRC has recommended that Venezuela take further measures pursuant to Article 27 in order to guarantee Indigenous peoples their own cultural life and the use of their own language.[12]

- When the United States presented its first report, the HRC was concerned that Aboriginal rights of Native Americans may, in law, be extinguished by Congress.[13] It was also concerned by the high incidence of poverty, sickness and alcoholism amongst Native Americans. Notwithstanding some improvements achieved with the Self-Governance Demonstration Project, the HRC recommended that steps be taken to ensure that previously recognised Aboriginal Native American rights cannot be extinguished. It urged the United States government to ensure that there is full judicial review in respect of determinations of Federal recognition of tribes. The Self-Governance Demonstration Project and similar programs should be

---

9   Note 8 above, para 89.

10 Note 8 above, paras 166-177.

11 Note 8 above, paras 166-182.

12 Human Rights Committee, *Report of the Human Rights Committee*, UN Doc A/48/40 (1993), paras 301-310.

13 Human Rights Committee, *Report of the Human Rights Committee*, UN Doc A/50/40 (1995), para 37.

strengthened to continue the fight against the high incidence of poverty, sickness and alcoholism amongst Native Americans.

• With respect to New Zealand's third report, the HRC regretted that, despite improvements, Maoris still experience disadvantages in access to health, education and employment. The HRC was also concerned that the proportion of Maoris in parliament and other high public offices, in liberal professions and in the senior rank of civil service remains low.[14] The HRC expressed hope that any decisions to be taken about future limitations to the entitlement of Maoris to advance claims before the Waitangi Tribunal will fully take account of Maori interests under the Treaty of Waitangi.

Form of the submission

Be concise, or if not, make an executive summary. Be precise with details of alleged violations: identities, dates, times and places. Include reference to and citation of relevant authorities and sources of evidence, including court cases, official reports, statistics, academic research and surveys. Keep in mind what kind of recommendation the HRC could make.

How can written submissions be put to the HRC?

As mentioned, the members of the HRC and the CEDAW Committee are willing to receive and consider documents provided by NGOs or individuals. There is no formal provision in the ICCPR for NGO material to be received by the HRC, but in practice there are two ways to do it:

1. Sending documents to individual members. Their names and their countries, but not their addresses, are published in the reports of the HRC.

2. The other way is by sending material to the Secretary of the HRC at Geneva[15] with a request that it be distributed. The HRC has endorsed formally an arrangement under which the Secretariat distributes documents submitted by NGOs to all members in the languages received. The Secretariat will be more willing to copy and distribute material if it is concise. Also material should be received in good time, some weeks at least before the session in which the report is to be

---

14 Human Rights Committee, *Report of the Human Rights Committee*, UN Doc A/50/40 (1995), paras 22, 25.

15 Secretary, Human Rights Committee, UN Centre for Human Rights, Palais des Nations, 1211 Geneva, Switzerland.

considered. Otherwise it will not be fully reflected in the preparation of written questions. If you choose to distribute via the Secretary, you could confirm, after a reasonable period of time, that distribution has actually occurred.

Observing the meetings of the HRC

The HRC meets three times a year for three to four weeks. The dates are set well in advance and always follow the same pattern:

- mid-March to early April   New York
- last three weeks of July   Geneva
- mid-October to early November   Geneva

Another development in recent years has been the presence of NGOs and individuals from the States whose reports are under consideration. When the Irish report was considered by the HRC in July 1993, the government had encouraged the NGOs in Ireland to take an interest in the proceedings. They attended in large numbers and provided considerable information on current human rights problems in Ireland to the members of the HRC. When Japan presented its second report to the HRC in October 1993, wide publicity had been given to the presentation in Japan, and so many Japanese citizens came to the Centre for Human Rights in Geneva that an additional room had to be made available to them, connected by sound to the main room. The members were overwhelmed by information from more than 20 organisations in Japan, in addition to the information provided by international NGOs. Similarly, the United States NGOs were present in large numbers when their country's report was considered in March 1995, and they provided a massive amount of material to the HRC.

Attending the meeting makes it easier to get a summary record of the proceedings, or to make notes. The Japanese made a tape of the whole proceedings before the HRC and had it transcribed later. Their government had provided Japanese interpretation, so they were able to listen and to record the proceedings in their own language. Being present makes it easier to get messages out to the media back home. This can help to build understanding of the process and support for the changes which the HRC considers necessary to ensure compliance with the standards of the ICCPR. It is somewhat easier to gain access to the UN building in Geneva than in New York. In New York, membership or sponsorship by an accredited NGO is usually the only way to get in. In Geneva, the Secretary of the HRC may help to get the necessary passes.

The main objective

The main objective of supporting the HRC's work is to ensure that it asks specific and relevant questions and that it makes Concluding Comments on the report of the State which will be useful to those working for better implementation of human rights standards. The better the information available to the HRC about law and practice, the more useful may be the result. Too much material of a disorganised, unfocused nature is likely to swamp the process and diffuse the thrust of the dialogue. Keep to a few main issues and focus on them from angles relevant to the ICCPR.

Then what? After the meeting

When the HRC has done its work there is, eventually, a Summary Record of the discussions. Immediately available is the Concluding Comment, and that should be the focus of attention. It can be used to attract media attention. For example, when Australia was criticised by the Committee on the Elimination of Racial Discrimination for not fulfilling its promise to implement the provision on racial vilification, this gained media attention and put pressure on the government.

If media action does not yield results, there may be other opportunities to draw public attention to the views expressed by the HRC and to the areas where Australia has been said to have failed in its obligations.

12

The Committee on the Elimination of Racial Discrimination: non-governmental input and the early warning and urgent procedure

Michael O'Flaherty

The Committee on the Elimination of Racial Discrimination

The Committee on the Elimination of Racial Discrimination is established pursuant to the provisions of Article 8 of the Convention on the Elimination of All Forms of Racial Discrimination. There are eighteen members, elected by the States parties for terms of four years.[1] Members, though all nationals of States parties, serve in their private capacities and take an oath of impartiality upon taking up office. The Committee presently meets twice each year, in March and August for sessions of

---

* The views in this chapter are the author's own and he does not purport to represent those of treaty bodies, their members or the UN Secretariat.

1 Membership as of January 1996: Mahmoud Aboul-Nasr (Egypt), Hamzat Ahmadu (Nigeria), Michael Parker Banton (United Kingdom of Great Britain and Northern Ireland), Theodoor van Boven (Netherlands), Andrew Chigovera (Zimbabwe), Ion Diaconu (Romania), Eduardo Ferrero Costa (Peru), Ivan Garvalon (Bulgaria), Régis de Gouttes (France), Carlos Lechuga Hevia (Cuba), Yuri A Rechetov (Russian Federation), Shanti Sadiq Ali (India), Agha Shahi (Pakistan), Michael E Sherifis (Cyprus), Deci Zou (China), Luis Valencia Rodriguez (Ecuador), Rudiger Wolfrum (Germany) and Mario Jorge Yutzis (Argentina).

three working weeks each. All sessions now take place in Geneva. Secretariat services are provided by the UN Centre for Human Rights.[2]

The reporting procedure

The obligation on the State[3]

Under Article 9 of the Convention, States are obliged to submit reports to the Committee one year after the Convention comes into effect for the State and thereafter every two years, on the legislative, judicial, administrative or other measures which they have adopted and which give effect to the provisions of the Convention.[4]

States which are overdue in submitting a number of reports may consolidate these in one document for submission to the Committee.[5]

---

2   Secretariat of CERD, International Instruments Branch, Centre for Human Rights, United Nations, Palais des Nations, 1211 – Geneva – Switzerland (Tel 41 22 917 1234).

3   International Convention on the Elimination of Racial Discrimination, Article 9; *Procedure of the Committee on the Elimination of Racial Discrimination*, Rules 63-68, UN Doc CERD/C/65/Rev 3. See S Guillet, *Nous, Peuples des Nations Unies – L'action des ONG au sein du système de protection international des droits de l'homme*, Paris, 1995, pp 70-71; K English and A Stapleton, *The Human Rights Handbook – A Practical Guide to Monitoring Human Rights*, Human Rights Centre, University of Essex, 1995, pp 179-180; M R Burrowes, "Implementing the UN Racial Convention: Some Procedural Aspects", (1981) 7 *Australian YB Int'l L* 236; I Dore, "United Nations Measures to Combat Racial Discrimination: Progress and Problems in Retrospect", (1981) 10 *Den J Int'l L & Pol* 299; T Buergenthal, "Implementing the UN Racial Convention", (1977) 12 *Tex Int'l LJ* 187; K Das, Measures of Implementation of the International Convention on the Elimination of All Forms of Racial Discrimination with Special Reference to the Provisions Governing Reports from States Parties to the Convention, (1971) 4 *Rev des droits de l'homme* 313.

4   See also L Valencia Rodriguez, "The International Convention on the Elimination of All Forms of Racial Discrimination" in UN Centre for Human Rights and UN Institute for Training and Research, *Manual on Human Rights Reporting Under Six Major International Human Rights Instruments*, United Nations, New York, 1991.

5   See, for example, Committee on the Elimination of Racial Discrimination, *Report of the Committee on the Elimination of Racial Discrimination*, UN Doc A/50/18 (1995) at para 693.

Also, the Committee has attempted to ameliorate the two-year periodicity rule by occasionally stipulating, on the occasion of the examination of a report, that the next report be of an updating rather than a comprehensive nature.[6]

Consonant with the State's implementation obligation as stated in the Convention, the Committee has indicated that the reporting requirement is a substantial one requiring that the report provide exhaustive information on a very wide range of government activities and that it comprehensively indicate the actual situation within the State even with regard to issues and circumstances which may appear to be beyond the appropriate or normal purview of governmental interference.[7] In July of 1993 the Committee stated that reports, to be comprehensible, must also contain detailed information concerning the racial and ethnic configuration of society.[8]

The scheduling process

Reports once submitted can be expected to be taken up by the Committee within the calendar year. Some three months before each session the list of reports to be considered is settled.[9] It is unusual, though not unknown, for the scheduling to be changed after this point. More common, however, are adjustments in the timetabling within sessions. Such changes sometimes occur during sessions and with very little advance notice.

---

6 At its thirty-eighth session in 1988, CERD decided to accept the proposal of the States parties that States parties submit a comprehensive report every four years and a brief updating report in the two-year interim (see L Valencia Rodriguez, note 4 above, p 141). However, this practice has not been followed in all cases.

7 *General Guidelines for the Preparation of State Reports*, UN Doc CERD/C/70/Rev 3. See K Partsch, "The Racial Discrimination Committee", in P Alston (ed), *The United Nations and Human* Rights, Oxford University Press, Oxford, 1992 at pp 350-351. The Committee also provides guidance to States in implementing their reporting obligations in the series of General Recommend-ations which it has issued which serve to explicate the content of the various substantive and other articles of the Convention.

8 *General Guidelines for the Preparation of State Reports*, note 7 above, at para 8

9 Available on request from the Secretariat.

Before the session

Each report receives the attention of a member designated as Country Rapporteur.[10] The Country Rapporteur is expected to undertake a detailed analysis of the report in preparation for the consideration by the Committee and to both identify key issues and prepare questions and comments to be put to the representatives of the government. Country Rapporteurs base their analysis on the report itself, previous reports of the State, the records of the Committee's consideration of previous reports, and any other information, regardless of source, which the Country Rapporteur considers to be of use.

Occasionally, Country Rapporteurs make their lists of issues and questions available to the States concerned and to interested NGOs prior to the Committee's consideration. There is, however, no standard practice in this regard.

Consideration by the Committee

Reports are considered by the Committee in public session and in dialogue with representatives of the State.[11] Reports are introduced by representatives of the government who will often use the occasion to provide further information or elaborate on aspects of the report. The Country Rapporteur then takes the floor and usually presents an exhaustive analysis regarding the entire report and all provisions of the Convention. Members then pose their questions or make comments. Once the members have spoken the representative has the opportunity to reply. Usually, representatives will reply to a number of the questions posed and undertake to provide outstanding answers either in the form of additional information or in the next report. The exchange between Committee and representatives ends with the concluding remarks of the Country Rapporteur and the members. At the end of the scrutiny, which usually extends over two consecutive three-hour meetings, the Committee adopts its "Concluding Observations". The Concluding Observations comprise a critique of the State report and of the response of the State representative

---

10 See Michael O'Flaherty, "The Committee on the Elimination of Racial Discrimination as an Implementation Agency" in M MacEwan (ed), *Anti-Discrimination Law Enforcement Agencies – A European and Comparative Perspective*, Edinburgh, 1996.

11 Rules of Procedure of the Committee on the Elimination of Racial Discrimination, Rules 63-68, UN Doc CERD/C/65/Rev 3.

to the scrutiny of the Committee, noting positive factors, drawing attention to matters of concern and making suggestions and recommendations. Concluding Observations are issued as public documents at the end of each session of the Committee and are included in the annual report to the General Assembly of the UN.[12]

The role of NGOs

NGOs do not have formal standing under the reporting procedure. Thus they may not have their documents received and processed as "UN documents" and they may not formally address the proceedings. NGOs do however have a wide range of opportunities to convey information informally to committee members and thus to influence proceedings. Independent submissions are accepted by members of the Committee as an aid towards the carrying out of the scrutiny of the State reports.[13] The submissions, therefore, should be prepared in the context of the purposes of State reporting. Submissions which stray beyond the boundaries dictated by this context are unhelpful to the Committee.

It is essential to study the text of the Convention in order to identify the precise articles which are of relevance to a particular concern. The Convention should be read in conjunction with the General Recommendations of the Committee. These comments are the Committee's interpretation of the meaning of most of the substantive articles. They are useful in indicating whether an article is apposite and also in showing the extent of affirmative action which the Committee expects of a State. Very often, also, they serve to expand the effective parameters and influence of a provision.[14]

---

12 Annual reports to the General Assembly of the UN are cited as "A" (which symbolises the General Assembly), the number of the session of the General Assembly, and the number attributed to the specific Committee, which for the Committee for the Elimination of Racial Discrimination is 18. Thus the 1995 report is UN Doc A/50/18.

13 See Decision 1(XI) of 1991 in which the Committee stated that, "members of the Committee must have access, as independent experts, to all (other) available sources of information, governmental and non-governmental".

14 For an analysis of the substantive provisions of the Convention see chapter 13 by M O'Flaherty, "Substantive Provisions of the International Convention on the Elimination of All Forms of Racial Discrimination", in the present volume.

In the search for articles to support a cause, account should be taken of the reservations entered by the State.[15] The entering of a reservation does not preclude the Committee from questioning the State as to the probity of its position. It may, for instance, inquire as to the reason for the maintenance of the reservation or as to any steps being taken towards the withdrawal of a reservation. Accordingly, an NGO is not precluded from adverting to matters which arise under an article which is subject to a reservation, and indeed, may well be doing the service of informally drawing attention to that reservation.

In preparing submissions it is useful to observe how the Committee last dealt with the country in question and to identify the key concerns which preoccupied it on that occasion.[16]

In the drafting of a submission[17] matters should be categorised with reference to articles of the Covenant. Echo the State report by dealing with matters article-by-article rather than issue-by-issue. Thus, for instance, if a submission is being made with regard to a particular matter, the approach should not be taken of discussing the issue in general, with inclusion of reference to specific articles only in the body of the text. Instead, it would be advisable to make reference, article by article, to the relevant provisions of the Convention and to highlight matters as they arise in the context of each of the relevant articles. This approach is very helpful to the Committee and assists its members in categorising the points which they may wish to raise during the scrutiny. The article-by-article method of preparation will, of course, give rise to a considerable amount of cross-referencing. This should be kept as clear and simple as possible.

Submissions should be kept succinct. Elaborate and lengthy submissions may never be read by busy members of the Committee. Regardless of the length of submissions, they should be prefaced with a

---

15 With regard to Australia, see O'Flaherty, note 14 above.

16 In this regard, reference may be had to the report of the Committee for the year when the State was last before the Committee and to the relevant summary records. The document symbol numbers for the summary records may be obtained from the entry in the annual report. Since 1991 the Committee has adopted Concluding Observations following its examination of reports. These can be found in the relevant annual report.

17 See, further, M O'Flaherty, *UN Covenant on Civil and Political Rights, A Guide to Making an Independent Submission*, Irish Commission for Justice and Peace, Dublin, 1991.

one-page summary of the key points. One can be reasonably confident that all members of the Committee will at least acquaint themselves with the contents of this page.

Submissions will be most highly valued if they indicate the actual circumstances "on the ground". The anecdotal should be avoided in the making of points. Submissions should include reference to and citation of relevant authorities and sources of evidence: court cases, official reports, statistics, academic research, and surveys. It is permissible to make reference to and discuss individual cases which serve to illustrate a point being made. This opportunity serves as an informal but valuable way to raise a particular case before the Committee. The UN provides no financial assistance for the preparation of submissions.

Once a State's report has been scheduled for consideration, NGOs should indicate their interest to the Secretariat and send a preliminary submission for transmission to the Country Rapporteur and other members. Rather than rely on the Secretariat to copy these, multiple copies should be sent. Certain Country Rapporteurs and members may also be happy to establish direct contact with NGOs. Some weeks before the session NGOs can send to the Secretariat a final version of their written submission with the request that it be distributed to members. At least 20 copies should be provided.

NGOs may also choose to send copies of their submissions to a specialised NGO in Geneva, the Anti Racism Information Service (ARIS),[18] which exists to facilitate the transmission of information to and from the Committee. This NGO summarises information made available to it and furnishes the summaries to members together with a clear citation of the source of the information. The existence of ARIS, however, in no way precludes NGOs from directly approaching Committee members.

If at all possible, NGOs should send representatives to meet with the members of the Committee when they assemble in Geneva. Most members are happy to meet informally with NGOs and experience confirms that such contacts greatly enhance the impact of submissions. In direct meetings it is possible to emphasise certain matters, provide background briefings, correct misapprehensions, and otherwise direct the thoughts of Committee members. Being present at the meetings of the Committee when the State report is considered also ensures that

---

18 ARIS (Anti-Racist Information Service), 14, Avenue Trembley – 1209 Geneva – Switzerland.

information can be relayed back to the media at home while it is still current and newsworthy, and affords the opportunity to contest any comments made by government representatives with which an NGO might wish to take issue. Finally, attendance at the meetings permits the taking of extensive notes on the proceedings – a useful practice given the fact that written transcripts of the proceedings are not provided.[19]

Access to the UN buildings in Geneva can be arranged in advance with the Secretary of the Committee.

The procedure for examining States whose reports are seriously overdue

The Committee has developed a procedure whereby it will proceed with consideration of the situation in a State which is seriously overdue in its reporting obligation.[20] In order to comply with Article 9 of the Convention, the Committee states that the basis for the consideration is the last report submitted. The procedure was devised by the Committee to indicate to recalcitrant States that they could not totally avoid the Committee's scrutiny and it has been surprisingly successful in drawing States back into the reporting cycle. Thus of 50 States examined up to 1995, some 25 percent had recommenced a dialogue with the Committee.[21]

The role of NGOs in this procedure is no different to that under the regular reporting process. Indeed, information provided by them may have even greater impact in that the State will not have made its contribution and the members will, in general, have access to a rather small range of information sources.

A number of considerations are scheduled in each session and the identity of the countries and the assigned dates usually become available at the same time as the list of States to be considered under the regular report procedure. Timetabling is, however, uncertain in that deferrals may

---

19 Summary records are provided within days of the meetings concerned in either in English or French but never both languages.

20 Committee on the Elimination of Racial Discrimination, *Report of the Committee on the Elimination of Racial Discrimination*, UN Doc A/50/18 (1995) at para 693.

21 Michael O'Flaherty, *The Committee on the Elimination of Racial Discrimination as an Implementation Agency*, note 10 above.

occur on short notice either because a State promises to speedily send a report or due to pressure of the Committee's other business.

Each State is assigned a Country Rapporteur who fulfils a similar role to that under the regular reporting procedure both in closely examining the situation of the country and in leading the discussion in the Committee. The discussion itself is usually confined to just one meeting. Brief Concluding Observations are subsequently issued.

The early warning and urgent procedure [22]

Commencing in 1993, the Committee has developed a procedure whereby it examines the situation in States parties where it considers that there is particular cause for concern on the basis of actual or potential circumstances.[23] The procedure has two defining elements: (a) it is not dependent on the State having submitted a report for consideration, and (b) there are as yet no relevant rules of procedure and matters are dealt with on a case-by-case basis.

By the end of 1995, the procedure has been invoked for eleven States parties.[24] In each case, members named the States in a public session of the Committee and then or later in the session the situation was considered. Consideration has taken place in both public and private sessions and, on occasion, the Committee has invited participation in the discussion of State representatives and experts such as Rapporteurs of the Commission on Human Rights. On occasion, the consideration by the Committee has included examination of the question of whether a particular situation actually raises issues under the Convention or not, and requests for further information have been made to States with a view to clarifying the matter.[25]

---

22 Michael O'Flaherty, *The Committee on the Elimination of Racial Discrimination as an Implementation Agency*, note 10 above.

23 Committee on the Elimination of Racial Discrimination, *Annual Report of the Committee on the Elimination of Racial Discrimination*, UN Doc A/48/18 (1993) at paras 15-19 and annex 3.

24 Papua New Guinea, Rwanda, Burundi, Israel, Mexico, the Former Yugoslav Republic of Macedonia, the Russian Federation, Algeria, Bosnia and Herzegovina, Croatia and the Federal Republic of Yugoslavia (Serbia and Montenegro).

25 See, for example, the case of Algeria: Committee on the Elimination of Racial Discrimination, *Report of the Committee on the Elimination of Racial Discrimination*, UN Doc A/50/18 (1995) at para 29.

Amongst the outcomes of the consideration by the Committee have been:

- formal decisions expressing the views of the Committee and usually requesting the immediate submission by the State of a report,[26]
- the bringing of particular situations to the attention of the High Commissioner for Human Rights, the Secretary-General,[27] the General Assembly and the Security Council,[28] and
- the undertaking, with the consent of the governments concerned, of missions to the territory concerned.[29]

Once a State is placed under the procedure it remains indefinitely on the agenda of the Committee and may receive attention at forthcoming sessions. Accordingly there has been a series of Committee initiatives concerning a number of the named States.

NGOs have not as yet played a large part in the development of the procedure. However, they have a potentially important role in bringing actual or potentially egregious situations of racial discrimination to the attention of Committee members and suggesting that the States concerned be considered under the procedure. NGOs can also play a useful role in providing information concerning States already under consideration and in suggesting the appropriate form of action or decision for the Committee to take. Finally, NGOs can draw public attention to whatever actions have been taken by the Committee and use this information in their own activities.

---

26 Such decisions have been adopted in almost all cases so far considered.
27 In 1995 this action was taken with regard to situations in the Russian Federation, Rwanda, Bosnia and Herzegovina, and Papua New Guinea.
28 Burundi and Bosnia and Herzegovina (1995).
29 Missions have taken place to Croatia and the Federal Republic of Yugoslavia (Serbia and Montenegro).

Part V

Indigenous peoples and some relevant human rights standards

13

Substantive provisions of the International Convention on the Elimination of All Forms of Racial Discrimination

Michael O'Flaherty

Introduction

The International Convention on the Elimination of All Forms of Racial Discrimination is one of the key instruments of the international community in the legal protection and promotion of human rights. With regard to its precise purpose, the combating of racial and related discrimination, it has been described as:

> the international community's only tool . . . which is at one and the same time universal in reach, comprehensive in scope, legally binding in character, and equipped with built-in measures of implementation.[1]

The Convention was drafted over a remarkably short period of time[2] and adopted in 1965, and it entered into force on 4 January 1969. By June

---

* The author does not purport to represent the views of the Committee on the Elimination of Racial Discrimination, its members or the UN Secretariat.

1 Committee on the Elimination of Racial Discrimination, *Report of the Committee on the Elimination of Racial Discrimination*, UN Doc A/33/18 (1978).

2 See E Schwelb, "The International Convention on the Elimination of All Forms of Racial Discrimination" (1966) 15 *ICLQ* 996; N Lerner, "Curbing Racial Discrimination – Fifteen Years CERD" (1983) 13 *Israel Yearbook on Human Rights* 170; N Lerner, *The UN Convention on the Elimination of All Forms of Racial Discrimination*, Sijthoff and Noordhoff, Alphen aan den Rijn, 1980.

1996, it had been ratified or acceded to by 150 States, making it, next to the International Convention on the Rights of the Child, the most widely ratified of the principal human rights international instruments.

The Convention comprises seven substantive articles and a further 18 addressing matters such as international supervision and dispute settlement. At the heart of the supervision system is the Committee on the Elimination of Racial Discrimination (CERD) which, pursuant to the provisions of Article 8, was established in 1970. This body has three principal functions:

- examination of periodic reports submitted by States parties describing implementation of the Convention in the respective countries,[3]

- consideration of communications from individuals or groups alleging violation of their Convention-protected rights in States which have accepted the right for such people to petition CERD,[4] and

- examination of inter-State complaints.

An understanding of the work of CERD is essential if one is to have a full grasp of the contents of the various substantive provisions of the Convention. Over the past 25 years, but particularly since 1992, in the course of report examination and in the very small number of individual cases dealt with, CERD has elaborated a form of jurisprudence which serves to clarify the content of the rights protected.[5] This jurisprudence of CERD is to be found in the records of its consideration of reports and communications and also in the series of decisions and General Recommendations which it continues to issue.

The present chapter examines all seven of the substantive articles: Article 1 which defines "racial discrimination", Article 2 which states the obligations on States parties to combat racial discrimination, Article 3

---

3   See chapter 12 by M O'Flaherty, "The Committee on the Elimination of Racial Discrimination: non-governmental input and the early warning and urgent procedure" in the present volume.

4   See chapter 9 by M O'Flaherty, "Individual communications: the Convention against Torture and the Convention on the Elimination of All Forms of Racial Discrimination" in the present volume.

5   This chapter does not address the question of the precise legal status of the "jurisprudence" of treaty bodies such as CERD but presumes that, given the absence of other bodies actually engaged in interpreting the instruments, their analysis carries a particular weight.

referring to racial segregation and apartheid, Article 4 comprising an obligation to prohibit by criminal law racist groups and acts of "hate speech", Article 5 which seeks to ensure non-discriminatory enjoyment of a range of human rights, Article 6 which concerns the right of redress of all victims of acts of racial discrimination, and Article 7 containing an obligation to promote respect for human rights through education and cultural activities.

A State party is bound by all of these provisions of the Convention unless, at the time it becomes a party, it enters a reservation excluding itself from certain of the obligations. A State is free to enter whatever reservations it wishes, subject to Article 20 which reflects a principle of international law that a reservation is illicit if it subverts the meaning and purpose of the instrument being ratified,[6] by stating that, "a reservation incompatible with the object and purpose of [the] Convention shall not be permitted". The article further states that it is impermissible to make a reservation which would, "inhibit the operation of any of the bodies established by [the] Convention" and "[a] reservation shall be considered incompatible or inhibitive if at least two-thirds of the States Parties . . . object to it". With regard to human rights instruments in general the issue of which reservations might be illicit remains unclear[7] and, in the context of the Convention, the issue is complicated by the provisions of Article 20. No less uncertain is the appropriate role of supervisory committees in addressing the issue of reservations.[8] In this regard the position of CERD remains to be clarified. However it may be noted that CERD is willing to question States parties as to whether they might consider withdrawing specific reservations.[9]

Another way for States to evade responsibility under certain human rights instruments, that of derogation from certain provisions in times of emergency, is not provided for in the Convention.

---

6   Article 19(3) of the Vienna Convention on the Law of Treaties, which is considered to be a statement of the position in international customary law.

7   See the very important General Comment 24(52) of the Human Rights Committee issued on 11 November 1994: UN Doc CCPR/C/21/Rev 1/Add 6.

8   Note 7 above, and see Comments of the Human Rights Committee concerning the initial report of the United States of America, UN Doc CCPR/C/79/Add 50.

9   See for instance consideration of a report of Australia by CERD in Committee on the Elimination of Racial Discrimination, *Report of the Committee on the Elimination of Racial Discrimination*, UN Doc A/49/18 (1994), para 549.

Article 1

The definition of racial discrimination in Article 1 has a very wide scope encompassing, as it does, issues of race, colour, descent, and national or ethnic origin.[10] This breadth is such that the Convention is actually restrictively and misleadingly named. An unfortunate consequence is that various individuals and groups remain unaware that the Convention may be relevant to their concerns even though these do not have a racial dimension in the commonly understood sense of the term. CERD has not been afraid to take full advantage of the wide definition contained in Article 1. Illustrative of its practice is the range of discrimination categories which it addressed at its forty-sixth session: distinctions based on colour, against Roma Gypsies, Indigenous peoples, linguistic and national minorities, religious groups which are culturally distinct, immigrants, and so on.[11] From time to time however, CERD is unsure as to whether discriminatory practices fall within its competence and has postponed action pending the receipt of further information.[12]

The wording of Article 1(1) seems to leave open the possibility that certain forms of discrimination are acceptable if they do not have an invidious purpose. This possible interpretation has engaged the attention of a number of commentators.[13] They have asked, first, whether there can be acceptable policies of racial discrimination, and secondly, whether unintentional discrimination falls within the purview of the definition in Article 1(1). Uncertainty in these regards is compounded by other provisions of the Convention, such as the forcefully worded anti-

---

10 See generally N Lerner, *The UN Convention on the Elimination of All Forms of Racial Discrimination*, note 2 above, pp 25-33.

11 Committee on the Elimination of Racial Discrimination, *Report of the Committee on the Elimination of Racial Discrimination*, UN Doc A/46/18 (1995).

12 See for instance CERD Decision 1(46) *Report Requested Urgently from the Russian Federation*, adopted on 14 March 1995, and the related debate in which it was acknowledged that no action could be taken concerning the Chechnya situation until CERD had a better grasp of the facts, including the extent to which the matter fell within the terms of Article 1. See UN Doc CERD/C/SR 1086 (1995).

13 For a review of the literature and analysis of the issues see T Meron, "The Meaning and Reach of the International Convention on the Elimination of All Forms of Racial Discrimination" (1985) 79 *American Journal of International Law* 283.

discrimination provisions in Articles 2 and 5 (and the declarations of intent contained in the preamble). CERD in its General Recommendation XIV[14] has provided some guidance and indicated that not all forms of discrimination are automatically invidious and that the measure of acceptability is their actual effect (or, in the words of CERD, "discrimination" is always invidious, but "differentiation" may be acceptable). Furthermore, instances of non-intentional discrimination do fall within the purview of Article 1(1). In practice CERD has carried this understanding a long way and will critique State practices, however socially significant and well intended, which unintentionally discriminate within the terms of Article 1(1).

It is not always apparent that a person or group of persons belong to a distinct ethnic or racial group. Indeed, given the sociopolitical significance of the acknowledgment of such groups it may not even be agreed that they themselves exist. To address the first of these problems CERD has, in General Recommendation VIII,[15] stated that membership of a group "shall, if no justification exists to the contrary, be based upon self-identification by the individual concerned". From the debate in CERD it is clear that the bare denial by a State that an individual is a member of a group would not constitute a "justification to the contrary".[16]

On a first reading it would seem that non-citizens are excluded from protection under the terms of Article 1 other than where they are subject to certain categories of legislation which discriminate against particular nationalities. This exclusion clause is not as wide-ranging as it at first appears in that (subject to the proviso in Article 1(3))[17] it does not extend to discriminatory practices directed against non-nationals which are based on categories other than citizenship/non-citizenship.[18] Furthermore it is

---

14 UN Doc HRI/GEN/1/Rev 2 (1996), p 95.

15 Note 14 above, p 92.

16 See UN Doc CERD/C/SR 883. For an interesting application of the "self-identification" principle see Concluding Observations adopted concerning a report of Greece, Committee on the Elimination of Racial Discrimination, *Report of the Committee on the Elimination of Racial Discrimination*, UN Doc A/47/18, p 37.

17 For a helpful analysis of the relevant *travaux preparatoire* see Schwelb, note 3 above, p 1009.

18 CERD has decided one case under Article 14 directly on this distinction between citizens and non citizens. *Diop v France*, Communication No 2/1989, Committee on the Elimination of Racial Discrimination, *Report of the Committee on the Elimination of Racial Discrimination*, UN Doc A/46/18 (1995), p 131.

not clear that the exclusion has the effect of depriving non-citizens of the benefit of Articles 5 and 6 in that these articles guarantee the relevant rights "to everyone".[19] It has however been argued that principles of treaty interpretation determine that "everyone" must be understood subject to the express provisions of Article 1.[20] Whatever the precise legal effects of the provisions, CERD has proved itself willing to inquire into the treatment of non-nationals and to criticise a wide range of discriminatory practices directed against them. Indeed in a number of instances there are references in CERD's reports suggesting that non-citizens are fully covered by Article 5. Thus, for instance, in the record of the consideration of a periodic report of Nigeria we find the following:

> [H]aving emphasised that under article 5 of the Convention the State had an obligation to guarantee the civil, political, economic, social and cultural rights of the whole population and not just of citizens, members wished to receive more detailed information on the implementation of all its provisions.[21]

In the course of consideration of a report of Luxembourg in 1994, members again seemed to assume that a wide range of Article 5 rights apply to non-nationals. The context in which the matter was addressed also raises important questions concerning the legitimacy under the Convention of various regional inter-State arrangements. The relevant portion of the record reads:

> [M]embers of the Committee observed that generally a distinction was made between nationals of States members of the European Union and those of other countries with regard to the enjoyment of the rights provided under Article 5(e)(i) of the Convention; and that such a practice was common to all States members of the European Union in view of the trend towards European

---

19 Though issues under Article 5 were also argued in the *Diop* case CERD did not address the issue of applicability of Article 5 in a situation of discrimination on the basis of citizenship/non-citizenship, and indeed seemed to assume that the provisions of Article 5 (in this case concerning the right to work and the right to family life) were applicable.

20 See Meron, note 13 above. However Schwelb, note 2 above, p 1008, notes that one of the rights listed in Article 5, "to leave any country, including ones own", must logically include the right to leave countries other than ones own, that is, in which one is a non-national.

21 Committee on the Elimination of Racial Discrimination, *Report of the Committee on the Elimination of Racial Discrimination*, UN Doc A/48/18 (1993), para 314.

integration. It was also noted other regulations existed in the State party which placed nationals of specified third party States on the same footing as European Union citizens. Members of the Committee asked for a clarification on those matters and indicated that further studies on the issue of European Union policy as to the treatment of non-nationals and on freedom of movement and its relationship to the Convention was required.[22]

The matter has also been the subject of General Recommendation XI which addresses certain of the issues.[23] Therein CERD reminds States that they are under an obligation to report fully on all legislation affecting foreigners and that nothing in the Convention may be construed as limiting those human rights obligations to non-citizens which have been undertaken pursuant to other international instruments.[24] In General Recommendation XIII[25] CERD restates the obligation in Article 5 as being to ensure rights "to everyone" and makes no reference to limits imposed by Article 1. In General Recommendation XX adopted by CERD at its forty-eighth session (March 1996) the Committee confirmed that the protection of Article 5 extends to non citizens ("all persons living in a given State") when categories of rights which could be deemed

---

22 K Partsch however states the view that, "In the light of the discussions during drafting, it seems clear that, according to Article 1(2), which has to be applied in interpreting the word 'everyone' in Article 5, the concession of privileges to the citizens of a certain foreign State on the grounds of nationality is not incompatible with the provisions of the Convention . . . If all aliens were to have been treated in the same way, which would exclude the application of the most favoured nation clause, this should have been expressly stated in the Convention in order to exclude the application of a general principle of international law." (K Partsch, "Elimination of Racial Discrimination in the Enjoyment of Civil and Political Rights" (1979) 14 *Tex Int'l LJ* 191, at 228)

23 UN Doc HRI/GEN/1/Rev 2 (1996), p 94.

24 This General Recommendation has two curious aspects. The first is that its first paragraph selectively cites Article 1.3 by omitting the phrase "concerning nationality, citizenship or naturalisation". The second is the affirmation in paragraph 3 that Article 1.2 must "not be interpreted to detract in any way from the rights and freedoms recognised and enunciated in other instruments, especially the *Universal Declaration of Human Rights*, the *International Covenant on Economic, Social and Cultural Rights* and the *International Covenant on Civil and Political Rights*". This statement seems to overlook both the different categories of instrument listed (2 legal instruments and one non-binding declaration) and the fact that the legal instruments only bind States parties to the respective instruments.

25 Note 23 above, p 95.

"universal" are at issue. The one example of such a right cited was that of the right to equal treatment before tribunals.[26]

According to Article 1, the Convention only addresses issues of racial discrimination within the domain of "public life". It is not at all clear what is the extent of "public life" and at what point matters enter into a private domain beyond the reach of the Convention. However, from a reading of a range of articles of the Convention it is clear that its concerns extend to situations where the State itself is not an actor: for example, there is an obligation on the State to intervene to prevent, punish, or redress acts of racial discrimination perpetrated by non-State actors. This extension of concern is also reflected in a number of General Recommendations of CERD and in its practice. The extent of this obligation is not clear and we must await the considered views of CERD as to obligations on the State to intrude into the affairs of those under its jurisdiction, notwithstanding rights such as those of privacy.[27]

In October 1994 the United States, in ratifying the Convention, lodged a number of reservations and declarations, including reservations concerning the public/private distinction and the related parameters for Convention-protected rights. The position of the United States has yet to be scrutinised by CERD and may yet be formally objected to by other States parties. The consideration by CERD of the first United States report will afford an opportunity to clarify uncertainties noted in this chapter.[28]

Article 2

Article 2(1)[29] contains the central obligation the Convention places on States parties to eradicate all vestiges of racial discrimination (as defined in Article 1) within their jurisdictions. The scope of the obligations imposed by Article 2(1) is such that even in the absence of subsequent articles of the Convention it would be a formidable weapon in the struggle against racial discrimination. Frequently matters addressed in

---

26 Committee on the Elimination of Racial Discrimination, *Report of the Committee on the Elimination of Racial Discrimination*, UN Doc A/51/18 (1996), p 124.

27 See Meron, note 13 above.

28 Due for submission on 19 November 1995, but as at 10 June 1996, had not been received.

29 See N Lerner, *The UN Convention on the Elimination of All Forms of Racial Discrimination*, note 2 above, pp 33-39.

Article 2(1) also arise under other articles. While the effect of such double or multiple treatment may be one of complementarity it can also give rise to problems of interpretation, some of which have been addressed already in this chapter. A general area of overlap is that between Articles 2(1) and 5. Article 5 will be analysed below. At this juncture it suffices to observe that CERD in its consideration of State reports frequently raises matters under Articles 2 and 5 taken together or in a manner in which either article might well be referred to.

The obligation in Article 2(1) and the other substantive provisions of the Convention is an immediate one[30] and no State may plead that it requires time before undertaking implementation.[31] This clear principle stated in the article and consonant with general principles of international law requires restating given the recent practice of CERD of adopting Concluding Observations at the end of its consideration of State reports in which it draws attention uncritically to "factors and difficulties which impede implementation of the Convention".[32] Comments of Committee members suggesting a certain tolerance for delays in full implementation of the Convention in newly established or otherwise disadvantaged States may also be noted.[33]

---

30 In the case of *Diop v France*, note 18 above, CERD noted that certain of the rights addressed in Article 5(e) are of a type requiring progressive implementation. This statement is probably best understood as not compromising the basic principle requiring immediate implementation of the Convention in that (a) in the particular instance of Article 5 rights (see below) CERD merely insists on non-discriminatory enjoyment of the rights rather than on their actual implementation, and (b) the fact that a right calls for progressive implementation need not preclude an obligation for immediate implementation of at least a minimum core content of that right.

31 The provision for "immediate" implementation contained in Article 2 and elsewhere, such as Article 4, might in other circumstances suggest that provisions which lacked the reference to immediate implementation called for a gradualist interpretation. For a discussion of the issue as concerning the International Covenant on Civil and Political Rights see M O'Flaherty and L Heffernan, *The International Covenant on Civil and Political Rights: International Human Rights Law in Ireland*, Brehon, Dublin, 1995, chapter 2.

32 A number of Concluding Observations adopted at the forty-sixth session (February/March 1995) include this category of comment. See for instance those concerning a report of Croatia, Committee on the Elimination of Racial Discrimination, *Report of the Committee on the Elimination of Racial Discrimination*, UN Doc A/46/18 (1995).

33 See for instance comments of a member during consideration of a report of Croatia, UN Doc CERD/C/SR 1087.

Though the obligation to implement is an immediate one, the Convention does not dictate the manner in which the State must set about implementing its obligations. Thus there is no obligation on the State to directly incorporate the Convention into its domestic law rendering it citable in national courts.[34] This has not stopped CERD members, in the context of queries about implementation of Article 2, from inquiring of States parties whether such direct incorporation might not be appropriate.

While a State's method of implementation may be discretionary it does not have freedom to limit implementation to certain layers of the country's government. Thus it is unacceptable to cite a federal structure for failure to ensure full implementation of the Convention. On a number of occasions CERD has insisted that national governments are under an obligation to overcome whatever internal problems there may be in ensuring full respect for the Convention throughout their territories and in all relevant areas of activity.[35]

While Article 1(4) allows for the continuation in a State party of certain affirmative programs for groups which have suffered from discriminatory practices, Article 2(2) actually imposes an obligation to undertake such affirmative actions. This provision is of immense importance for racial or ethnic groups and, given the extent to which it surpasses the obligations in Article 27 of the International Covenant on Civil and Political Rights in creating a regime of minority group rights, it is surprising that it has received so little attention from academics and NGOs.[36]

States must take Article 2(2) action "when the circumstances so warrant". From an analysis of the practice of CERD and the wording of the relevant section of its General Guidelines for the Preparation of State Reports[37] it would appear that the measure of necessity for the taking of affirmative action is an objective one and not dependent on the subjective view of the government.

At its forty-sixth session (March 1995), CERD gave consideration to a draft decision focusing on the nature of the right to self-determination of ethnic or religious groups or minorities. In the course of a protracted

---

34 In accordance with principles of law affecting the various human rights instruments. See O'Flaherty and Heffernan, note 31 above.

35 For an illustration see the case of Australia noted below.

36 However see Meron, note 13 above, who draws attention to the importance of the provision.

37 UN Doc CERD/C/70/Rev 3 at p 3.

debate the draft went through five revisions. A final text, General Recommendation XX, was adopted by CERD at its forty-eighth session. It provides that:

> In accordance with Article 2(2) of the [Convention] and other relevant international documents, Governments should be sensitive towards the rights of persons belonging to ethnic groups, particularly their right to lead lives of dignity, to preserve their culture, to share equitably in the fruits of national growth and to play their part in the Government of the country of which they are citizens. Also, Governments should consider, within their respective constitutional frameworks, vesting persons belonging to ethnic or linguistic groups comprised of their citizens, where appropriate, with the right to engage in activities which are particularly relevant to the preservation of the identity of such persons or groups.[38]

The General Recommendation goes on to state the opposition of CERD to the fragmentation of States and its adherence to principles of international law concerning secession.[39]

Questions remain as to the applicability of Article 2(2) in situations where the government concerned denies the very identity or existence of a particular group. In such a case General Recommendation VIII, mentioned above, may be indicative. Committee practice would also suggest that broad criteria of assessment should be applied and that the view of the government alone would not be considered as determinative. Of course the problem of elaborating objective criteria remains highly problematic and beyond the scope of this chapter. Another issue which has engaged commentators is whether a government might ever be obliged to undertake affirmative programs for a disadvantaged group which constitutes a numerical majority of its population.[40] Recent Committee practice has clearly answered this matter in the affirmative.[41]

In order for a government to carry out its obligations under Article 2 and other provisions of the Convention, it must be acutely aware of the actual situation within its own jurisdiction, including the identity,

---

38 Committee on the Elimination of Racial Discrimination, *Report of the Committee on the Elimination of Racial Discrimination*, UN Doc A/51/18 (1996), at pp 125-126.

39 The debate is recorded in UN Doc CERD/C/SR 1084, 1085 (1995).

40 See Meron, note 13 above, p 307.

41 See Concluding Observations concerning Guatemala, which focused attention on the rights of Indigenous peoples as an undifferentiated group, Committee on the Elimination of Racial Discrimination, *Report of the Committee on the Elimination of Racial Discrimination*, UN Doc A/50/18 (1995).

characteristics, circumstances and requirements of all ethnic or racial groups. While this might seem a commonplace matter it has instead been the experience of CERD that many governments have not put in place the research and analysis tools for such work. Often also States operate systems of census which fail to identify crucial characteristics of the population. The rectification of such situations would, despite the reluctance to conform of certain States, appear to be obligatory under the Conventions.[42]

In considering State reports CERD tends to inquire about a wide range of issues under the rubric of Article 2. The practice is well illustrated by its consideration of Australia's most recent report, in 1994.[43] Members asked for more information on how the concept of Aboriginal was defined with respect to land rights; on the status of the Convention in the national legal order including the Federal level; on the implementation of the *Mabo* decision and the *Native Title Act* 1993 (Cth); on the relationship between the Federal and State governments in implementing the Convention; on recognition of the right to mineral royalties; and on the functions and activities of the Council for Aboriginal Reconciliation. In their Concluding Observations CERD:

> noted with concern that, although the Commonwealth Government is responsible for ratifying international human rights instruments, the implementation of their provisions requires the active participation of states and territories which have almost exclusive jurisdiction over many of the matters covered by the Convention and cannot be compelled to change their laws.

Article 3

One of the more significant controversies surrounding the work of CERD for many years was its approach to this article, regarding racial segregation and apartheid.[44] A General Recommendation issued in 1972[45] states that it:

---

42 See the General Guidelines, note 37 above.

43 Committee on the Elimination of Racial Discrimination, *Report of the Committee on the Elimination of Racial Discrimination*, UN Doc A/49/18 (1994) paras 512-551.

44 See N Lerner, *The UN Convention on the Elimination of All Forms of Racial Discrimination*, note 2 above, pp 40-43.

45 UN Doc HRI/GEN/1/Rev 2 (1996), p 61.

welcomed the inclusion in the reports submitted . . . by any State party which chooses to do so, of information regarding the status of its diplomatic, economic and other relations with the racist regimes in southern Africa.

Though the General Assembly acknowledged the right of CERD to seek such information pursuant to Article 3,[46] a number of States either refused to comply,[47] or did so while indicating their view that they were under no legal obligation.[48] The factual situation in southern Africa giving rise to this controversy is now of course of no more than historical interest. The implications for international law are more enduring in that this is the clearest instance of a number of States parties to an instrument choosing to reject a position taken by a treaty monitoring body and thus drawing attention to the limits on the ability of such a body to definitively interpret the instrument in question.

At its forty-sixth session CERD again turned to Article 3 and continued the debate on a new General Recommendation.[49] The draft would invite States parties to control all tendencies likely to provoke racial segregation, to address all the negative consequences which arise from racial segregation, and to report fully on these matters in their periodic reports to CERD. During the short debate on the issue a number of members expressed disquiet with the draft in that they were of the view that some instances of segregation were voluntary and harmless. Examples were cited of phenomena such as the "Chinatowns" found in many big cities across the world, and the Muslim quarter in Beijing. General Recommendation XIX was adopted at the forty-seventh session in August 1995.[50]

---

46 General Assembly Res 31/81 (1976).

47 The United Kingdom, Committee on the Elimination of Racial Discrimination, *Report of the Committee on the Elimination of Racial Discrimination*, UN Doc A/38/18 (1983), para 173.

48 See with regard to Venezuela, France and the Federal Republic of Germany, Committee on the Elimination of Racial Discrimination, *Report of the Committee on the Elimination of Racial Discrimination*, UN Doc A/38/18 (1983).

49 For the draft and debate see UN Doc CERD/C/SR 1078 (February/March 1995.

50 General Recommendation XIX, in Committee on the Elimination of Racial Discrimination, *Report of the Committee on the Elimination of Racial Discrimination*, UN Doc A/50/18 (1995), annex VII.

Despite an understandable hesitancy and delay in formulating the new General Recommendation, CERD had, in its examination of reports, expressed concern regarding certain tendencies towards segregation. Thus, for instance, when scrutinising a report of France, members expressed disquiet regarding social trends towards residential and educational segregation.[51] In their 1994 examination of a report of Australia, members asked for information on segregation in housing and education which "seemed to exist in some parts of Australia, such as Toomelah and Goonawindi".[52]

Article 4

The formulation of Article 4, containing the obligation to prohibit racist groups and hate speech, is sturdy.[53] Its force is generally underpinned by both the practice of CERD and the formulation of its relevant General Recommendations. The article goes beyond Article 1 in that it addresses situations in which racial discrimination may not be incited or occur and it may thus be seen to have a wide preventative role. This aspect is also to be noted in the obligation on States parties to put in place a range of criminal legislation even if the State can argue that the problems addressed are not relevant for that country.

Application of Article 4 may require severe restraints on such human activities as expression and assembly and thus raise issues of the relationship of the obligation to the protection of the related human rights of freedom of expression and assembly. In attempting to determine the nature of this relationship, commentators have argued that the reference in Article 4(1) to "due regard to the principles embodied in the Universal Declaration of Human Rights and the rights expressly set forth in Article 5 of this Convention" should be taken to indicate that the article must be applied with due regard to Article 30 of the Universal Declaration of Human Rights whereby no person or State may, "engage in any activity or . . . perform any act aimed at the destruction of any of the rights and freedoms set forth herein", such rights to include those of freedom of

---

51 Committee on the Elimination of Racial Discrimination, *Report of the Committee on the Elimination of Racial Discrimination*, UN Doc A/49/18 (1994), para 123.

52 Note 51 above, para 522.

53 See N Lerner, *The UN Convention on the Elimination of All Forms of Racial Discrimination*, note 2 above, pp 43-55.

expression and assembly. They argue that Article 30 of the Universal Declaration would thus serve to temper an absolutist reading of the article.[54] CERD has not followed this line of reasoning. In an authoritative paper prepared by its Special Rapporteur and published under its authority, the focus of the relationship with the Universal Declaration is instead directed to Article 29, whereby rights may be limited, "for the purpose of securing due recognition and respect of the rights and freedoms of others and of meeting the just requirements of morality, public order and the general welfare in a democratic society", and "rights and freedoms may in no case be exercised contrary to the purposes and principles of the United Nations".[55]

CERD's understanding of Article 4 is forcefully stated in General Recommendation XV[56] where States are reminded both of the mandatory nature of the article and of the obligation not only to establish certain criminal laws but also to ensure that the laws are effectively enforced. The General Recommendation also explains the reasoning behind the view of CERD and reaffirms the legal analysis of its one-time Special Rapporteur while adding a reference to Article 20 of the International Covenant on Civil and Political Rights which demands prohibition by law of advocacy of national, racial or religious hatred that constitutes incitement to discrimination, hostility or violence. This latter reference may be construed as somewhat disingenuous as the reference in the Covenant is considerably narrower than that in the Convention, containing as it does the requirement that the impugned activity constitute an actual incitement to discrimination, hostility or violence.

CERD's view is also reflected in the opinion adopted in the case of *LK v The Netherlands*[57] where it was stated that the State must prosecute persons who act in a manner inconsistent with Article 4.[58]

---

54 See K Partsch, "The Racial Discrimination Committee" in P Alston (ed), *The United Nations and Human Rights*, Oxford University Press, Oxford, 1992, 359-360. There are references in the *travaux preparatoires* supporting this understanding, UN Docs A/C 3/SR 1315, 1318, 1373 (statements of United States and United Kingdom representatives).

55 UN Doc CERD/2 (1986) (prepared for the Committee by Mr Ingles).

56 UN Doc HRI/GEN/1/Rev 2 (1996), p 68.

57 Communication No 4/1991, Committee on the Elimination of Racial Discrimination, *Report of the Committee on the Elimination of Racial Discrimination*, UN Doc A/48/18 (1993).

58 But see the inconsistent decision in *Yimaz-Dogan v Netherlands*, note 72 below.

Recently the European Court of Human Rights had to reflect on the nature and effect of Article 4 in the course of a case, *Jersild v Denmark*,[59] which concerned the question whether a criminal prosecution taken in Denmark pursuant to legislation enacted to implement Article 4 might be in contravention of the terms of the freedom of expression article of the European Convention on Human Rights. Though the Court did struggle to avoid declaring that full application of both articles might cause them to conflict with each other, it reiterated that, under the European Convention, actions taken to limit or punish the exercise of speech or other forms of expression must be proportionate to the goal of protecting the rights or reputations of others. Bearing in mind CERD's own understanding of Article 4, this judgement suggests that a fact situation may possibly arise in the future where a State may have to choose between complying with the European Convention on Human Rights or the Convention on the Elimination of All Forms of Racial Discrimination. Australia has entered a reservation to Article 4 wherein it:

> declares that [it] is not at present in a position specifically to treat as offences all the matters covered by article 4(a) of the Convention. Acts of the kind there mentioned are punishable only to the extent provided by the existing criminal law dealing with such matters as the maintenance of public order, public mischief, assault, riot, criminal libel, conspiracy and attempts. It is the intention of the Australian Government, at the first suitable moment, to seek from Parliament legislation specifically implementing the terms of article 4(a).

During CERD's consideration of the 1994 Australian report,[60] the government's representative was asked to explain the reservation. In his reply he indicated that enactment of proposed national legislation on racial vilification would make it easier for Australia to withdraw the reservation, although other factors would have to be taken into account. Subsequently in its Concluding Observations on the Australian report, CERD recommended that the necessary legislation be adopted and the reservation withdrawn.

Article 5

This article[61] is a primary focus for the concern of CERD in its consideration of State reports as it actually identifies a wide range of

---

59 Case 36/1993/431/510. Judgment of 23 September 1994.

60 Note 43 above.

61 See N Lerner, *The UN Convention on the Elimination of All Forms of Racial Discrimination*, note 2 above, pp 55-60.

specific human rights and states the obligation to ensure that they are enjoyed "before the law" in a non-discriminatory manner. The article presents a range of problems of interpretation[62] some of which have been discussed above, such as the rights of non-citizens and aspects of the relationship between it and Articles 1 and 2.

A central problem regarding Article 5 is whether it obligates States parties to honour the listed rights or more modestly confines itself to stipulating that the rights, to the extent that the State recognises them, be enjoyed before the law in a non-discriminatory fashion. Committee practice would seem to follow the latter understanding[63] and this is certainly the view of one former Committee member.[64] There have however been instances where formulations by CERD suggest that it is its view that Article 5 both confers rights and imposes obligations to ensure their enjoyment before the law in a non-discriminatory fashion. In this regard see, for instance, the Concluding Observations adopted following examination of a periodic report of Austria where it is stated that, "under article 5(e)(i) of the Convention, everyone in Austria must be guaranteed the right, without distinction as to race, to equality before the law in the enjoyment of the right to work".[65]

A related problem has been that of whether the list of rights contained in the article is exhaustive or indicative. If it is merely indicative the question would then arise of how the non-enumerated rights might be identified, that is, can they include locally recognised rights not contained in international instruments? If it is the latter, is the list confined to rights in legally binding instruments or may it extend to matters covered by "soft law" such as UN declarations? The answer to the first of these uncertainties is suggested both by the open-ended language of the text of

---

62 See the extensive analysis of K Partsch in "Elimination of Racial Discrimination in the Enjoyment of Civil and Political Rights", note 22 above.

63 See *Diop v France*, note 18 above.

64 K Partsch, "The Racial Discrimination Committee", note 54 above, p 360. However the same commentator in "Elimination of Racial Discrimination in the Enjoyment of Civil and Political Rights", note 22 above, draws attention to indications in the *travaux preparatoires*, and in State practice in making reservations upon accession, to the effect that Article 5 confers substantive rights other than that of non-discriminatory equality before the law.

65 Committee on the Elimination of Racial Discrimination, *Report of the Committee on the Elimination of Racial Discrimination*, UN Doc A/47/18 (1992), p 57.

the article and the long-standing practice of CERD supporting the contention that the list is no more than indicative.[66] With regard to the second and third questions, the inclusion of rights in the Article 5 list which are not noted in the other international instruments, such as a "right to inherit", should be borne in mind. Also, the general obligations under the Convention for States to eradicate all forms of racial discrimination would suggest that Article 5, both alone and in conjunction with Article 2, addresses the enjoyment of all rights regardless of source.

At its forty-eighth session (February/March 1996) CERD adopted a General Recommendation XX on Article 5. It was obvious from the debate that members of CERD considered that Article 5 does not create rights but rather ensures their non-discriminatory enjoyment, and that the protection of the article extends to all rights recognised by the State regardless of source. Thus for instance, one member suggested that, in a State which conferred the right to kindergarten attendance, the provisions of Article 5 would come into play. Amongst other elements of the Recommendation was the clarification concerning non-citizens discussed above and the stipulation that, where a State had restricted any given rights, even if the restriction was universally applied the State would be obliged in its reports to CERD to indicate both the proportionality of the restriction to the intended goal and its conformity with Article 1(1) of the Convention.[67]

CERD considered the application of Article 5 in the case of *Narrainen v Norway*,[68] where it was alleged that the applicant's rights pursuant to Article 5 had been violated when his criminal trial was allowed to proceed despite a racist remark being directed towards him by a juror. The opinion of CERD, in which it rejected the contentions of the applicant in a rather summary and thinly argued fashion, does not add to an understanding of the article.

---

66 See K Partsch, "Elimination of Racial Discrimination in the Enjoyment of Civil and Political Rights", note 22. Amongst the un-enumerated rights cited is that of *habeas corpus*: Committee on the Elimination of Racial Discrimination, *Report of the Committee on the Elimination of Racial Discrimination*, UN Doc A/47/18, p 43 (1992).

67 For the text of the General Recommendation see Committee on the Elimination of Racial Discrimination, *Report of the Committee on the Elimination of Racial Discrimination*, UN Doc A/51/18 (1996) p 124.

68 Communication No 3/1991, Committee on the Elimination of Racial Discrimination, *Report of the Committee on the Elimination of Racial Discrimination*, UN Doc A/49/18 (1994), p 119.

In its 1994 examination of the report of Australia,[69] CERD focused a lot of attention on implementation of Article 5. The relevant paragraph of the record reads as follows:

> members asked for further information on the government policy to promote multi-culturalism launched in 1989; on measures taken to implement the recommendations of the Royal Commission into Aboriginal Deaths in Custody and the difficulties encountered in that regard at state or territory level; on the participation of Aboriginals in the electoral process and, in general, in the conduct of public affairs; on measures taken with regard to such phenomena as infant mortality, disease, street violence, poverty and unemployment, to which Aboriginal were particularly exposed, especially those living in urban areas; on the number of Aboriginals in the criminal justice services, on prison staff, and in the police forces and social services; and on the recognition of Aboriginal customary law by the Australian courts. Additionally, clarification was requested of the treatment of refugees or asylum seekers, particularly "boat people", who were detained for long periods of time in unsatisfactory conditions in camps while their applications were being processed.[70]

A number of these concerns were also reflected in the Concluding Observations adopted by CERD.

Article 6

The wording of this article indicates a certain overlap with other provisions such as Articles 2, 4 and 5 of the Convention concerning the rights to "effective protection". What sets Article 6 apart however is the attention paid to the right to effective remedies in cases of discrimination.[71] The right is not confined to the court system but extends to all relevant redress procedures, including tribunals, labour dispute settlement procedures, the work of ombudsmen, and parliamentary inquiries.

Remedies must not only exist but be effective and so CERD has drawn attention to such matters as the accessibility of the procedures, the extent to which they are conducted in the language of claimants, the independence of judges and arbiters, and the time required to process

---

69 Note 43 above.

70 Note 43 above, para 524.

71 See N Lerner, *The UN Convention on the Elimination of All Forms of Racial Discrimination*, note 2 above, pp 60-62.

cases. On numerous occasions CERD has also emphasised that the article requires that judges, lawyers and all others involved in relevant dispute settlement procedures be aware of the provisions of the Convention.

Article 6 has received the consideration of CERD in the case of *Yimaz-Dogan v The Netherlands*,[72] where it was stated that "the terms of Article 6 do not impose upon States parties the duty to institute a mechanism of sequential remedies, up to and including the Supreme Court level, in cases of alleged racial discrimination". It is beyond the scope of the present chapter to analyse this rather timid decision. However, in the case of *LK v The Netherlands* the State was considered to have violated Article 6 by failing to prosecute racist actions which were contrary to Article 4.[73]

CERD has not as yet addressed the issue of whether Article 6 includes a right to financial assistance for indigent claimants.

Article 6 states that its provisions are for the benefit of "everyone within their (the States parties) jurisdiction". As an aid to the interpretation of this provision reference may be made to the discussion above on the relationship between Articles 1 and 5 and the possible future view of CERD as reflected in the text of the draft General Recommendation on Article 5.[74]

In its consideration of the 1994 Australian report,[75] CERD, in the Concluding Observations, stated regarding compliance with, inter alia, Article 6, that:

> legal proceedings for the recognition of native title and for responding to land claims have been protracted. The necessity for claimants to prove that they have maintained their connection with the land and that their title has not been extinguished can be an exigent condition. That persons who identify as Aboriginal but whose ancestors are predominantly non-Aboriginal may not qualify as Aboriginal with respect to land rights may become a further matter of concern.[76]

---

72 Communication No 1/1984, Committee on the Elimination of Racial Discrimination, *Report of the Committee on the Elimination of Racial Discrimination*, UN Doc A/43/18 (1988).

73 Communication No 4/1991, Committee on the Elimination of Racial Discrimination, *Report of the Committee on the Elimination of Racial Discrimination*, UN Doc A/48/18 (1993), p 130.

74 And see Schwelb, note 2 above, p 1028.

75 Note 43 above.

76 Note 43 above, para 544.

Article 7

Article 7[77] has an exceptionally wide scope obligating the States parties to take a range of actions to combat prejudice, promote understanding and friendship and propagate the purposes and principles of the UN and its human rights regime including particularly the standards of the Convention. As an explicit and binding international commitment the article is without parallel and its implementation calls for the development in each State party of a culture of human rights protection and promotion which would pervade all aspects of government and society. Remarkably the obligation also extends to the foreign policy of the States parties with the stipulation that they must each promote "understanding, tolerance and friendship among nations".

CERD has considered Article 7 in two General Recommendations, a decision and its General Guidelines.[78] General Recommendation V[79] reminds States of the mandatory nature of the article even in States which hold that they experience no problems of racial discrimination. In General Recommendation XIII,[80] States parties were called upon to "review and improve the training of law enforcement officials so that the standards of the Convention as well as the Code of Conduct for Law Enforcement Officials (1979) are fully implemented". The General Guidelines[81] draw attention to the crucial role played by the media in achieving the objectives of the article.

In its consideration of State reports the focus of CERD's attention has tended to be on the aspect of the article addressing issues of racial discrimination. It has for instance inquired about school curricula, the policy of the mass media, and the dissemination of the Convention, especially amongst "at risk" groups, and its translation into minority languages.[82] CERD has also asked whether its own work was given

---

77 See N Lerner, *The UN Convention on the Elimination of All Forms of Racial Discrimination*, note 2 above, pp 63-64.

78 Article 7 has also been the subject of a study prepared by its then Special Rapporteur, Mr Tenekides: *Teaching, Education, Culture and Information as a means of Eliminating Racial Discrimination*, UN Doc CERD/3 (1985).

79 UN Doc HRI/GEN/1/Rev 2 (1996), page 62.

80 Note 25 above.

81 Note 37 above, pp 6-7.

82 There are occasional instances of a broader approach: *Report of the Committee on the Elimination of Racial Discrimination*, UN Doc A/47/18 (1992), p 53 (consideration of a report of Yemen).

adequate public attention through, for instance, the publication by respective governments of Concluding Observations. Accordingly, following its consideration of Australia's report,[83] it:

> recommend[ed] that the report submitted by the State party to the Committee and the concluding comments of the Committee be disseminated as widely as possible in Australia in order to encourage the involvement of all sectors concerned in the elimination of all forms of racial discrimination.

---

83 Committee on the Elimination of Racial Discrimination, *Report of the Committee on the Elimination of Racial Discrimination*, UN Doc A/49/18 (1994), para 550.

14

The International Covenant on Civil and Political Rights and Indigenous peoples

Sarah Pritchard

Introduction

The International Covenant on Civil and Political Rights was adopted by the UN General Assembly on 16 December 1966 and entered into force on 23 March 1976. As at 30 June 1996, there were 132 States parties to the Covenant.[1] In the following remarks it is proposed to consider some of the provisions of the Covenant which may be particularly relevant to the needs and aspirations of Aboriginal and Torres Strait Islander peoples in Australia.

The Covenant is drafted in fairly general, open-ended language. Where can we seek guidance in interpreting the provisions of the Covenant? In domestic legal systems, we refer to the decisions of courts and tribunals. In the case of human rights treaties, we refer to the work of the human rights treaty bodies. These are the bodies established to supervise implementation of human rights instruments. In the case of the Covenant, this is the Human Rights Committee. In accordance with Article 28, a Human Rights Committee was established to supervise implementation of the International Covenant on Civil and Political Rights. The Committee consists of 18 members of high moral character and recognised competence in the field of human rights. In its supervision

---

1 United Nations, *Human Rights International Instruments: Chart of Ratifications as at 30 June 1996*, UN Doc ST/HR/4/Rev 14.

of the implementation of the rights recognised in the Covenant, the Committee follows a number of procedures. In order to make some observations upon the obligations of States under the Covenant, it is necessary to review briefly the procedures of the Human Rights Committee.

Supervisory procedures

The Human Rights Committee supervises implementation of the Covenant pursuant to three main procedures:

1. **Reporting Procedure**. Pursuant to Article 40, States parties are required to submit periodic reports to the Human Rights Committee on measures they have adopted to give effect to the rights recognised in the Covenant and on progress made in the enjoyment of those rights. The periodicity for submission of reports, other than initial reports, is five years.[2]

2. **Inter-State Communications Procedure**. Pursuant to Articles 41 and 42, States parties can recognise the competence of the Human Rights Committee to receive communications from States parties claiming that other States parties are not fulfilling their obligations under the Covenant (Articles 41 and 42). Unlike the equivalent procedure under the International Convention on the Elimination of All Forms of Racial Discrimination, the competence of the Human Rights Committee to receive inter-State complaints does not result automatically upon ratification or accession. A State party must declare that it recognises the competence of the Committee to receive such communications. To date, no State party has submitted an inter-State complaint to the Human Rights Committee.

3. **Individual Communications Procedure**. By becoming a party to the First Optional Protocol to the Covenant, a State can recognise the competence of the Human Rights Committee to receive individual communications. The Protocol was adopted by the General Assembly on 16 December 1966. It entered into force on 23 March 1976. As at 30 June 1996, there were 89 States parties to the Protocol. By becoming a party to the Protocol, a State party to the Covenant recognises the competence of the Committee to receive and consider communications from individuals claiming to be victims of violations of any of the rights

---

2   UN Doc CCCPR/C/19/Rev 1.

contained in the Covenant. The Committee cannot receive communications concerning States parties to the Covenant not parties to the Protocol (Article 1(2)). Individuals claiming that their rights in the Covenant have been violated may submit a written communication to the Committee once "all available domestic remedies" have been exhausted (Article 2). Communications which are anonymous, an abuse of the right of submission or incompatible with the provisions of the Covenant are inadmissible (Article 3).[3]

Accession by Australia to the Optional Protocol took place with the deposit of an instrument of accession with the Secretary-General of the UN on 25 September 1991. The Protocol entered into force for Australia on 25 December 1991, in accordance with Article 9(2).

In addition to these procedures, the Committee has developed a practice of adopting "General Comments". These address specific articles of the Covenant or issues concerning the implementation of the Covenant generally. They reflect the experience gained by the Committee in considering a large number of States reports, representative of diverse geographical regions, religious and cultural traditions, and political, legal and economic systems. The Human Rights Committee's General Comments provide a valuable body of material relevant to the interpretation of the Covenant.[4]

Some substantive provisions

Article 1: The right of self-determination

Article 1(1) of the Covenant provides:

> All peoples have the right of self-determination. By virtue of that right they freely determine their political status and freely pursue their economic, social and cultural development.

---

3   See generally S Pritchard and N Sharp, *Communicating with the Human Rights Committee: A Guide to the Optional Protocol to the International Covenant on Civil and Political Rights* Australian Human Rights Information Centre, University of New South Wales, Human Rights Booklet No 1, July 1996.

4   These are reproduced in *Compilation of General Comments and General Recommendations adopted by the Human Rights Treaty Bodies*, UN Doc HRI/GEN/1/Rev 2 (1996).

The Human Rights Committee has consistently reaffirmed self-determination as a right of all peoples. In a General Comment on Article 1(1), the Committee asks States parties to describe the constitutional and political processes which in practice allow the exercise of this right.[5] Pursuant to the State-reporting procedure under Article 40, the Committee has adopted a robust view of the applicability of self-determination to post-colonial situations. In this practice, it has made clear that the right of self-determination has significance for the internal constitutional and political order of States. A former member of the Committee, Roslyn Higgins, has summarised this practice:

> What then is this right of self-determination that the peoples of an independent country are entitled to? It is the right to determine their own political and economic and social destiny. . . . [T]he idea of self-determination as the right to determine one's own destiny, and not to have it imposed from above, goes right back to the beginning of the Committee's work.[6]

Higgins has noted that this view finds widespread acceptance amongst the States parties appearing before the Committee. She cites the third

---

5   General Comment No 12 (21) (Art 1), para 4. The Committee's General Comment on Article 1 also refers to "other international instruments concerning the right of all peoples to self-determination, in particular the *Declaration on Principles of International Law Concerning Friendly Relations and Co-operation Among States in Accordance with the Charter of the United Nations*, adopted by the General Assembly on 24 October 1970 (General Assembly Resolution 2625 (XXV)", General Comment No 12 (21) (Art 1), para 7. The Friendly Relations Declaration provides that, inter alia, free association with an existing State or "any other political status freely determined by a people constitute modes of implementing the right of self-determination of that people". The Friendly Relations Declaration also seeks to clarify the relationship between the principle of self-determination and those of territorial integrity and national unity. It provides that inviolability of territorial integrity will be enjoyed by those States "conducting themselves in accordance with the principles of equal rights and self-determination of peoples . . . and thus possessed of a government representing the whole people belonging to the territory without distinction as to race, creed or colour". See also *Vienna Declaration and Programme of Action*, adopted by the World Conference on Human Rights, Vienna, 25 June 1993, para 3; also Michael O'Flaherty's discussion of the Committee on the Elimination of Racial Discrimination's approach to self-determination in chapter 13, above.

6   R Higgins, "Postmodern Tribalism and the Right to Secession" in C Brolmann, R Lefeber, M Zieck, *Peoples and Minorities in International Law* Martinus Nijhoff, Dordrecht, 1993, pp 29-35 at p 32.

periodic report of Colombia as "a graphic example", reporting on how all the peoples of its country had the opportunity to participate in the political and social structures, to change the government through elections, to contribute to the formulation of policy, and to determine events.[7] In its comments on the report, the Human Rights Committee expressed satisfaction that the approach of the State party to the right of peoples to self-determination "has been in line with the development of participatory democracy and that Colombia is making real efforts to achieve full equality for minority groups".[8]

The Committee's summary records in relation to Article 1 frequently refer to representative forms of government, with possibilities for participation and representation, and more exceptionally to self-government and autonomy for groups within States. Under the heading "Self-determination (article 1)", in the list of issues prepared by the Committee for consideration in connection with the third periodic report of Iraq,[9] the State party was asked to clarify "proposals aimed at enhancing the autonomy of Iraqi Kurdistan", as well as "the actual state of the relationship between the Government of Iraq and the Kurds". Noting that the right of self-determination applied not only to colonial situations but to other situations as well and that the people of a given territory should be allowed to determine their economic and political destiny, members also requested clarification of the position of the authorities concerning the autonomy of Iraqi Kurdistan.[10]

During the Committee's consideration of the report, Committee member Higgins commented that in the opinion of the Committee, self-determination is applicable not only to colonial situations. According to Higgins, a problem in relation to self-determination is often discernible in States in which the Constitution accords a particular party a privileged position. In her view, recognition of a right to autonomy can offer a solution to such problems. Although, in her opinion, the right of self-

---

7   UN Doc CCPR/C/64/Add 3.

8   See Human Rights Committee, *Report of the Human Rights Committee*, UN Doc A/47/40 (1992), para 391. See also summary record of Human Rights Committee's examination of the report at its 1136th-1139th meetings: UN Doc CCPR/C/SR 1136-1139 (1992).

9   UN Doc CCPR/C/64/Add 6.

10 See Human Rights Committee, *Report of the Human Rights Committee*, UN Doc A/47/40 (1992), para 195. See also summary records of 1106th-1108th meetings, held 30-31 October 1991.

determination is not a right of all minorities, "all peoples, including minorities, had the right to take part in the political system and social destiny; if that was not the case they did not enjoy the right to self-determination".[11]

In its concluding comments on the initial report of Azerbaijan, the Human Rights Committee regretted the position adopted in the report regarding the principle of self-determination. In that connection, it recalled that: "under article 1 of the Covenant, that principle applies to all people and not merely to colonized peoples".[12]

For procedural reasons, the Human Rights Committee has declined to entertain complaints of violations of Article 1 pursuant to the individual communications procedure of the Optional Protocol to the Covenant. In the 1990 case of *Chief Ominayak v Canada*, the Committee expressed the view that the Optional Protocol provides a procedure pursuant to which individuals or groups of individuals similarly affected can complain that their individual rights under Part III, Articles 6-27 of the Covenant have been violated. The question whether the Lubicon Lake Band constituted a "people" was not an issue for the Committee to address under the Optional Protocol.[13]

Article 2: Measures to give effect to the Covenant

Part II contains a number of general provisions relevant to all the rights in the Covenant. Pursuant to Article 2, States parties undertake to adopt legislative and other measures to give effect to the rights recognised in the Covenant and to ensure effective remedies for persons whose rights have been violated. In its General Comment on Article 2, the Human Rights Committee states that the obligation contained in Article 2 is of both a negative and a positive nature:

---

11 See Higgins, note 6 above.

12 See Human Rights Committee, *Report of the Human Rights Committee*, UN Doc A/47/40 (1992), para 296. See also summary records of 1332nd and 1336th meetings, held 12 and 14 July 1994.

13 Communication No 167/1984, Human Rights Committee, *Report of the Human Rights Committee*, UN Doc A/45/40, vol 2, para 32.1 (1990). See also the 1990 decision in *AB v Italy* in which the Committee declined to consider whether the ethno-German population of Italian South Tirol constitutes a "people" within the terms of Article 1: Communication No 413/1990, Human Rights Committee, *Report of the Human Rights Committee*, UN Doc A/46/40, para 3.2 (1991). See also *EP v Colombia*, Communication No 318/1988, Human Rights Committee, *Report of the Human Rights Committee*, UN Doc A/45/40, vol 2, para 8.2 (1990).

The Committee considers it necessary to draw to the attention of States parties the fact that the obligation under the Covenant is not confined to the respect of human rights, but that States parties have also undertaken to ensure the enjoyment of these rights to all individuals under their jurisdiction. This aspect calls for specific activities by the States parties to enable individuals to enjoy their rights.[14]

Article 3: Equal rights of men and women

In Article 3 States parties undertake to ensure the equal right of men and women to the enjoyment of the civil and political rights enumerated in the Covenant. In a General Comment, the Human Rights Committee indicates that implementation of this article:

> requires not only measures of protection, but also affirmative action designed to ensure the positive enjoyment of rights. This can not be done simply by enacting laws.[15]

Article 6: The inherent right to life

Article 6 proclaims the "inherent right" of every human being to life: "This right shall be protected by law. No-one shall be arbitrarily deprived of his life." In a General Comment on Article 6, adopted on 27 July 1992, the Human Rights Committee notes:

> that the right to life has been too often narrowly interpreted. The expression "inherent right to life" cannot properly be understood in a restrictive manner, and the protection of this right requires that States adopt positive measures. In this connection, the Committee considers that it would be desirable for States parties to take all possible measures to reduce infant mortality and to increase life expectancy, especially in adopting measures to eliminate malnutrition and epidemics.[16]

---

14 General Comment No 3 (13) (Art 2), para 1.

15 General Comment No 4 (3) (Art 3), para 2.

16 General Comment No 6 (16) (Art 6), para 5. In 1989 a Second Optional Protocol to the ICCPR was adopted with the objective of eliminating the death penalty. Article 1 of the Protocol requires States parties to ensure that no capital punishment is ever imposed on anyone anywhere in their territory. Australia is one of 30 States parties to the Second Optional Protocol.

Articles 7-10, 14

Numerous provisions of the Covenant provide scope for examination of the impact of the Australian criminal justice system on Aboriginal and Torres Strait Islander peoples. Article 7 contains a prohibition of torture and cruel, inhuman or degrading treatment or punishment; Article 8 a prohibition of slavery, servitude and forced or compulsory labour. Article 9 proclaims the right to liberty and security of the person and freedom from arbitrary arrest or detention. In a General Comment on Article 9, the Human Rights Committee points out that the prohibition of arbitrary arrest and detention applies to all deprivation of liberty, whether in criminal cases or other cases, such as mental illness, vagrancy, drug addiction, educational purposes, immigration control, and so on.[17] In relation to Articles 7, 8 and 9, it might be appropriate to raise, amongst others, issues of police violence, juvenile justice, diversion from police custody, over-representation in custody and implementation of the recommendations of the Royal Commission into Aboriginal Deaths in Custody.

Article 10 recognises the right of all persons deprived of their liberty to be treated with humanity and with respect for the inherent dignity of the human person. This provision is relevant to conditions and standards of care and treatment in police lockups and custodial facilities. Article 14 contains a guarantee of a fair trial, under which some Indigenous advocates might wish to raise questions relating to the differential employment of sentencing and other options, and the availability of interpreters and appropriate legal services.

Other provisions of the Covenant

Other provisions of the Covenant include:
- freedom of movement and choice of residence (Article 12);
- prohibition of the retroactive application of criminal law (Article 15);
- right to recognition as a person before the law (Article 16);
- prohibition of interference with privacy, family and home (Article 17);
- freedom of opinion and expression (Article 19);
- prohibition of propaganda for war and advocacy of national, racial or religious hatred (Article 20);
- right of peaceful assembly (Article 21); and
- freedom of association, including the right to form and join trade unions (Article 22).

---

17 General Comment No 8 (16) (art 9), para 1.

Article 18 contains a guarantee of freedom of thought, conscience and religion. This might well assist in securing access to and control of sacred sites, skeletal remains, burial artefacts and other items of religious or cultural significance to Indigenous Australians.[18] In UN practice, the concept of religion has been interpreted extensively. The 1967 draft UN Convention on the Elimination of All Forms of Religious Intolerance defined "religion or belief" to include "theistic, non-theistic and atheistic beliefs". A Special Rapporteur on Religious Intolerance has described religion as "an explanation of the meaning of life and how to live accordingly": "Every religion has at least a creed, a code of action and a cult."[19] Pursuant to procedures for examining State reports, both the Committee on the Elimination of Racial Discrimination and the Human Rights Committee seek information concerning the protection of the religions of indigenous peoples.[20]

Articles 23 and 24 contain rights relating to the family, marriage and children. Article 24 recognises the right of every child to such measures of protection as required by the child's status as a minor. In a General Comment on this provision, the Human Rights Committee notes that the measures to be adopted:

> although intended primarily to ensure that children fully enjoy the other rights enunciated in the Covenant, may also be economic, social and cultural. For example, every possible economic and social measure should be taken to reduce infant mortality and to eradicate malnutrition among children and to prevent them from being subjected to acts of violence and cruel and inhuman treatment or from being exploited by means of forced labour or prostitution, or by their use in the illicit trafficking of narcotic drugs, or by any other means.[21]

Together with the prohibition on racial discrimination in Articles 2(1) and 26, Articles 23 and 24 might be interpreted to require recognition of

---

18 In a section dealing with freedom of religion, Australia's second periodic report to the Human Rights Committee refers to measures to protect Aboriginal sacred sites: Human Rights Committee, *Consideration of Reports Submitted by States Parties Under Article 40 of the Covenant, Second Periodic Reports of States Parties Due in 1986: Australia*, UN Doc CCPR/C/42/Add 2, (1987) para 459.

19 United Nations, *Elimination of All Forms of Intolerance and of Discrimination Based on Grounds of Religion or Belief* (*Odio Benito Report*), New York, 1989, para 19.

20 *Odio Benito Report*, p 68 f.

21 General Comment No 17 (35) (Art 24).

Aboriginal law in relation to marriage, kinship[22] and the care of children, as well as family arrangements and kinship obligations in social security and family services.

Article 25: Participatory rights

Article 25 recognises the right of the citizen to take part in the conduct of public affairs, to vote and be elected, and to have access to public service. If a substantive understanding of Article 25 were adopted, the enjoyment of participatory rights might require appropriate institutional arrangements to ensure effective participation by Aboriginal and Torres Strait Islander communities in Australian public life.[23] The Human Rights Committee, however, appears to have endorsed a formal, rather than substantive approach to the issue of participatory rights. In *Mikmaq Tribal Society v Canada* the Committee found that the failure of Canada to invite representatives of the Mikmaq Tribal Society to constitutional conferences on Aboriginal matters did not violate the right in Article 25 to participate in public affairs. In the view of the Committee, participation and representation at these conferences had not been subjected to unreasonable restrictions.[24]

Article 26: Equality before the Law

Article 26 contains a guarantee of the equality of all persons before the law and of the equal protection of the law. In its General Comment on this provision, the Human Rights Committee notes that: "the application

---

22 Human Rights Committee, *Report of the Human Rights Committee*, UN Doc A/43/40 (1988), para 418.

23 S Pritchard, "Aborigines: International Law", *Laws of Australia*, Law Book Co, Sydney, 1993, Subtitle 1.7, para 25. In relation to Article 25, Australia's second periodic report to the Human Rights Committee refers to incorporated community-based Aboriginal organisations, national Aboriginal organisations which act as a medium for policy consultation for governments and Aboriginal Land Councils: Human Rights Committee, *Consideration of Reports Submitted by States Parties Under Article 40 of the Covenant, Second Periodic Reports of States Parties Due in 1986: Australia*, UN Doc CCPR/C/42/Add 2 (1987), para 629.

24 Communication No 205/1986, UN Doc CCPR/C/43/D/205/1986 (1991).

of the principle of non-discrimination contained in Article 26 is not limited to those rights provided for in the Covenant":

> [T]he Committee believes that the term "discrimination" as used in the Covenant should be understood to imply any distinction, exclusion, restriction or preference which is based on any ground, . . . and which has the purpose or effect of nullifying or impairing the enjoyment or exercise by all persons, on an equal footing, of all rights and freedoms.

The Committee also pointed out that the principle of equality sometimes requires States parties "to take affirmative action in order to diminish or eliminate conditions which cause or help to perpetuate discrimination prohibited by the Covenant":

> For example, in a State where the general conditions of a certain part of the population prevent or impair their enjoyment of human rights, the State should take specific action to correct those conditions. Such action may involve granting for a time to a part of the population concerned certain preferential treatment in specific matters as compared with the rest of the population. However, as long as such action is needed to correct discrimination in fact, it is a case of legitimate differentiation under the Covenant.[25]

It is clear that the principle of non-discrimination in Article 26 prohibits governmental and corporate actions which have a disproportionate impact on the enjoyment of the rights of Aborigines and Torres Strait Islanders. In particular, it is now established in Australian law that the prohibition of discrimination limits the effect of legislative or executive power to extinguish native title or otherwise interfere with the property rights of Indigenous Australians.[26] In its consideration of the initial report submitted by the United States under Article 40, the Committee recommended that the United States take steps "to ensure that previously recognised Native American rights not be extinguished."[27] It might also be argued that Article 26 places an obligation on governments to remove barriers to access and equity in government services and to take measures to eliminate inadequate provision to Aboriginal and Torres Strait Islander communities of essential services, such as housing, water, sanitation and electricity.

---

25 General Comment No 18 (37) (Art 26), paras 12, 10.

26 *Mabo v Queensland (No 1)* (1988) 166 CLR 186; *Western Australia v Commonwealth* (*Native Title Act* case) (1995) 183 CLR 373.

27 UN Doc CCPR/C/79/Add 50, 6 April 1995, para 37.

Article 27:   Rights of minorities

Article 27 provides that:

> Members of ethnic, religious or linguistic minorities shall not be denied the right, in community with the other members of their group, to enjoy their own culture, to profess and practise their own religion, or to use their own language.

The Human Rights Committee has rejected a minimalist interpretation of Article 27 as imposing an obligation on States parties merely to refrain from activities interfering in the enjoyment of the rights under Article 27. It has emphasised the obligation of States to take positive measures to ensure the survival and development of the cultures, languages and religions of the minorities concerned. In a General Comment on Article 27 adopted on 6 April 1994, the Committee stated that the article "does recognise the existence of a 'right'" and that:

> [P]ositive measures by States may . . . be necessary to protect the identity of a minority and the rights of its members. In their reports, States parties should indicate the measures they have adopted to ensure the full protection of these rights. . . . Although the rights protected under article 27 are individual rights, they depend in turn on the ability of the minority group to maintain its culture, language or religion. Accordingly, positive measures by States may also be necessary to protect the identity of the minority and the rights of its members to enjoy and develop their culture and language and to practise their religion, in community with other members of the group.[28]

The General Comment affirms the relevance of Article 27 for Indigenous peoples:

> [T]he Committee observes that culture manifests itself in many forms, including a particular way of life associated with the use of land resources, specially in the case of indigenous peoples. That right may include such traditional activities as fishing or hunting and the right to live in reserves protected by law. The enjoyment of those rights may require positive legal measures of protection and measures to ensure the effective participation of members of minority communities in decisions which affect them.[29]

In the context of the standard-setting activities of the UN Working Group on Indigenous Populations, Indigenous peoples have rejected

---

28   General Comment No 23 (50) (Art 27), para 6.2.
29   General Comment No 23 (50) (Art 27), para 7.

attempts to equate their rights with those of ethnic minorities. They have argued that the status of ethnic minorities in integrated national settings is incompatible with their right of self-determination. The distinction has been accepted in the practice of the UN, which has established separate procedures to elaborate standards on minority and on Indigenous rights, and separate working groups to review developments relating to minority and Indigenous groups. At the same time, however, there is growing consensus that these are neither coextensive nor mutually exclusive categories. The jurisprudence of the Human Rights Committee suggests that Article 27 can be of assistance in compelling States parties to recognise and secure the special relationship of Indigenous peoples with their land, and to recognise the cultural importance and protect the enjoyment of Indigenous economic activities.

A series of "views" pursuant to the Optional Protocol has demonstrated how Article 27 might be invoked by Indigenous peoples to secure a measure of autonomy in their traditional territories. In these decisions, the Human Rights Committee has confirmed the legitimacy of systems of special rights to ensure the cultural survival of Indigenous collectivities.[30] In light of the Committee's reluctance to receive complaints of violations of the right to self-determination (Article 1), the value of these decisions should not be underestimated.

In *Lovelace v Canada*,[31] Sandra Lovelace, a Maliseet Indian, complained that Canadian legislation, under which she lost her Indian status and right to residence on the reserve on which she had been raised upon her marriage to a non-Indian, violated Article 27. The Committee observed:

> Persons who are born and brought up on a reserve, who have kept ties with their community and wish to maintain these ties must normally be considered belonging to a minority within the meaning of the Covenant.

The Committee noted that not every interference could be regarded as a denial of rights in Article 27. However, it did not seem that to deny Lovelace the right to reside on the reserve was "reasonable, or necessary to preserve the identity of the tribe." The Committee found that there had

---

30 See D Sanders, "Collective Rights" (1991) 13 *Human Rights Quarterly* 368 at 379-80.

31 Communication No 24/1977, *Selected Decisions of the Human Rights Committee under the Optional Protocol*, UN Doc CCPR/C/OP/1 (1988), pp 86-90.

been an interference with Lovelace's "right of access to her native culture and language in community with other members of her group".

In *Kitok v Sweden*, Ivan Kitok, a Saami, challenged Swedish legislation which sought to secure the existence of reindeer husbandry by restricting reindeer breeding to members of Saami communities. By pursuing other employment, Kitok had lost his breeding rights. The Saami community could have restored these rights but declined to do so. In *Kitok's* case, the Human Rights Committee affirmed that economic activities may come within the ambit of Article 27 where they are an essential element of the culture of an ethnic community. The Human Rights Committee found reindeer husbandry to be an essential element of Saami culture. The "right to enjoy one's own culture in community" could not be determined in abstract, but had to be placed in context. The Committee was required to find a balance between the rights of Kitok, an Indigenous individual, and the rights of the Saami community to which he belonged. The Committee noted that:

> [A] restriction upon the right of an individual member of a minority must be shown to have a reasonable and objective justification and to be necessary for the continued viability and welfare of the minority as a whole.

On the facts of *Kitok's* case, restricting the number of reindeer breeders for economic and ecological reasons, and to secure the wellbeing of the Saami community, was reasonable and consistent with Article 27. Accordingly, there was no violation of Kitok's rights under that article.[32]

In *Ominayak v Canada*, Chief Ominayak complained that the expropriation of the Lubicon Lake Band's territories for the purpose of granting leases for forestry and for oil and gas exploration violated the Band's rights under the Covenant.[33] The Human Rights Committee declined to consider whether the Lubicon Lake Band constituted a people under Article 1 of the Covenant. Instead, the Committee found a violation of Article 27, recognising that:

> [T]he rights protected by article 27, include the right of persons, in community with others, to engage in economic and social activities which are part of the culture of the community to which they belong.[34]

---

32 Communication No 197/1985, UN Doc CCPR/C/33/D/197/1985 (1988), paras 9.2, 9.3, 9.8.

33 Communication No 167/1984, Human Rights Committee, *Report of the Human Rights Committee*, UN Doc A/45/40 (1990). See D McGoldrick, "Canadian Indians, Cultural Rights and the Human Rights Committee" (1991) 40 *ICLQ* 658.

34 Communication No 167/1984, Human Rights Committee, *Report of the Human Rights Committee*, UN Doc A/45/40 (1990), para 32.2.

In considering the Lubicon Lake Band's claim the Committee noted that:

> Historical inequities, to which the State party refers, and certain more recent developments threaten the way of life and culture of the Lubicon Lake Band, and constitute a violation of article 27 so long as they continue. The State party proposes to rectify the situation by a remedy that the Committee deems appropriate within the meaning of article 2 of the Covenant.

The decision in Ominayak was based upon Rule 86 of the Committee's Rules of Procedure. This allows the Committee to inform a State party as to the desirability of interim measures to avoid irreparable damage to the victim prior to forwarding its final views.

In its most recent decision concerning Article 27, *Lansmann v Finland*, the Human Rights Committee recalled that economic activities may come within the ambit of Article 27 where they are an essential element of the culture of an ethnic community. The Committee reiterated the view it had earlier expressed in *Kitok's* case that "the right to enjoy one's culture cannot be determined *in abstracto* but has to be placed in context". In *Lansmann's* case, Saami reindeer-breeders challenged the decision of the Central Forestry Board to award a contract allowing the quarrying of stone on the flank of the Etela-Riutusvaara Mountain, a sacred place of the old Saami religion. They contended that the quarrying and transport of stone would disturb their reindeer breeding activities and the complex system of reindeer fences determined by the natural environment. The Human Rights Committee rejected the submission of Finland that Article 27 only protects traditional means of livelihood of national minorities. The fact that the authors "may have adapted their methods of reindeer herding over the years and practice it with the help of modern technology" did not prevent them from invoking Article 27.[35] Moreover, Riutusvaara Mountain continued to have "a spiritual significance relevant to their culture."

On the facts of the case, however, the Committee did not consider the impact of quarrying to be so substantial that it effectively denied to the authors "their right to enjoy their cultural rights in that region". In reaching this conclusion, the Committee noted that the interests of the Herdsmen's Committee of the authors were taken into account in the proceedings leading to the delivery of the quarrying permit, that the authors had been consulted during the proceedings, and that reindeer

---

35 Communication No 511/1992, UN Doc CCPR/C/52/D/511/1992 (8 November 1994), para 9.3.

herding in the area did not appear to have been adversely affected by such quarrying as had occurred. The Committee concluded by noting that significant expansion of mining activities might constitute a violation of the authors' rights under Article 27.

Indigenous peoples have begun exploring the limits of the right of their members, "in community with the other members of their group, to enjoy their own culture". *Kitok's* case is authority for a contextual approach to the right to culture. *Ominayak's* case suggests that expropriation of Indigenous land for the granting of forestry leases and exploration licences constitutes a violation of Article 27. *Lansmann's* case supports the proposition that development which adversely affects Indigenous cultural rights — including places of spiritual significance and economic activities — will be similarly contrary to Article 27. In the *Lovelace*, *Kitok*, *Ominayak* and *Lansmann* cases, Article 27 was invoked in an essentially defensive manner, with varying degrees of success. It remains to be seen whether the positive actions required of States parties to implement their obligations under Article 27 will address the land needs of dispossessed Indigenous peoples and support Indigenous aspirations for political rights and the recognition of their law and customs.

Consideration by the Human Rights Committee of Australia's second report

The Covenant entered into force for Australia on 13 November 1980. Australia's initial report to the Committee was submitted in November 1981 and considered in October 1982. A second report[36] was submitted in February 1987 and considered by the Committee in April 1988.[37] Australia's third report was due on 12 November 1991 and has not yet been finalised. Australia's fourth report, due on 12 November 1996, is also overdue. At its fifty-first session in 1994, the Committee expressed

---

36 Human Rights Committee, *Consideration of Reports Submitted by States Parties Under Article 40 of the Covenant, Second Periodic Reports of States Parties Due in 1986: Australia*, UN Doc CCPR/C/42/Add 2 (1987).

37 Human Rights Committee, *Summary Record of the 806th Meeting*, UN Doc CCPR/C/SR 806 (1988); Human Rights Committee, *Summary Record of the 807th Meeting*, UN Doc CCPR/C/SR 807 (1988); Human Rights Committee, *Summary Record of the 808th Meeting*, UN Doc CCPR/C/SR 808 (1988); Human Rights Committee, *Summary Record of the 809th Meeting*, UN Doc CCPR/C/SR 809 (1988).

concern that despite appeals and reminders so many States parties are in default of their reporting obligations. Accordingly, it decided to mention in the core of its report to the General Assembly States parties that have more than one report overdue. In the Committee's 1994 report to the General Assembly, the following States were named as in serious default of their obligations under the Covenant: Gabon, Syrian Arab Republic, Gambia, Lebanon, Suriname, Kenya, Mali, Jamaica, Guyana, Democratic People's Republic of Korea, Equatorial Guinea, Central African Republic, Mauritius, Saint Vincent and the Grenadines, Panama and Madagascar.[38] On present indications, Australia will be similarly named in the Committee's 1997 report to the General Assembly.

In comments on Australia's second report, Committee members raised, amongst others, the following issues:

- According to one Committee member, the "disconcerting" implication of the place given to conciliation in the work of the Human Rights and Equal Opportunity Commission was "that the wealthy had legal remedies while the poor had conciliation".

- Opposition to the bill of rights proposal, it was suggested, indicated that the population was not aware of its own human rights. Serious efforts to bring the Covenant to the attention of the Australian public might result in a bill of rights being passed by the Federal Parliament. The passage of Federal legislation, for which constitutional powers did exist, might need to be considered.

- The comments of a number of members referred to the cumbersome amalgam of measures adopted in implementation of the Covenant. Concern was expressed at the failure to incorporate the Covenant into Australian law through legislation, and the inability of courts to invoke its provisions.[39]

- One Committee member sought information on whether instruction on the rights under the Covenant and other human rights instruments was provided in Aboriginal education.

---

38 Human Rights Committee, *Report of the Human Rights Committee*, UN Doc A/49/40 (1994), para 67.

39 See Human Rights Committee, *Summary Record of the 806th Meeting*, UN Doc CCPR/C/SR 806 (1988), paras 30-32, 34-35, 38-39; Human Rights Committee, *Summary Record of the 809th Meeting*, UN Doc CCPR/C/SR 809 (1988), paras 49-50, 63.

- Australia's reservation to Article 20 was considered by at least one Committee member to be completely contrary to the Covenant.[40] According to this reservation, the prohibition of propaganda for war and advocacy of national, racial or religious hatred (Article 20) is interpreted as consistent with rights of freedom of opinion, expression and assembly (Articles 19, 21, 22).[41]

- In connection with the prohibition of discrimination in Articles 2(1), 3 and 26, one Committee member referred to the *Affirmative Action (Equal Employment Opportunity for Women) Act* 1986 (Cth) and asked why it was thought appropriate to employ affirmative action measures to deal with discrimination against women and not against Aborigines.[42]

---

40 Human Rights Committee, *Summary Record of the 806th Meeting*, UN Doc CCPR/C/SR 806 (1988), para 39. See also Human Rights Committee, *Summary Record of the 809th Meeting*, UN Doc CCPR/C/SR 809 (1988), para 51.

41 According to Australia's 1994 *National Action Plan*, the government has not been in a position to remove this reservation. Legislation relating to racial vilification lapsed when the House of Representatives dissolved for the 1993 Federal elections: "The Government is currently considering submissions and responses to the draft Bill, and the most appropriate legislative response to race hatred laws for each Australian jurisdiction". *National Action Plan: Australia*, AGPS, Canberra, 1994, p 9. In 1994, a *Racial Hatred Bill* 1994 (Cth) was tabled, which proposed amendments to the *Racial Discrimination Act* 1975 (Cth) to make racial vilification unlawful, as well as amendments to the *Crimes Act* 1914 (Cth) to make racial incitement a criminal offence. During 1995, the Bill was amended in the Senate, with the criminal provisions being removed. A new part, Part IIA, was inserted into the *Racial Discrimination Act* 1975 (Cth) to enable the Human Rights and Equal Opportunity Commission to deal with complaints of offensive behaviour based on racial hatred. The Act, as amended, makes it unlawful to do any act that is reasonably likely "to offend, insult, humiliate or intimidate another person or a group of people" because of the race of that person or group. In the Senate, the Coalition and Greens voted down the proposed amendments to the *Crimes Act* 1914 (Cth) that would have created federal offences in relation to threats to cause physical harm or to destroy or damage property because of race, as well as the intentional incitement of racial hatred. The previous government issued a media release on 30 August 1995 indicating that it would accept the amendments as an interim measure, but remained committed to the introduction of further legislation to impose criminal sanctions for extreme racist behaviour.

42 Human Rights Committee, *Summary Record of the 807th Meeting*, UN Doc CCPR/C/SR 807 (1988), para 38.

- In connection with the right to life in Article 6, further information was sought on regulations relating to the use of firearms by police, infant mortality and life expectancy rates for Aborigines,[43] the results of the Royal Commission into Aboriginal Deaths in Custody,[44] and the lack of recognition of Aboriginal customary laws, in particular on the problem of double jeopardy, which is considered to contravene Article 14(7) of the Covenant.[45]

- Also in connection with the rights of liberty and security of the person in Articles 7-10, further information was sought on legislative follow-up to the Australian Law Reform Commission's report on *Recognition of Aboriginal Customary Laws.*[46]

- In relation to Article 27, Committee members sought further information on affirmative action measures in the economic and cultural spheres adopted in favour of Aborigines living both inside and outside Aboriginal communities, and on plans for establishing an elected Aboriginal Commission and for addressing the issue of land rights.[47]

---

43 Human Rights Committee, *Summary Record of the 807th Meeting*, UN Doc CCPR/C/SR 807 (1988), para 42.

44 Human Rights Committee, *Summary Record of the 807th Meeting*, UN Doc CCPR/C/SR 807 (1988), para 53. See also *Summary Record of the 809th Meeting*, UN CCPR/C/SR 809, para 57.

45 Human Rights Committee, *Summary Record of the 807th Meeting*, UN Doc CCPR/C/SR 807, paras 49, 57. See also *Summary Record of the 808th Meeting*, UN Doc CCPR/C/SR 808, paras 9, 11.

46 Human Rights Committee, *Summary Record of the 807th Meeting*, UN Doc CCPR/C/SR 807, para 61.

47 Human Rights Committee, *Summary Record of the 809th Meeting*, UN Doc CCPR/C/SR 809, para 24.

Select bibliography

The UN and human rights

Alston, P (ed), *The United Nations and Human Rights: A Critical Appraisal*, Clarendon Press, Oxford; Oxford University Press, New York, 1992

Bayefsky, A, "Making the Human Rights Treaties Work" in L Henkin and JL Hargrave (eds), *Human Rights: An Agenda for the Next Century*, Studies in Transnational Legal Policy, No 26, American Society of International Law, 1994

Centre for Human Rights, *United Nations Action in the Field of Human Rights*, United Nations, New York, 1995

Dimitrievic, V, "The Monitoring of Human Rights and the Prevention of Human Rights Violations through Reporting Procedures" in A Bloed et al (eds), *Monitoring Human Rights in Europe*, Dordrecht, Boston, 1993

Farer, T J, "The United Nations and Human Rights: More than a Whimper Less than a Roar" (1987) 9 *Human Rights Quarterly* 550

Forsythe, D, "The United Nations and Human Rights, 1945-1985" (1985) 100 *Political Science Quarterly* 249

Hannum, H (ed), *Guide to International Human Rights Practice,* 2nd edn, University of Pennsylvania Press, Philadelphia, 1992

Henkin, L and Hargrave, JL, *Human Rights: An Agenda for the Next Century*, American Society of International Law, Studies in Transnational Legal Policy, No 26, Washington DC, 1994

Herndl, K, "The Role of the United Nations in the Development of Human Rights" (1986) 2 *UN Bulletin of Human Rights* 1

Humphrey, JP, *Human Rights and the United Nations: A Great Adventure*, Transnational Publishers, New York, 1984

Johnson, L, "The United Nations System for the Protection of Human Rights" (1990) 20 *Georgia Journal of International and Comparative Law* 363

Lawson, E (ed), *Encyclopedia of Human Rights*, Taylor & Francis, New York, 1991

Meron, T, *Human Rights in Internal Strife: Their International Protection*, Grotius, Cambridge, 1987

Meron, T, *Human Rights Law-Making in the United Nations*, Oxford University Press, New York, 1986

O'Flaherty, M, *Human Rights and the UN: Practice before the Treaty Bodies*, Sweet & Maxwell, London, 1996

Robertson, A and Merrills, J, *Human Rights in the World*, 3rd edn, Manchester University Press, New York, 1989

Steiner, HJ and Alston, P, *International Human Rights in Context: Law, Politics*, Morals, Clarendon Press, Oxford, 1996

Thomson, P, "Human Rights Reporting from a State Party's Perspective" in Alston, P (ed), *Towards an Australian Bill of Rights*, Centre for International and Public Law, Australian National University, Canberra, and Human Rights and Equal Opportunity Commission, Sydney, 1994

United Nations Centre for Human Rights and United Nations Institute for Training and Research, *Manual on Human Rights Reporting Under Six Major International Human Rights Instruments*, New York, 1991

The UN Commission on Human Rights

Alston, P, "The Commission on Human Rights" in Alston, P (ed), *The United Nations and Human Rights: A Critical Appraisal*, Clarendon Press, Oxford, 1992

Bossuyt, MJ, "The Development of Special Procedures of the United Nations Commission on Human Rights" (1985) 6 *Human Rights Law Journal* 179

Brody, R, Parker, P and Weissbrodt, W, "Major Developments in 1990 at the UN Commission on Human Rights" (1990) 12 *Human Rights Quarterly* 559

Brody, R and Weissbrodt, D, "Major Developments at the 1989 Session of the UN Commission on Human Rights" (1989) 11 *Human Rights Quarterly* 586

Tolley, H, *The UN Commission on Human Rights*, Westview Press, Boulder CO, 1987

The Human Rights Committee

Bayefsky, AF, "The Human Rights Committee and the Case of Sandra Lovelace" (1982) 20 *Canadian Yearbook of International Law* 244

Brar, PS, "The Practice and Procedures of the Human Rights Committee under the Optional Protocol of the International Covenant on Civil and Political Rights" (1986) 26 *Indian Journal of International Law* 506

Caleo, C, "Implications of Australia's Accession to the First Optional Protocol" (1993) 4 *Public Law Review* 175

Charlesworth, H, "Australia's Accession to the First Optional Protocol to the International Covenant on Civil and Political Rights" (1991) 18 *Melbourne University Law Review* 428

Chinkin, C, "Using the Optional Protocol: The Practical Issues" (1993) 3 *Aboriginal Law Bulletin* 6

Ghandi, PR, "The Human Rights Committee and the Right of Individual Communication" (1987) 57 *British Yearbook of International Law* 201

Gomez del Prado, J, "United Nations Conventions on Human Rights: The Practice of the Human Rights Committee and the Committee on the Elimination of Racial Discrimination in Dealing with Reporting Obligations of States Parties" (1985) 7 *Human Rights Quarterly* 492

Graefrath, B, "Human Rights and International Cooperation – Ten Years in the Human Rights Committee" (1988) 14 *Bulletin of the GDR Committee for Human Rights* 5

Human Rights Committee, *Selected Decisions under the Optional Protocol*, vol 1, United Nations, New York, 1985, UN Doc CCPR/C/OP/1

Human Rights Committee, *Selected Decisions of the Human Rights Committee under the Optional Protocol*, vol 2, United Nations, New York, 1990, UN Doc CCPR/C/OP/2

International Human Rights Reports (IHRR), commenced in 1994 by Nottingham University. Includes decisions and comments of the Human Rights Committee and other treaty bodies.

McGoldrick, D, *The Human Rights Committee: Its Role in the Development of the International Covenant on Civil and Political Rights,* Clarendon Press, Oxford; Oxford University Press, New York, 1991

Opsahl, T, "The Human Rights Committee" in Alston, P (ed), *The United Nations and Human Rights: A Critical Appraisal*, Clarendon Press, Oxford, 1992

Pocar, F, "The International Covenant on Civil and Political Rights" in United Nations Centre for Human Rights and United Nations Institute for Training and Research, *Manual on Human Rights Reporting Under Six Major International Human Rights Instruments*, United Nations, New York, 1991

Pritchard, S and Sharp, N, *Communicating with the Human Rights Committee: A Guide to the Optional Protocol to the International Covenant on Civil and Political Rights*, Australian Human Rights Centre, University of New South Wales, Human Rights Booklet No 1, July 1996

Schmidt, M, "Individual Human Rights Complaints Procedures based on United Nations Treaties and the Need for Reform" (1992) 41 *International and Comparative Law Quarterly* 645

Shelton, DL, "Supervising Implementation of the Covenants: The First Ten Years of the Human Rights Committee" (1986) 80 *Proceedings of the American Society of International Law* 413

The Committee on the Elimination of Racial Discrimination

Banton, M, *International Action Against Racial Discrimination*, Clarendon Press, Oxford, 1996

Lerner, N, *The United Nations Convention on the Elimination of Racial Discrimination*, 2nd edn, Sijthoff and Noordhoff, Alphen aan den Rijn, 1980

McKean, W, *Equality and Discrimination under International Law*, Clarendon Press, Oxford, 1983

Meron, T, "The Meaning and Reach of the International Convention on the Elimination of All Forms of Racial Discrimination" (1985) 79 *American Journal of International Law* 283

Partsch, KJ, "The Committee on the Elimination of Racial Discrimination" in Alston, P (ed), *The United Nations and Human Rights: A Critical Appraisal*, Clarendon Press, Oxford, 1992

Valencia Rodriguez, L, "The International Convention on the Elimination of All Forms of Racial Discrimination" in United Nations Centre for Human Rights and United Nations Institute for Training and Research, *Manual on Human Rights Reporting under Six Major International Human Rights Instruments*, United Nations, New York, 1991

The Committee on the Elimination of Discrimination against Women

Byrnes, A, "Australia and the Convention on Discrimination against Women" (1988) 62 *Australian Law Journal* 478

Byrnes, A, "The 'Other' Human Rights Treaty Body: The Work of the Committee on the Elimination of Discrimination against Women" (1989) 14 *Yale Journal of International Law* 1

Cook, R (ed), *Human Rights of Women: National and International Perspectives*, University of Pennsylvania Press, Philadelphia, 1992

Evatt, E, "Discrimination against Women: The United Nations and CEDAW" in L Spender (ed), *Human Rights: The Australian Debate*, Redfern Legal Centre Publishing, Sydney, 1987

Ilic, Z, "The Convention on the Elimination of All Forms of Discrimination against Women" in United Nations Centre for Human Rights and United Nations Institute for Training and Research, *Manual on Human Rights Reporting Under Six Major International Human Rights Instruments*, United Nations, New York, 1991

International Women's Rights Action Watch, *Assessing the Status of Women: A Guide to Reporting Using the Convention on the Elimination of All Forms of Discrimination against Women*, International Women's Rights Action Watch, New York, 1988

Jacobson, R, "The Committee on the Elimination of Discrimination against Women" in Alston, P (ed), *The United Nations and Human Rights: A Critical Appraisal*, Clarendon Press, Oxford, 1992

Wadstein, M, "Implementation of the UN Convention on the Elimination of All Forms of Discrimination against Women" (1988) 6 *Netherlands Quarterly of Human Rights* 5

The Committee against Torture

Burgers, JH and Danelius, H, *The United Nations Convention against Torture: A Handbook on the Convention against Torture and Other Cruel, Inhuman or Degrading Treatment or Punishment*, Martinus Nijhoff, Boston, 1988

Byrnes, A, "The Committee against Torture" in Alston, P (ed), *The United Nations and Human Rights: A Critical Appraisal*, Clarendon Press, Oxford, 1992

Cassese, A, (ed), *The International Fight against Torture,* Nomos Verlagsgesellschaft, Baden-Baden, 1991

Dormenval, A, "UN Committee against Torture: Practice and Perspectives" (1990) 8 *Netherlands Quarterly of Human Rights* 26

Tardu, M, "The Convention against Torture and Other Cruel Inhuman or Degrading Treatment or Punishment" (1987) 4 *Nordic Journal of International Law* 303

Voyame, J, "The Convention against Torture and Other Cruel, Inhuman or Degrading Treatment or Punishment" in United Nations Centre for Human Rights and United Nations Institute for Training and Research, *Manual on Human Rights Reporting Under Six Major International Human Rights Instruments*, United Nations, New York, 1991

The Committee on Economic, Social and Cultural Rights

Alston, P, "The United Nations' Specialized Agencies and Implementation of the International Covenant on Economic Social and Cultural Rights" (1979) 10 *Colombia Journal of Transnational Law* 79

Alston, P, "Out of the Abyss: The Challenges Confronting the New UN Committee on Economic Social and Cultural Rights" (1987) 9 *Human Rights Quarterly* 332

Alston, P, "The Committee on Economic, Social and Cultural Rights" in Alston, P (ed), *The United Nations and Human Rights: A Critical Appraisal*, Clarendon Press, Oxford, 1992

Alston, P and Simma, B, "First Session of the UN Committee on Economic Social and Cultural Rights" (1987) 81 *American Journal of International Law* 747

207

Alston, P, and Simma, B, "Second Session of the UN Committee on Economic Social and Cultural Rights" (1988) 82 *American Journal of International Law* 603

Alston, P, "The International Covenant on Economic, Social and Cultural Rights" in United Nations Centre for Human Rights and United Nations Institute for Training and Research, *Manual on Human Rights Reporting Under Six Major International Human Rights Instruments*, United Nations, New York, 1991

Craven, M, *International Covenant on Economic Social and Cultural Rights: A Perspective on Development*, Clarendon Press, Oxford, 1995

Craven, M and Dommen, C, "Making Room for Substance: Fifth Session of the Committee on Economic, Social and Cultural Rights" (1991) 9 *Netherlands Quarterly of Human Rights* 83

Eide, A, C Krause and Rosas, A, *Economic Social and Cultural Rights: A Textbook*, Nijhoff, Dordrecht, 1995

Sohn, L (ed), *Guide to Interpretation of the International Covenant on Economic Social and Cultural Rights*, Transnational Publishers, Irvington NY, 1993

Symposium, "The Implementation of the International Covenant on Economic, Social and Cultural Rights" (1987) 9 *Human Rights Quarterly* 121

Committee on the Rights of the Child

Alston, P (ed), *The Best Interests of the Child: Reconciling Culture and Human Rights*, Clarendon Press, Oxford, 1994

Alston, P, Parker, S and Seymour, J (eds), *Children, Rights and the Law*, Clarendon Press, Oxford, 1992

Alston, P, *The Convention on the Rights of the Child: A Commentary*, 2 vols, United Nations and UNICEF, Geneva, 1995

Bennett, WH Jr, "A Critique of the Emerging Convention on the Rights of the Child" (1987) 20 *Cornell International Law Journal* 1

International Commission of Jurists, "The Convention on the Rights of the Child: Time for a New Look at Implementation" (1986) 36 *International Commission of Jurists Review* 30

Appendix 1

Model communication

Communication to:

The Human Rights Committee
c/o Centre for Human Rights
United Nationals Office
8-14 avenue de la Paix
1211 Geneva 10, Switzerland

Submitted for consideration under the First Optional Protocol to the to the International Covenant on Civil and Political Rights

1. Information concerning the author of the communication

Name .... First names ....

Nationality .... Profession ....

Date and place of birth ....

Present address ....

Address for exchange of confidential correspondence (if other than present address)

....

Submitting the Communication as:

(a) .... Victim of the violation or violations set forth below   ☐
(b) .... Appointed representative / legal counsel of alleged victim   ☐
(c) .... Other   ☐

If box (c) is marked the author should explain:

(i) In what capacity he or she is acting on behalf of the victim (eg family relationship or other personal links with the alleged victim):

....

....

(ii) Why the victim is unable to submit the communication him or herself:

....

....

An unrelated third party having no link to the victim cannot submit a communication on his or her behalf

2. Information concerning the alleged victim(s) *(if other than the author)*

Name .... First names ....

Nationality .... Profession ....

Date and place of birth ....

Present address or whereabouts ....

....

**3. State concerned / articles violated / domestic remedies /
other international proceedures**

Name of the State party (country) to the ICCPR and First Optional Protocol against which the communication is directed:

....

Article(s) of the ICCPR allegedly violated:

....

Steps taken by or on behalf of the alleged victim to exhaust domestic remedies - recourse to the courts or other public authorities, when and with what results (if possible, enclose copies of all relevant judicial or administrative decisions):

....

....

If domestic remedies have not been exhausted, explain why:

....

....

Has the same matter been submitted for examination under another proceedure of international investigation or settlement? If so, when and with what results?

....

4. Facts of the claim

Detailed description of the facts of the alleged violation or violations (including relevant dates):

....

....

....

....

Author's signature: ....

Date: ....

Appendix 2

Example of Secretariat reply to an individual communication

OFFICE DES NATIONS UNIES A GENEVE	UNITED NATIONS OFFICE AT GENEVA
POUR LES DROITS DE L'HOMME	CENTRE FOR HUMAN RIGHTS

Telefax: (41 22) 9170213
Telegrammes: UNATIONS, GENEVE
Telephone: (41 22) 9173456
Email: secrt.hchr@unog.ch
Website: www.hchr.ch
REF NO:

Dear

This is to acknowledge the receipt of your undated letter, postmarked . . . , in which you seek advice from the Human Rights Committee.

For the sake of clarity, first let me explain to you that, with respect to . . . , a procedure came into force on . . . , under which individuals who claim to be victims of a violation of any of the rights set forth in the International Covenant on Civil and Political Rights, may submit a communication for consideration under the procedure governed by the Optional Protocol to the International Covenant on Civil and Political Rights.

For your information, I enclose herewith the text of the Covenant and of the Optional Protocol thereto, as well as a Model Communication and Guidelines which have been prepared to assist those who intend to submit communications to the Human Rights Committee under the Optional Protocol. Also enclosed is a publication explaining the communications procedures serviced by the Centre for Human Rights.

In this connection, I wish to point out that a communication submitted to the Human Rights Committee must fulfil a number of admissibility criteria, which are set out in articles 1, 2, 3 and 5(2) of the Optional Protocol and have been further developed in the jurisprudence of the Human Rights Committee. In particular, I should like to draw your attention to the following:

(a) All domestic remedies must have been exhausted before the case is submitted to the Human Rights Committee. This does not apply, however, if it is demonstrated that the application of domestic remedies has been unduly prolonged, or if it can be demonstrated that they would be ineffective. [. . .]

(b) As mentioned above, the Optional Protocol entered into force for . . . on . . . This means that the Human Rights Committee is precluded from considering alleged violations of human rights occurring before . . . unless these violations continue or have effects which in themselves constitute a violation of any of the provisions of the Covenant after that date;

(c) The right to property is not protected by the International Covenant on Civil and Political Rights. However, discrimination is prohibited by article 26 of the Covenant. If you wish to submit a communication to the Human Rights Committee relating to the denial of your right to . . . purchase property, you would be required to substantiate your allegations about discriminatory treatment by the local authorities in this respect. [. . .]

Yours sincerely,

Chief, Communications Section
Centre for Human Rights

Appendix 3

Extract from the Rules of Procedure of the
Human Rights Committee

(UN Doc CCPR/C/3/Rev 3)

XVI. PROCEDURE FOR THE CONSIDERATION OF COMMUNICATIONS RECEIVED UNDER ARTICLE 41 OF THE COVENANT

Rule 72

1. A communication under article 41 of the Covenant may be referred to the Committee by either State party concerned by notice given in accordance with paragraph 1(b) of that article.
2. The notice referred to in paragraph 1 of this rule shall contain or be accompanied by information regarding:
   (a) Steps taken to seek adjustment of the matter in accordance with article 41, paragraphs (a) and (b), of the Covenant, including the text of the initial communication and of any subsequent written explanations or statements by the States parties concerned which are pertinent to the matter;
   (b) Steps taken to exhaust domestic remedies;
   (c) Any other procedure of international investigation or settlement resorted to by the States parties concerned.

Rule 73

The Secretary-General shall maintain a permanent register of all communications received by the Committee under article 41 of the Covenant.

Rule 74

The Secretary-General shall inform the members of the Committee without delay of any notice given under rule 72 of these rules and shall transmit to them as soon as possible copies of the notice and relevant information.

Rule 75

1. The Committee shall examine communications under article 41 of the Covenant at closed meetings.

2. The Committee may, after consultation with the States parties concerned, issue communiques, through the Secretary-General, for the use of the information media and the general public regarding the activities of the Committee at its closed meetings.

Rule 76

A communication shall not be considered by the Committee unless:

    (a) Both States parties concerned have made declarations under article 41, paragraph 1, of the Covenant which are applicable to the communication;

    (b) The time-limit prescribed in article 41, paragraph 1(b), of the Covenant has expired;

    (c) The Committee has ascertained that all available domestic remedies have been invoked and exhausted in the matter in conformity with the generally recognized principles of international law, or that the application of the remedies is unreasonably prolonged.

Rule 77A

Subject to the provisions of rule 76 of these rules, the Committee shall proceed to make its good offices available to the States parties concerned with a view to a friendly solution of the matter on the basis of respect for human rights and fundamental freedoms as recognized in the Covenant.

Rule 77B

The Committee may, through the Secretary-General, request the States parties concerned or either of them to submit additional information or observations orally or in writing. The Committee shall indicate a time-limit for the submission of such written information or observations.

Rule 77C

1. The States parties concerned shall have the right to be represented when the matter is being considered in the Committee and to make submissions orally and/or in writing.

2. The Committee shall, through the Secretary-General, notify the States parties concerned as early as possible of the opening date, duration and place of the session at which the matter will be examined.

3. The procedure for making oral and/or written submissions shall be decided by the Committee, after consultation with the States parties concerned.

Rule 77D

1. Within 12 months after the date on which the Committee received the notice referred to in rule 72 of these rules, the Committee shall adopt a report in accordance with article 41, paragraph 1(h), of the Covenant.
2. The provisions of paragraph 1 of rule 77C of these rules shall apply to the deliberations of the Committee concerning the adoption of the report.
3. The Committee's report shall be communicated, through the Secretary-General, to the States parties concerned.

Rule 77E

If a matter referred to the Committee in accordance with article 41 of the Covenant is not resolved to the satisfaction of the States parties concerned, the Committee may, with their prior consent, proceed to apply the procedure prescribed in article 42 of the Covenant.

XVII. PROCEDURE FOR THE CONSIDERATION OF COMMUNICATIONS RECEIVED UNDER THE OPTIONAL PROTOCOL

A. TRANSMISSION OF COMMUNICATIONS TO THE COMMITTEE

Rule 78

1. The Secretary-General shall bring to the attention of the Committee, in accordance with the present rules, communications which are or appear to be submitted for consideration by the Committee under article 1 of the Protocol.
2. The Secretary-General, when necessary, may request clarification from the author of a communication as to his wish to have his communication submitted to the Committee for consideration under the Protocol. In case there is still doubt as to the wish of the author, the Committee shall be seized of the communication.
3. No communication shall be received by the Committee or included in a list under rule 79 if it concerns a State which is not a party to the Protocol.

Rule 79

1. The Secretary-General shall prepare lists of the communications submitted to the Committee in accordance with rule 78 above, with a brief summary of their contents, and shall circulate such lists to the members of the Committee at regular intervals. The Secretary-General shall also maintain a permanent register of all such communications.

2. The full text of any communication brought to the attention of the Committee shall be made available to any member of the Committee upon his request.

Rule 80

1. The Secretary-General may request clarification from the author of a communication concerning the applicability of the Protocol to his communication, in particular regarding:

    (a) The name, address, age and occupation of the author and the verification of his identity;

    (b) The name of the State party against which the communication is directed;

    (c) The object of the communication;

    (d) The provision or provisions of the Covenant alleged to have been violated;

    (e) The facts of the claim;

    (f) Steps taken by the author to exhaust domestic remedies;

    (g) The extent to which the same matter is being examined under another procedure of international investigation or settlement.

2. When requesting clarification or information, the Secretary-General shall indicate an appropriate time-limit to the author of the communication with a view to avoiding undue delays in the procedure under the Protocol.

3. The Committee may approve a questionnaire for the purpose of requesting the above-mentioned information from the author of the communication.

4. The request for clarification referred to in paragraph 1 of the present rule shall not preclude the inclusion of the communication in the list provided for in rule 79, paragraph 1, above.

Rule 81

For each registered communication the Secretary-General shall as soon as possible prepare and circulate to the members of the Committee a summary of the relevant information obtained.

B. GENERAL PROVISIONS REGARDING THE CONSIDERATION OF COMMUNICATIONS BY THE COMMITTEE OR ITS SUBSIDIARY BODIES

Rule 82

Meetings of the Committee or its subsidiary bodies during which communications under the Protocol will be examined shall be closed. Meeting during which the Committee may consider general issues such as procedures for the application of the Protocol may be public if the Committee so decides.

Rule 83

The Committee may issue communiqués, through the Secretary-General, for the use of the information media and the general public regarding the activities of the Committee at its closed meeting.

Rule 84

1. A member shall not take part in the examination of a communication by the Committee:

    (a) If he has any personal interest in the case; or

    (b) If he has participated in any capacity in the making of any decision on the case covered by the communication.

2. Any question which may arise under paragraph 1 above shall be decided by the Committee.

Rule 85

If, for any reason, a member considers that he should not take part or continue to take part in the examination of a communication, he shall inform the Chairman of his withdrawal.

Rule 86

The Committee may, prior to forwarding its final views on the communication to the State party concerned, inform the State of its views whether interim measures may be desirable to avoid irreparable damage to the victim of the alleged violation. In doing so, the Committee shall inform the State party concerned that such expression of its views on interim measures does not imply a determination on the merits of the communication.

C. PROCEDURE TO DETERMINE ADMISSIBILITY

Rule 87

1. The Committee shall decide as soon as possible and in accordance with the following rules whether the communication is admissible or is inadmissible under the Protocol.

2. A Working Group established under rule 89, paragraph 1, may also declare a communication admissible when it is composed of five members and all the members so decide.

Rule 88

1. Communications shall be dealt with in the order in which they are received by the Secretariat, unless the Committee or a Working Group established under rule 89, paragraph 1, decides otherwise.

2. Two or more communications may be dealt with jointly if deemed appropriate by the Committee or a Working Group established under rule 89, paragraph 1.

Rule 89

1. The Committee may establish one or more Working Groups of no more than five of its members to make recommendations to the Committee regarding the fulfilment of the conditions of admissibility laid down in articles 1, 2, 3 and 5(2) of the Protocol.
2. The rules of procedure of the Committee shall apply as far as possible to the meetings of the Working Group.
3. The Committee may designate Special Rapporteurs from among its members to assist in the handling of communications.

Rule 90

With a view to reaching a decision on the admissibility of a communication, the Committee, or a Working Group established under rule 89, paragraph 1, shall ascertain:

(a) That the communication is not anonymous and that it emanates from an individual, or individuals, subject to the jurisdiction of a State party to the Protocol;

(b) That the individual claims, in a manner sufficiently substantiated, to be a victim of a violation by that State party of any of the rights set forth in the Covenant. Normally, the communication should be submitted by the individual himself or by his representative; a communication submitted on behalf of an alleged victim may, however, be accepted when it appears that he is unable to submit the communication himself;

(c) That the communication is not an abuse of the right to submit a communication under the Protocol;

(d) That the communication is not incompatible with the provisions of the Covenant;

(e) That the same matter is not being examined under another procedure of international investigation or settlement;

(f) That the individual has exhausted all available domestic remedies.

Rule 91

1. The Committee or a Working Group established under rule 89, paragraph 1, or a Special Rapporteur designated under rule 89, paragraph 3, may request the State party concerned or the author of the communication to submit additional written information or observations relevant to the question of the admissibility of the communication. To avoid undue delays, a time-limit for the submission of such information or observations shall be indicated.

2. A communication may not be declared admissible unless the State party concerned has received the text of the communication and has been given an opportunity to furnish information or observation as provided in paragraph 1 of this rule.

3. A request addressed to a State party under paragraph 1 of this rule shall include a statement of the fact that such a request does not imply that any decision has been reached on the question of admissibility.

4. Within fixed time-limits, each party may be afforded an opportunity to comment on submissions made by the other party pursuant to this rule.

Rule 92

1. Where the Committee decides that a communication is inadmissible under the Protocol it shall as soon as possible communicate its decision, through the Secretary-General, to the author of the communication and, where the communication has been transmitted to a State party concerned, to that State party.

2. If the Committee has declared a communication inadmissible under article 5, paragraph 2, of the Protocol, this decision may be reviewed at a late by the Committee upon a written request by or on behalf of the individual concerned containing information to the effect that the reasons for inadmissibility referred to in article 5, paragraph 2, no longer apply.

3. Any member of the Committee may request that a summary of his individual opinion shall be appended to the Committee's decision declaring a communication inadmissible under the Optional Protocol.

D. PROCEDURE FOR THE CONSIDERATION OF COMMUNICATIONS ON MERITS

Rule 93

1. As soon as possible after the Committee or a Working Group acting under rule 87, paragraph 2, has taken a decision that a communication is admissible under the Protocol, that decision and the text of the relevant documents shall be submitted, through the Secretary-General, to the State party concerned. The author of the communication shall also be informed, through the Secretary-General, of the decision.

2. Within six months, the State party concerned shall submit to the Committee written explanations or statements clarifying the matter under consideration and the remedy, if any, that may have been taken by that State

3. Any explanations or statements submitted by a State party pursuant to this rule shall be communicated, through the Secretary-General, to the author of the communication who may submit any additional written information or observations within fixed time-limits.

4. Upon consideration of the merits, the Committee may review its decision that a communication is admissible in the light of any explanation or statements submitted by the State party pursuant to this rule.

Rule 94

1. If the communication is admissible, the Committee shall consider the communication in the light of all written information made available to it by the individuals and by the State party concerned and shall formulate its reviews thereon. For this purpose the Committee may refer the communication to a Working Group of not more than five of its members or to a Special Rapporteur to make recommendations to the Committee.

2. The views of the Committee shall be communicated to the individual and to the State party concerned.

3. Any member of the Committee may request that a summary of his individual opinion shall be appended to the views of the Committee.

Appendix 4

Extract from the Rules of Procedure of the Committee against Torture

(UN Doc CAT/C/3/Rev 1)

XIX. PROCEDURE FOR THE CONSIDERATION OF COMMUNICATIONS RECEIVED UNDER ARTICLE 22 OF THE CONVENTION

A. GENERAL PROVISIONS

Declaration by States parties

Rule 96

1. The Secretary-General shall transmit to the other States parties copies of the declarations deposited with him by States parties recognizing the competence of the Committee, in accordance with article 22 of the Convention.

2. The withdrawal of a declaration made under article 22 of the Convention shall not prejudice the consideration of any matter which is the subject of a communication already transmitted under that article; no further communication by or on behalf of an individual shall be received under that article after the notification of withdrawal of the declaration has been received by the Secretary-General, unless the State party has made a new declaration.

Transmission of communication to the Committee

Rule 97

1. The Secretary-General shall bring to the attention of the Committee, in accordance with the present rules, communications which are or appear to be submitted for consideration by the Committee under paragraph 1 of article 22 of the Convention.

2. The Secretary-General, when necessary, may request clarification from the author of a communication as to his wish to have his communication submitted to the Committee for consideration under article 22 of the Convention. In case there is still doubt as to the wish of the author, the Committee shall be seized of the communication.

3. No communication shall be received by the Committee or included in a list under rule 98 if it concerns a State which has not made the declaration provided for in article 22, paragraph 1, of the Convention.

List and register of communications

Rule 98

1. The Secretary-General shall prepare lists of the communications brought to the attention of the Committee in accordance with rule 97 above, with a brief summary of their contents, and shall circulate such lists to the members of the Committee at regular intervals. The Secretary-General shall also maintain a permanent register of all such communications.

2. The full text of any communication brought to the attention of the Committee shall be made available to any member of the Committee upon his request.

Request for clarification or additional information

Rule 99

1. The Secretary-General may request clarification from the author of a communication concerning the applicability of article 22 of the Convention to his communication, in particular regarding:

   (a) The name, address, age and occupation of the author and the verification of his identity;

   (b) The name of the State party against which the communication is directed;

   (c) The object of the communication;

   (d) The provision or provisions of the Convention alleged to have been violated;

   (e) The facts of the claim;

   (f) Steps taken by the author to exhaust domestic remedies;

   (g) The extent to which the same matter is being examined under another procedure of international investigation or settlement.

2. When requesting clarification or information, the Secretary-General shall indicate an appropriate time-limit to the author of the communication with a view to avoiding undue delays in the procedure under article 22 of the Convention.

3. The Committee may approve a questionnaire for the purpose of requesting the above-mentioned information from the author of the communication.

4. The request for clarification referred to in paragraph 1 of the present rule shall not preclude the inclusion of the communication in the list provided for in rule 98, paragraph 1.

223

Summary of the information

Rule 100

For each registered communication the Secretary-General shall, as soon as possible, prepare and circulate to the members of the Committee a summary of the relevant information obtained.

Meetings

Rule 101

1. Meetings of the Committee or its subsidiary bodies during which communications under article 22 of the Convention will be examined shall be closed.
2. Meetings during which the Committee may consider general issues, such as procedures for the application of article 22 of the Convention, may be public if the Committee so decides.

Issue of communiqués concerning closed meetings

Rule 102

The Committee may issue communiqués, through the Secretary-General, for the use of the information media and the general public regarding the activities of the Committee under article 22 of the Convention.

Inability of a member to take part in the examination of a communication

Rule 103

1. A member shall not take part in the examination of a communication by the Committee or its subsidiary body:
    (a) If he has any personal interest in the case; or
    (b) If he has participated in any capacity in the making of any decision on the case covered by the communication.
2. Any question which may arise under paragraph 1 above shall be decided by the Committee without the participation of the member concerned.

Withdrawal of a member

Rule 104

If, for any reason, a member considers that he should not take part or continue to take part in the examination of a communication, he shall inform the Chairman of his withdrawal.

B. PROCEDURE FOR DETERMINING ADMISSIBILITY OF COMMUNICATIONS

Method of dealing with communications

Rule 105

1. In accordance with the following rules, the Committee shall decide as soon as possible whether or not a communication is admissible under article 22 of the Convention.

2. The Committee shall, unless it decides otherwise, deal with communications in the order in which they have been placed before it by the Secretariat.

3. The Committee may, if it deems it appropriate, decide to consider jointly two or more communications.

4. The Committee may, if it deems it appropriate, decide to join the consideration of the question of admissibility of a communication to the consideration of the communication on its merits.

Establishment of a Working Group

Rule 106

1. The Committee may, in accordance with rule 61, set up a Working Group to meet shortly before its sessions, or at any other convenient time to be decided by the committee in consultation with the Secretary-General, for the purpose of making recommendations to the Committee regarding the fulfilment of the conditions of admissibility of communications laid down in article 22 of the Convention and assisting the committee in any manner which the Committee may decide.

2. The Working Group shall not comprise more than five members of the Committee. The Working Group shall not comprise more than five members of the Committee. The Working Group shall elect its own officers, develop its own working methods, and apply as far as possible the rules of procedure of the Committee to its meetings.

Conditions for admissibility of communications

Rule 107

1. With a view to reaching a decision on the admissibility of a communication, the Committee or its Working Group shall ascertain:

   (a) That the communication is not anonymous and that it emanates from an individual subject to the jurisdiction of a State party recognizing the competence of the Committee under article 22 of the Convention;

225

(b) That the individual claims to be a victim of a violation by the State party concerned of the provisions of the Convention. The communication should be submitted by the individual himself or by his relatives or designated representatives or by others on behalf of an alleged victim when it appears that the victim is unable to submit the communication himself, and the author of the communication justifies his acting on the victim's behalf;

(c) That the communication is not an abuse of the right to submit a communication under article 22 of the Convention;

(d) That the communication is not incompatible with the provisions of the Convention;

(e) That the same matter has not been and is not being examined under another procedure of international investigation or settlement;

(f) That the individual has exhausted all available domestic remedies. However, this shall not be the rule where the application of the remedies is unreasonable prolonged or is unlikely to bring effective relief to the person who is the victim of the violation of this Convention.

2. The Committee shall consider a communication, which is otherwise admissible, whenever the conditions laid down in article 22, paragraph 5, are met.

Additional information, clarifications and observations

Rule 108

1. The Committee or the Working Group established under rule 106 may request, through the Secretary-General, the State party concerned or the author of the communication to submit additional written information, clarifications or observations relevant to the question of admissibility of the communication.

2. Requests referred to in paragraph 1 of this rule which are addressed to the State party shall be accompanied by the text of the communication.

3. A communication may not be declared admissible unless the State party concerned has received the text of the communication and has been given an opportunity to furnish information or observations as provided in paragraph 1 of this rule, including information relating to the exhaustion of domestic remedies.

4. The Committee or the Working Group may adopt a questionnaire for requesting such additional information or clarifications.

5. The Committee or the Working Group shall indicate a time-limit for the submission of such additional information or clarification with a view to avoiding undue delay.

6. If the time-limit is not respected by the State party concerned or the author of a communication, the Committee or the Working Group may decide to consider the admissibility of the communication in the light of available information.

7. If the State party concerned disputes the contention of the author of a communication that all available domestic remedies have been exhausted, the State party is required to give details of the effective remedies available to the alleged victim in the particular circumstances of the case and in accordance with the provisions of article 22, paragraph 5(b), of the Convention.

8. Within such time-limit as indicated by the Committee or the Working Group, the State party or the author of a communication may be afforded an opportunity to comment on any submission received from the other party pursuant to a request made under the present rule. Non-receipt of such comments within the established time-limit should, as a rule, not delay the consideration of the admissibility of the communication.

9. In the course of the consideration of the question of the admissibility of a communication, the Committee or the Working Group may request the State party to take steps to avoid a possible irreparable damage to the person or persons who claim to be victim(s) of the alleged violation. Such a request addressed to the State party does not imply that any decision has been reached on the question of the admissibility of the communication.

Inadmissible communications

Rule 109

1. Where the Committee decides that a communication is inadmissible under article 22 of the convention, or its consideration is suspended or discontinued, the Committee shall as soon as possible transmit its decision, through the Secretary-General, to the author of the communication and, where the communication has been transmitted to a State party concerned, to that State party.

2. If the Committee has declared a communication inadmissible under article 22, paragraph 5, of the Convention, this decision may be reviewed at a later date by the Committee upon a written request by or on behalf of the individual concerned. Such written request shall contain documentary evidence to the effect that the reasons for inadmissibility referred to in article 22, paragraph 5, of the Convention no longer apply.

3. Consideration of communications on their merits

Method of dealing with admissible communications

Rule 110

1. When it has decided that a communication is admissible under article 22 of the Convention, the Committee shall transmit to the State party, through the Secretary-General, the text of its decision together with any submission received from the author of the communication not already transmitted to the State party under rule 108, paragraph 2. The Committee shall also inform the author of the communication, through the Secretary-General, of its decision.

2. Within six months, the State party concerned shall submit to the Committee written explanations or statements clarifying the case under consideration and the remedy, if any, that may have been taken by it. The Committee may indicate, if it deems it necessary, the type of information it wishes to receive from the State party concerned.

3. In the course of its consideration, the Committee may inform the State party of its views on the desirability, because of urgency, of taking interim measures to avoid possible irreparable damage to the person or persons who claim to be victim(s) of the alleged violation. In doing so, the Committee shall inform the State party concerned that such expression of its views on interim measures does not prejudge its final views on the merits of the communication.

4. Any explanations or statements submitted by a State party pursuant to this rule shall be transmitted, through the Secretary-General, to the author of the communication who may submit any additional written information or observations within such time-limit as the Committee shall decide.

5. The Committee may invite the author of the communication or his represent-ative and representatives of the State party concerned to be present at specified closed meetings of the committee in order to provide further clarifications or to answer questions on the merits of the communication.

6. The Committee may revoke its decision that a communication is admissible in the light of any explanations or statements submitted by the State party pursuant to this rule. However, before the Committee considers revoking that decision, the explanations or statements concerned must be transmitted to the author of the communication so that he may submit additional information or observations within a time-limit set by the Committee.

Views of the Committee on admissible communications

Rule 111

1. Admissible communications shall be considered by the Committee in the light of all information made available to it by or on behalf of the individual and by the State party concerned. The Committee may refer the communication to the Working Group for assistance in this task.

2. The Committee or the Working Group may at any time, in the course of the examination, obtain through the Secretary-General any documentation that may assist in the disposal of the case from United Nations bodies or the specialized agencies.

3. After consideration of an admissible communication, the Committee shall formulate its views thereon. The views of the Committee shall be forwarded, through the Secretary-General, to the author of the communication and to the State party concerned.

4. Any member of the Committee may request that a summary of his individual opinion be appended to the views of the Committee when they are forwarded to the author of the communication and to the State party concerned.

5. The State party concerned shall be invited to inform the Committee in due course of the action it takes in conformity with the Committee's views.

Summaries in the Committee's annual report and inclusion of texts of final decisions

Rule 112

1. The Committee shall include in its annual report the text of its views under article 22, paragraph 7, of the Convention. It may also decide to include in its annual report the text of any decision declaring a communication inadmissible under article 22 of the Convention.

2. The Committee may decide to include in its annual report the text of its views under article 22, paragraph 7, of the Convention. It may also decide to include in its annual report the text of any decision declaring a communication inadmissible under article 22 of the Convention

Appendix 5

Extract from the Rules of Procedure of the Committee on the Elimination of Racial Discrimination

(01/01/89 CERD/C/35/Rev 3)

XVI. COMMUNICATIONS FROM STATES PARTIES UNDER ARTICLE 11 OF THE CONVENTION

Method of dealing with communications from States parties

Rule 69

1. When a matter is brought to the attention of the Committee by a State party in accordance with article 11, paragraph 1, of the Convention, the Committee shall examine it at a private meeting and shall then transmit it to the State party concerned through the Secretary-General. The Committee in examining the communications shall not consider its substance. Any action at this stage by the Committee in respect of the communication shall in no way be construed as an expression of its views on the substance of the communication.

2. If the Committee is not in session, the Chairman shall bring the matter to the attention of its members by transmitting copies of the communication and requesting their consent to transmit such communication on behalf of the Committee, to the State party concerned in compliance with article 11, paragraph 1. The Chairman shall also specify a time-limit of three weeks for their replies.

3. Upon receipt of the consent of the majority of the members, or, if within the specified time-limit no replies are received, the Chairman shall transmit the communication to the State party concerned, through the Secretary-General, without delay.

4. In the event of any replies being received which represent the views of the majority of the Committee, the Chairman, while acting in accordance with such replies, shall bear in mind the requirement of urgency in transmitting the communication to the State party concerned on behalf of the Committee.

5. The Committee, or the Chairman on behalf of the Committee, shall remind the receiving State that the time-limit for submission of its written explanations or statement under the Convention is three months.

6. When the Committee receives the explanations or statements of the receiving State, the procedure laid down above shall be followed with respect to the transmission of those explanations or statements to the State party submitting the initial communication.

Request for information

Rule 70

The Committee may call upon the States parties concerned to supply information relevant to the application of article 11 of the Convention. The Committee may indicate the manner as well as the time within which such information shall be supplied.

Notification to the States parties concerned

Rule 71

If any matter is submitted for consideration by the Committee under paragraph 2 of article 11 of the Convention, the Chairman, through the Secretary-General, shall inform the States parties concerned of the forthcoming consideration of this matter not later than 30 days in advance of the first meeting of the Committee, in the case of a regular session, and at least 18 days in advance of the first meeting of the Committee, in the case of a special session.

XVII. ESTABLISHMENT AND FUNCTIONS OF THE AD HOC CONCILIATION COMMISSION UNDER ARTICLES 12 AND 13 OF THE CONVENTION

Consultations on the composition of the Commission

Rule 72

After the Committee has obtained and collated all the information it thinks necessary as regards a dispute that has arisen under article 11, paragraph 2, of the Convention, the Chairman shall notify the States parties to the dispute and undertake consultations with them concerning the composition of the Ad Hoc Conciliation Commission (hereinafter referred to as "the Commission"), in accordance with article 12 of the Convention.

Appointment of members of the Commission

Rule 73

Upon receiving the unanimous consent of the States parties to the dispute regarding the composition of the Commission, the Chairman shall proceed to the appointment of the members of the Commission and shall inform the States parties to the dispute of the composition of the Commission.

Rule 74

1. If within three months of the Chairman's notification as provided in rule 72 above, the States parties to the dispute fail to reach agreement on all or part of the composition of the Commission, the Chairman shall then bring the situation to the attention of the Committee which shall proceed according to article 12, paragraph 1 (b), of the Convention at its next session.
2. Upon the completion of the election, the Chairman shall inform the States parties to the dispute of the composition of the Commission.

Solemn declaration by members of the Commission

Rule 75

Upon assuming his duties, each member of the Commission shall make the following solemn declaration at the first meeting of the Commission:

"I solemnly declare that I will perform my duties and exercise my powers as a member of the Ad Hoc Conciliation Commission honorably, faithfully, impartially and conscientiously."

Filling of vacancies in the Commission

Rule 76

Whenever a vacancy arises in the Commission, the Chairman of the Committee shall fill the vacancy as soon as possible in accordance with procedures laid down in rules 72 to 74. He shall proceed with filling such vacancy upon receipt of a report from the Commission or upon a notification by the Secretary-General.

Transmission of information to members of the Commission

Rule 77

The information obtained and collated by the Committee shall be made available by its Chairman, through the Secretary-General, to the members of the Commission at the time of notifying the members of the Commission of the date of the first meeting of the Commission.

Report of the Commission

Rule 78

1. The Chairman of the Committee shall communicate the report of the Commission referred to in article 13 of the Convention as soon as possible after its receipt to each of the States parties to the dispute and to the members of the Committee.

2. The States parties to the dispute, shall, within three months after the receipt of the Commission's report, inform the Chairman of the Committee whether or not they accept the recommendations contained in the report of the Commission. The Chairman shall transmit the information received from the States parties to the dispute to the members of the Committee.

3. After the expiry of the time-limit provided for in the preceding paragraph, the Chairman of the Committee shall communicate the report of the Commission and any declaration of States parties concerned to the other States parties to the Convention.

Keeping members of the Committee informed

Rule 79

The Chairman of the Committee shall keep the members of the Committee informed of his actions under rules 73 to 78.

Index